The 1992 Presidential Campaign

THE 1992 PRESIDENTIAL CAMPAIGN

A Communication Perspective

Edited by Robert E. Denton, Jr.

Praeger Series in Political Communication

PRAEGER

Westport, Connecticut
London

Library of Congress Cataloging-in-Publication Data

The 1992 presidential campaign : a communication perspective / edited
by Robert E. Denton, Jr.
    p.   cm. — (Praeger series in political communication, ISSN
1062–5623)
   Includes bibliographical references.
   ISBN 0–275–94559–6 (alk. paper : hc). — ISBN 0–275–94560–X (alk.
paper : pbk)
    1. Presidents—United States—Election—1992. 2. Electioneering—
United States. 3. Communication in politics—United States.
4. Mass media—Political aspects—United States. I. Denton, Robert
E., Jr. II. Series.
JK526   1992h
324.973'0928—dc20   93–50064

British Library Cataloguing in Publication Data is available.

Library of Congress Catalog Card Number: 93–50064
ISBN: 0–275–94559–6; 0–275–94560–X (pbk.)
ISSN: 1062–5623

First published in 1994

Praeger Publishers, 88 Post Road West, Westport, CT 06881
An imprint of Greenwood Publishing Group, Inc.

Printed in the United States of America

∞

The paper used in this book complies with the
Permanent Paper Standard issued by the National
Information Standards Organization (Z39.48-1984).

10 9 8 7 6 5 4 3 2 1

This book is dedicated to the late James D. McComas, a university president, a mentor, a colleague, and a friend, who always took time to share and care about the world, the nation, the state, the community, and individual people. He was a man of vision and hope, words and deeds. Such privileged associations define life. With my utmost admiration and appreciation.

Contents

Series Foreword

Those of us from the discipline of communication studies have long believed that communication is prior to all other fields of inquiry. In several other forums I have argued that the essence of politics is "talk" or human interaction.[1] Such interaction may be formal or informal, verbal or nonverbal, public or private, but it is always persuasive, forcing us consciously or subconsciously to interpret, to evaluate, and to act. Communication is the vehicle for human action.

From this perspective, it is not surprising that Aristotle recognized the natural kinship of politics and communication in his writings *Politics* and *Rhetoric*. In the former, he established that humans are "political beings [who] alone of the animals [are] furnished with the faculty of language."[2] In the latter, he began his systematic analysis of discourse by proclaiming that "rhetorical study, in its strict sense, is concerned with the modes of persuasion."[3] Thus, it was recognized over twenty-three hundred years ago that politics and communication go hand in hand because they are essential parts of human nature.

In 1981, Dan Nimmo and Keith Sanders proclaimed that political communication was an emerging field.[4] Although its origin, as noted, dates back centuries, a "self-consciously cross-disciplinary" focus began in the late 1950s. Thousands of books and articles later, colleges and universities offer a variety of graduate and undergraduate coursework in the area in such diverse departments as communication, mass communication, journalism, political science, and sociology.[5] In Nimmo and Sanders's early assessment, the "key areas of inquiry" included rhetorical analysis, propaganda analysis, attitude change studies, voting studies, government and the news media, functional and systems analyses, technological changes, media technologies, campaign techniques, and research techniques.[6] In a survey of the state of the field in 1983, the same authors and Lynda Kaid found additional, more specific areas of concerns such as the presidency, political polls, public opinion, debates, and advertising.[7] Since the first study, they have also noted a shift away from the rather strict behavioral approach.

A decade later, Dan Nimmo and David Swanson argued that "political communication has developed some identity as a more or less distinct domain of scholarly work."[8] The scope and concerns of the area have further expanded to include critical theories and cultural studies. Although there is no precise definition, method, or disciplinary home of the area of inquiry, its primary domain comprises the role, processes, and effects of communication within the context of politics broadly defined.

In 1985, the editors of *Political Communication Yearbook: 1984* noted that "more things are happening in the study, teaching, and practice of political communication than can be captured within the space limitations of the relatively few publications available."[9] In addition, they argued that the backgrounds of "those involved in the field [are] so varied and pluralist in outlook and approach, . . . it [is] a mistake to adhere slavishly to any set format in shaping the content."[10] More recently, Swanson and Nimmo have called for "ways of overcoming the unhappy consequences of fragmentation within a framework that respects, encourages, and benefits from diverse scholarly commitments, agendas, and approaches."[11]

In agreement with these assessments of the area and with gentle encouragement, in 1988 Praeger established the series entitled "Praeger Studies in Political Communication." The series is open to all qualitative and quantitative methodologies as well as contemporary and historical studies. The key to characterizing the studies in the series is the focus on communication variables or activities within a political context or dimension. As of this writing, nearly forty volumes have been published and numerous impressive works are forthcoming. Scholars from the disciplines of communication, history, journalism, political science, and sociology have participated in the series.

I am, without shame or modesty, a fan of the series. The joy of serving as its editor is in participating in the dialogue of the field of political communication and in reading the contributors' works. I invite you to join me.

Robert E. Denton, Jr.

NOTES

1. See Robert E. Denton, Jr., *The Symbolic Dimensions of the American Presidency* (Prospect Heights, IL: Waveland Press, 1982); Robert E. Denton, Jr., and Gary Woodward, *Political Communication in America* (New York: Praeger, 1985; 2d ed., 1990); Robert E. Denton, Jr., and Dan Hahn, *Presidential Communication* (New York: Praeger, 1986); and Robert E. Denton, Jr., *The Primetime Presidency of Ronald Reagan* (New York: Praeger, 1988).

2. Aristotle, *The Politics of Aristotle,* trans. Ernest Barker (New York: Oxford University Press, 1970), p. 5.

3. Aristotle, *Rhetoric,* trans. Rhys Roberts (New York: The Modern Library, 1954), p. 22.

4. Dan Nimmo and Keith Sanders, "Introduction: The Emergence of Political Communication as a Field," in *Handbook of Political Communication,* eds. Dan Nimmo and Keith Sanders (Beverly Hills, CA: Sage, 1981), pp. 11–36.

5. Ibid., p. 15.

6. Ibid., pp. 17–27.

7. Keith Sanders, Lynda Kaid, and Dan Nimmo, eds. *Political Communication Yearbook: 1984* (Carbondale, IL: Southern Illinois University: 1985), pp. 283–308.

8. Dan Nimmo and David Swanson, "The Field of Political Communication: Beyond the Voter Persuasion Paradigm," in *New Directions in Political Communication,* eds. David Swanson and Dan Nimmo (Beverly Hills, CA: Sage, 1990), p. 8.

9. Sanders, Kaid, and Nimmo, *Political Communication Yearbook: 1984,* p. xiv.

10. Ibid.

11. Nimmo and Swanson, "The Field of Political Communication," p. 11.

Preface

Every four years a gong goes off and a new Presidential campaign surges into the national consciousness: new candidates, new issues, a new season of surprises. But underlying the syncopations of change is a steady, recurrent rhythm from election to election, a pulse of politics, that brings up the same basic themes in order, over and over again.

James David Barber

For years, those of us in the discipline of communication studies have argued that the essence of politics is simply "talk" or human interaction. The interaction may be formal or informal, verbal or nonverbal, public or private, but it is always persuasive—forcing us as individuals to interpret, to evaluate, and to act.

Political campaigns are highly complex and sophisticated communication events, involving the communication of issues, images, social reality, and personas. They are essentially exercises in the creation, recreation, and transmission of "significant symbols" through human communication. As we attempt to make sense of our environment, "political bits" of communication influence our voting choices, world views, and legislative desires.

The 1992 presidential campaign was one of the most exciting and unique campaigns in recent history. Some scholars even characterize the campaign as a watershed in American presidential politics. The election signaled the end of the Reagan era, a revitalization of voter interest and participation, a generational shift of national leadership, the strongest third-party challenge since 1912, and the creative use of television and new communication technologies. Candidates were innovative in reaching the voters. Television talk shows replaced the stump speech; popular tabloids and talk radio overshadowed network evening news as important sources of political information.

The purpose of this volume is to review the 1992 presidential campaign from a communication perspective. The analyses go beyond the quantitative facts, electoral counts, and poll results of the election. Each chapter focuses on a specific area of political campaign communication: the communication functions and activities across the campaign phases, the nomination conventions, the debates, political advertising, the discussion and framing of issues, candidate images, the role and impact of network and local news, "electronic town hall" meetings, and C-SPAN.

In Chapter 1, Mary Stuckey and I provide an overview of the 1992 presidential campaign by presenting a communication model of campaigns. The model identifies six essential elements that are common to all candidates and that cut across all phases of a campaign. However, the rhetorical functions and impact of the elements differ dramatically across the four phases of campaigns. The model attempts to capture the dynamism of the elements and hence the campaign by exploring the interaction among the elements in the various stages.

In Chapter 2, Judith Trent examines the early campaign period. It was one of the most unique in American history. In addition to starting later than usual, the period was marked by a drastic drop in popularity for the president, an absence of noted Democratic candidates, challenges by a Texas billionaire and a well-known conservative journalist, and the use of new technologies and media outlets. The communication functions of this period set the stage for the general campaign.

In Chapter 3, David Timmerman and Larry David Smith analyze the nominating conventions whose purpose is not to nominate candidates as much as to orchestrate "cordial concurrence," to legitimize the candidates, and to provide a transition from intraparty confrontations to interparty contest. The authors use narrative principles to interpret the style and substance of the conventions' podium oratory, video presentations, and platforms. The narrative elements provide insight into how conventions characterize opponents, establish party values, and generate story lines for the general campaign. What was most noteworthy of the 1992 conventions was their striking contrast in style and content as well as the role reversal of the parties' convention stereotypes. The Democrats were positive and unified. The Republicans were fragmented and negative. From a narrative perspective, the Democrats were successful in establishing a "master plot" for the general campaign, whereas the Republicans were less successful. The authors conclude that the Republican convention represents the first failed convention of the "telepolitical era."

In Chapter 4, Robert Friedenberg provides an analysis of the debates. The 1992 presidential debates revealed candidate positions on issues as well as candidate personalities. Clinton was the general "winner" of the

debates because of his mastery of the seven criteria that characterize successful political debaters: (1) direct remarks at specifically targeted audiences, (2) develop an overall theme throughout the debates, (3) debate not
to lose by avoiding specifics and making use of proven safe responses, (4)
present themselves as vigorous, active leaders, (5) foster identification of
themselves with national aspirations, (6) foster identification of themselves with the dominant political party/philosophy, and (7) personify
themselves as exemplifying a desirable characteristic. Both Clinton and
Perot presented themselves as more vigorous and as better agents of
change than Bush. Friedenberg's analysis also suggests changes to the
debate formats of the 1992 presidential campaign.

In Chapter 5, Lynda Lee Kaid focuses on political advertising during
the primary and general campaigns. In addition to providing an overview
of the styles and strategies of the political ads, Kaid provides a content
analysis of the 1992 general election commercials and the results of
experimental tests of audience response data. The 1992 campaign marked
the greatest use of spot market buys, extensive use of cable television, and
the successful use of Perot's "infomercials." Overall, the ad campaigns
were the most expensive and the most negative in history.

In Chapter 6, Rachel Holloway examines the issues of the presidential
campaign by analyzing the strengths and weaknesses of key definitional
strategies employed by Bush and Clinton, and by providing an interpretation of what we can learn about political issues and campaigns from this
election. In addition to concerns with the economy, health care, crime, and
other issues, the election marked a shift in the cycles of political commitment. The shift created a rhetorical context that constrained presidential
discourse in unique ways. Ultimately, Bush's refusal to become the "agent
of change" cost him the election, whereas Clinton embraced the "change"
terminology that was appropriate to the shift in political commitments.
Holloway argues that the main issue of the campaign was the relationship
between the American people, their government, and their president.
Despite Bush's earlier popularity, his status quo rhetoric failed to meet the
rhetorical demands of the election. The central terms of the campaign,
Bush's "trust" and Clinton's "covenant," represent very different views of
government. "Covenant" implies a solemn agreement or contract between
two parties. "Trust" implies that one defers to another, mostly out of faith.
In 1992, the American people wanted a partnership with government to
address social and economic problems. A candidate's ability to give voice
to public hopes and desires is essential to political and electoral success.

In Chapter 7, Alan Louden challenges the prevailing academic
assumption—that because of the media circus associated with presidential
campaign coverage, it is nearly impossible for voters to reach "rational"

or "informed" electoral decisions. By using candidate image as the organizing construct, Louden argues that candidates and citizens negotiate and mutually participate in image construction and evaluation. Voters use interactive cues in appraising candidate character. Voters are "rational" by attending to candidate behavior and actions (including issues) as evidence of character, which reflects voter values and perceptions of candidate reliability. In 1992, candidates learned the art of utilizing free media and extended formats rather than being limited to a few seconds on the evening news. Thus, the candidates had greater opportunities to "interact" with voters in less formal settings. The issue is not evaluating past performances to predict future behavior, but how someone with a certain character would act as president. How candidate images emerged from the 1992 presidential campaign provides a study of contrast and irony.

In Chapter 8, Montague Kern and Robert Wicks explore the changing roles of network and local television news in presidential and statewide campaigns. Since 1988, the public, scholars, and even journalists have called for changes in covering campaigns. Networks were determined to focus more on issues, to provide greater context for issue discussion, to provide longer candidate "sound bites," and to provide more analyses of political ads and debates. The candidates, however, sought alternative ways to reach voters. The result was a decline in the role of journalists and a greater number of more entertainment-oriented forms of political expression. Increasing use of satellite technologies also heightened the importance of local news. Kern and Wicks describe the emergence of a "new mass media election": the coverage is more candidate-driven, relying on "sound bite" journalism and emotional political advertising. By polling and interviewing local news directors, the authors found that a significant number of news directors focused their coverage not just on campaign strategy and effectiveness but also on accuracy and underlying symbolic meanings of ads.

In Chapter 9, Dan Nimmo examines the impact and importance of another significant development of the 1992 presidential campaign, the "electronic town hall" meetings with voters. In his analysis, Nimmo looks at the uses, functions, and variations of the "televised interactive format" and whether or not the format resulted in "genuine" deliberation between candidates and citizens. He speculates about the future of electronic town hall meetings in American elections. Ultimately, Nimmo argues that the electronic town hall meetings of 1992 served the candidates well, especially Clinton, and generally reduced the boredom of more familiar and standard campaign tactics of the past. However, it was certainly a way for candidates to avoid difficult questions and play to the emotions of the audience and the melodrama of entertainment television. Nimmo also questions the value of the format in terms of audience education and the enhancement of "direct democracy."

In Chapter 10, Janette Kenner Muir reviews the role and importance of C-SPAN in the presidential campaign. It was during this election that the small Cable-Satellite Public Affairs Network came into its own. Muir provides an overview of the network and an analysis of the network's coverage of the campaign. With over 1,200 hours of coverage, Muir identifies three major benefits from C-SPAN's election focus. First, the network provides a unique perspective of the campaign by covering behind-the-scene activities or the "backstage" of daily campaigning. Second, through extended periods of viewer call-in programming, citizens get to question and interact with key players and experts of the campaign directly. Finally, because of C-SPAN's unique approach to covering events, it provides a more direct sense of viewer involvement and engagement in the campaign process. Candidates have not yet figured out how to best "use" or "manage" C-SPAN, so the challenge is how to keep the network free from excessive commercial demands and candidate manipulation.

Presidential campaigns communicate and influence, reinforce and convert, motivate as well as educate. Bruce Gronbeck (1984) argues that campaigns

get leaders elected, yes, but ultimately, they also tell us who we as a people are, where we have been and where we are going; in their size and duration they separate our culture from all others, teach us about political life, set our individual and collective priorities, entertain us, and provide bases for social interaction. (496)

Presidential campaigns are our national conversations. In 1992 the national conversation was intense and inclusive. After thirty years of voter alienation, millions of citizens finally entered the national dialog. However, still too many millions remain silent. We must remember that *more* communication does not mean *better* communication. More technology does not mean more *effective* communication. Perhaps by better understanding the role and process of communication in presidential campaigns, we may somehow improve the quality of our national conversations.

REFERENCES

Barber, James David. 1980. *The Pulse of Politics.* New York: W. W. Norton.

Gronbeck, Bruce. 1984. "Functional and Dramaturgical Theories of Presidential Campaigns." *Presidential Studies Quarterly* 14: 487–98.

Acknowledgments

Editing a book is risky business. Working with academics can be more difficult and challenging than herding cats. Luckily for me, the contributors made editing this project a most enjoyable and rewarding endeavor. Over the years I have learned from their analyses, discussions, and insights. It is a privilege to work with such outstanding colleagues. I appreciate their participation in this volume and their wonderful, insightful contributions.

I also want to thank my colleagues in the Department of Communication Studies at Virginia Polytechnic Institute and State University. I am most thankful for their support and encouragement to pursue projects of interest. In many ways they protect me from the bureaucratic abyss, sea of paper, and administrative minutiae of academic life. With this group, one can easily maintain a sense of humor and perspective.

In the end, of course, family members and close friends sustain us, encourage us, and provide a sense of belonging and security that allows the mental freedom to think, reflect, and write. They provide life beyond academe. Their support comes not from evaluation but from the heart. They understand that such projects are essential to my very being. "You know."

The 1992
Presidential
Campaign

1

A Communication Model of Presidential Campaigns: A 1992 Overview

Robert E. Denton, Jr., and Mary E. Stuckey

With the rise of the "public presidency" (Kernell, 1986) and the new style of election campaigns, public communication has become an increasingly important element in our understanding of the American presidency. Judith Trent and Robert Friedenberg (1991) assert that political campaigns are essentially campaigns of communication (12). Likewise, candidate communication helps to define the aim of the campaign (Kessel, 1988) and is increasingly directed at voters, not at other public officials or party elites (Polsby and Wildavsky, 1980).

In 1980, Sidney Blumenthal argued that one result of the new technology in the age of information is the "permanent campaign." This is a new kind of politics in which "issues, polls, and media are not neatly separate categories. They are unified by a strategic imperative. . . . the elements of the permanent campaign are not tangential to politics: they are the political process itself" (10). With the decline of party structure, discipline, and workers, television commercials and media appearances serve to mobilize voters and govern the nation once the election is over. Although the permanent campaign is recognizable and a dominant aspect of presidential politics, Blumenthal contends that the "permanent campaign will permeate politics down to the most remote legislative district as politicians feel the need to retain consultants to give them the advantage" (26).

Despite these changes and the increased importance of communication in the presidential election process, neither political scientists nor communication scholars have attempted to generate theories concerning the precise role of communication variables in presidential elections. The working model presented here is an attempt to formulate such a theory from a communication perspective. From this perspective, campaigns are exercises in the creation, re-creation, and transmission of "significant symbols." Communication activities are thus the vehicles for action. We need to locate, isolate, analyze, and describe the communication variables in the presidential campaign process.

The model presented here is only a beginning. It is not intended to serve as the final and definitive stage of the theory-building process, but as the necessary first step of that process. Our goal is to identify the important elements that constitute the model, not to provide the definitive formulation of such a model. Two basic assumptions direct this research. First, there are several essential elements of the campaign that are common to all candidates and that cut across all phases of a campaign. Second, these common elements differ dramatically in terms of rhetorical functions and impact across the phases of campaigns. Thus, although the elements remain the same, the roles they play and their impact upon strategy and outcome differ over time.

The model explores the interaction of six key elements over the four stages of a presidential campaign. Both campaigns and communication, more broadly understood, are *processes* rather than discrete events. Through this model we will examine the dynamic nature of communication within the evolving structure of a presidential campaign.

THE KEYS TO A PRESIDENTIAL CAMPAIGN

In our analysis of presidential campaigns, we found six elements that are crucial to understanding the presidential campaign process. These elements are (1) the strategic environment, (2) organization, (3) finance, (4) public opinion polls, (5) candidate image, and (6) media. Each of these functions independently as well as interactively. That is, they have an independent effect upon the rhetorical strategies and tactics of the candidates—as well as affecting one another and thus indirectly affecting those rhetorical strategies and tactics.

1. The Strategic Environment

The term "strategic environment" was coined by Nelson Polsby and Aaron Wildavsky in their seminal work, *Presidential Elections* (1980). For Polsby and Wildavsky, the strategic environment includes voters, interest groups, political parties, finances, control over information, television, and the issue of incumbency. Because our purposes are somewhat different from theirs, we define the strategic environment as the broad context within which the electoral process is played out. This context varies depending on the electoral phase. There are two general areas of concern: political and social (Wayne, 1992, 56–84). Political concerns include party identification, party nomination rules, number of likely opponents, incumbency, voter behavior, and attitudes. For example, elements of voter behavior such as turnout, group ties, and partisanship will have very different strategic implications during the primary versus the general election phase of a campaign. Social concerns include dominant social issues, issues "created" by candidates, and unforeseen or unexpected events. Some social issues that may dominate a campaign include the economy, crime, or abortion. Of course, candidates hope to "own" issues, or at least have unique positions on issues. While the broad issue of family values was salient in the presidential campaign of 1988, it was markedly less important in 1992, when the economy became the dominant issue.

Electoral laws are also important as broad determinants of candidate behavior. They are a factor in the preprimary period, as candidates decide which races to enter and which to avoid; getting on the ballot may require an organization strong enough to obtain requisite signatures and may require an early decision. In the primary period, electoral laws govern the allocation of delegates to state and national conventions. The allocation procedure is not neutral and will inevitably favor some candidates, or some types of candidacies, over others. Finally, in the general election, the electoral college is a crucial determinant of candidate strategy. All candidates naturally want the largest total vote they can amass, but because of the peculiar arithmetic required by the electoral college, candidates are inclined to spend less time in "safe" states or states they have given up for lost; instead, they concentrate their efforts on close state races or those where they are likely to succeed.

A candidate's rhetorical strategies will also be affected by the partisan structure of the race. This structure determines the strategy to the degree that it requires the candidate to appear centrist, right-wing, or left-wing. The structure during the preprimary and primary is clearly different from that of the general election. This is because the relevant electorate is also different. Similarly, the volatility and expected turnout will affect candidate strategy, since candidates design appeals to those most likely to vote. In a very real sense, support only matters to the extent that it can be measured in the voting booth.

Elections do not occur in a vacuum. Citizens bring their histories, beliefs, attitudes, and values to the voting booth. The social and political contexts of elections greatly influence strategic considerations.

2. Organization

In any campaign effort, candidate organization is vital. At the presidential level, campaign organizations are large, specialized, and complex. At a minimum, most campaigns have a director who coordinates all activities and acts as liaison among the candidate, the organization, and the party; a campaign manager who oversees the day-to-day activities; division chiefs for specialized tasks such as polling, media, issues, fund-raising; and geographic coordinators that encompass regional territories down to congressional district levels with states (Wayne, 1992, 173–80). From a macro-perspective, the organization plans, develops, and implements campaign strategies and tactics.

This organization is both internal and external. Internally, the organizations consist of all the advisors and strategists: those people who plan the strategy, coordinate the effort, and manage the overall campaign. According to political scientist John Kessel (1988), this internal organization can be broken up into two specific groups: the core group and the strategy group.

The core group consists of the candidate's own confidants, persons he has known well or worked closely with for some years. . . . The strategy group is made up of those persons who are making the basic decisions about the campaign. Its membership is quite restricted, and should not be confused with a publicly announced "strategy committee." (88)

The majority—and some would argue the most critical—members of a campaign staff are the paid political consultants (Chagall, 1981). Political consultants have come to dominate the presidential election scene, becoming, in the process, political actors of some note themselves. Consultants are important in their own right as well because of their input on other strategic considerations. Larry Sabato (1981) noted that

The consultants successfully recruited by a candidate have become status symbols. . . . Through the consultant he is purchasing acceptance from other politicians, insurance that his campaign will be taken seriously, and a favorable mention by journalists. He is also buying association with a consultant's past clientele, particularly the winners. He is securing access to the web of relationships that a consultant and his firm have developed. Finally, he is accepting the public services of a surrogate. (20)

Campaign professionals and consultants include pollsters, media consultants, direct-mail experts, lawyers, accountants, and marketers, to name only a few. Although consultants occupy the role that used to belong to the party bosses, they play that role very differently. They lack the party boss's loyalty to a larger institution, the boss's personal and individual connections to the electorate, and, most seriously, "The party boss might tell a candidate what to do, but he does not instruct him who to be" (Blumenthal, 1980, 4). The consultant, as we will see later, does.

The external candidate organization is also very important, although it is becoming less essential as the mass media increasingly dominates the electoral scene. Such organization is more important in some locations than others. The rule of thumb is that the larger, more urban, more heterogeneous the state, the more likely it is that candidates will rely on media appeals more heavily than the precinct workers of old.

3. Finance

Along with organization, campaign finance is a critical element. It is a long-standing maxim that money is the lifeblood of politics: the organization and other campaign accoutrements have to be paid for—"primary success, poll standing, and the ability to raise money are all interrelated" (Asher, 1980, 254). Financial concerns involve more than just raising funds. There are other considerations: where to obtain funds, how to obtain funds, how to allocate funds, and how to ensure compliance with complex legal requirements of political fund-raising. Such concerns have strategic and tactical implications. While one cannot simply assume that the candidate with the most money wins, "money contributes to success, but potential success also attracts money" (Wayne, 1992, 51). Money is most critical early in a campaign and for those less known to the general public. Edward Walsh (1992) has argued that "the more seed money, the better the harvest" (50). Early money is needed for candidates to hire consultants, conduct polls, and travel.

New regulations governing campaign finance ensure that raising money is increasingly problematic and time-consuming (DiClerico and Uslaner, 1984, 87–98; Edwards and Wayne, 1990, 30–32). Instead of relying on "fat cats" or political parties for money, candidates are turning ever more frequently to professional fund-raisers (Kessel, 1988, 147) and the technology of direct mail (Sabato, 1981, 224). These have virtually replaced large individual contributions with small, grass-roots contributors and political action committees.

No one can discuss modern campaign finance without including a discussion of political action committees (PACs). Because PACs can raise and disburse large amounts of money, it is hard for candidates to ignore them completely. Yet relying heavily on PAC money can reduce a candidate's strategic and rhetorical options, and the candidate risks being identified, as Walter Mondale was in 1984, as the "candidate of special interests."

4. Public Opinion Polls

Political public opinion polls have become an essential element of both campaign management and news coverage. Technology has increased the types, frequency, and sophistication of opinion polls. There are numerous data-collection techniques: phone surveys, door-to-door surveys, mail surveys, dial-900 surveys, and focus groups, to name a few (Selnow, 1991, 177).

From a campaign perspective, polls provide needed information about voters: who they are, what they think, how they feel, and how they will behave in the voting booth. In addition to providing information on voters, they provide valuable feedback to the campaign that allows for message adjustments and refinements. During the course of a campaign, the types of polls include (among others) benchmark, follow-up, panel surveys, tracking, and basic data analyses (Selnow, 1991, 177–78).

An increasing percentage of campaign funds go to the support of polls and pollsters. A candidate's standing in the polls is a crucial determinant of that candidate's ability to raise money (Asher, 1980, 254). Polls have several uses: they allow candidates to identify constituencies and issues, to tailor their image accordingly, to target their opponents' weak spots, and to influence media strategy (Caddell and Wirthlin, 1981, 2–12, 63–64; Edwards and Wayne, 1990, 34).

According to Larry Sabato (1981), one visible result of the importance of polls to campaigning is that

the onset of polling in an election campaign, like the campaign itself, has been moved steadily forward on the calendar. In past years, the benchmark survey for a campaign was usually scheduled in the spring of an election year, but now it is done in the prior autumn or even summer or spring of the previous year. (77)

The earlier a candidate begins, the more money must be invested, so the more important fund-raising becomes. The polls themselves are important; a solid standing early in those polls can be vital to getting a campaign off the ground.

In addition to candidate-sponsored polls, there has been an incredible growth of media public opinion polls. In the 1972 presidential campaign, there were only three media polls conducted. By 1988 the number had risen to 259. A 1990 Roper Center Survey revealed that 82 percent of large circulation newspapers and 56 percent of television stations were involved in news polling (Ladd and Benson, 1992, 22).

Polls have a dramatic impact on election coverage. According to Diana Owen (1991), the reporting of poll results "represent news manufactured by journalists themselves through the production of statistical data that can be reported as fact. News stories that contain polls gain a heightened aura of authenticity by assigning a numerical figure to a political trend" (91). Polls influence how candidates are covered, how much airtime they will receive, which reporter will be assigned to cover them, and how the candidate's campaign will be portrayed (Ratzan, 1989).

Beyond organizational strategic considerations, the impact of polls in campaigns is both direct and indirect. Polls influence voters, politicians, political elites, opinion leaders, and members of the media (Traugott, 1992, 126–46). For example, media polls influence candidate image, status, momentum, funding opportunities, candidate performance expectations, and volunteer help. From a voter perspective, polls may influence interest and support in a candidate and motivate voters to seek out additional candidate information. Polls may also influence voter turnout.

5. Candidate Image

For the purposes of this chapter, image is more than public perception of a candidate. As Stephen Wayne (1992) observed, "it is difficult to separate a candidate's image from the events of the real world" (207). Image includes a candidate's personal traits, job performance, and issue positions. Every American can cite a list of desirable traits that make a "good" president. Candidates compete to demonstrate that they meet public expectations of presidential performance.

A key factor in determining a candidate's standing in the polls is image, and designing a viable image is the chief and most controversial task of the political consultant. However, "Image-making, no matter how manipulative, doesn't replace reality; it becomes part of it. Images are not unreal simply because they are manufactured" (Blumenthal, 1980, 5).

There is at least some evidence that "perceptual defenses are lower during the primaries than in the general election, and hence images of the candidates formed during the primary season, especially early on, are more likely to be stimulus-determined" (Asher, 1980, 250). This means that the earlier the candidates begin to communicate an image, the more control they—and their organization—have over the image-building process. Obviously, however, this process does not occur in a vacuum, no matter how early the candidate begins, especially on the presidential level. Most presidential contenders have been in public life, and in the public eye, for many years. They cannot create new images out of whole cloth, but must design images that are appropriate for both a presidential bid and their public past.

Increasingly, character is becoming an important part of candidate image, as discovered by candidates as diverse as Robert Dole, Gary Hart, and Joseph Biden in 1988 and Bill Clinton in 1992 (Lichter et al., 1988, 7). The candidates' private lives are no longer considered sacrosanct by the media, and posing with the spouse, kids, and family dog no longer constitutes sufficient evidence of moral integrity. It is not enough to design a presidential image and hope for the best; the candidate must also be careful not to undermine that image through inappropriate or inconsistent behavior.

Once an image has been designed, it must be communicated. The mass media is one way of accomplishing this communication. As Larry Sabato (1981) said, this can be done in a variety of ways:

Commercials can be used to establish name identification and draw attention to a candidate, increasing his visibility. The candidate's personal image can be developed, evoking certain feelings about him based on selected personality characteristics. . . . Advertisements can link the candidate directly with his party or other groups, winning support for his cause through association. . . . Finally, campaign commercials can be used to attack opponents. (121)

But the mass media is not the only means through which a candidate communicates image. In fact, other forms of communication are important in preparing voters for television advertising, familiarizing them with campaign themes, and providing an element of fun. Bumper stickers, placards, and other campaign toys are useful campaign aids and should not be overlooked (Sabato, 1981, 192).

Candidate image is important, if not to create, at least to control through paid media, news coverage, campaign events, speeches, and debates. Most Americans do not cast their vote based on a single issue; Americans are more inclined to cast their vote based on the individual candidate.

6. Media

Presidential campaigns are essentially mass media campaigns. In fact, Diana Owen (1991) has argued that "the mass media are playing an increasingly pervasive and visible role in the American presidential election process" (xv). According to Jack Germond and Jules Witcover (1988), the media are becoming increasingly seen as one of, if not *the*, most important feature of a presidential election (54). So much so, in fact, that journalists have become "an alternative electorate" (Arterton, 1978, 4). As the influence of political parties decreases, and as the size of the potential electorate increases, campaign organizations increasingly rely on "durable communication structures in order to communicate with the electorate" (Arterton, 1978, 6). Without being too deterministic, at the very least the mass media provide substantial "political and candidate" information that works in conjunction with preexisting public political orientations that influence candidate images and issues (Owen, 1991, 173).

The mass media have caused both quantitative and qualitative changes in presidential elections (Denton, 1988, 35). Daily news coverage of the campaign, debates, political ads, and pseudo events produce more campaign messages than ever before. From a qualitative standpoint, the media demands more sophisticated techniques of presentation, message creation, and targeting.

Media coverage can make or break a candidacy, as candidate organizations are painfully aware. Although few if any candidacies are planned solely around media strategies, all candidate organizations plan with a view toward media interpretations of events. These interpretations are most important during the early stages of a campaign, when the standards of victory are less clear (as in multicandidate primary races) and the level of information is low (Asher, 1980, 252). As the level of information increases and as the structure of competition simplifies, making decisions easier, the role of the media as interpreter correspondingly diminishes.

Although the media's interpreter role diminishes, powerful roles are still played by the media throughout the election. These roles include agenda setting and defining candidate images. Much of their ability to perform these roles depends on access to the candidate, and campaigns can, within limits, control coverage by controlling access (Edwards and Wayne, 1990, 34–38). In addition, candidate organizations use techniques such as staged events in their effort to control and dominate the news.

Although candidates and elected officials are frequently criticized for "news management," it is equally true that candidates and elected officials who *fail to manage the news* are not likely to be candidates or elected officials very long. A presidential candidate, in particular, must communicate a strongly focused image to maintain an organization, raise needed funds, and gain success both in the polls and at the polls. No candidate can afford to rely on the media to safeguard his image; successful news management is essential to a successful campaign.

In summary, there are six elements that are essential to all phases of every presidential campaign: the strategic environment or context; the organization, both internal and external; finance and fund-raising; public opinion polls; candidate image; and finally, the mass media. Although each is important in its own right, their role and functions are affected by and affect one another. This dynamic process is played out over time in a roughly predictable fashion.

A COMMUNICATION MODEL OF PRESIDENTIAL CAMPAIGNS

Scholars have identified various stages or phases of presidential campaigns. For example, John Kessel divides prenomination politics into four phases: early days, initial contests, mist clearing, and the convention (1988, 7–12). Trent and Friedenberg (1991, 17–50) identify the stages as preprimary, primary, convention, and general election. They argue that various communication functions differ across the stages of a campaign. Likewise, the essential elements of a campaign differ in rhetorical functions and impact across campaign stages. So although the elements remain the same, the roles they play and their impact on strategy and outcome differ over time.

Although all the various elements are interactive and interdependent during each stage of a campaign, some are more "important" or dominant. The dominant elements for each campaign phase are essential not only in defining the strategy but also in influencing the other elements. (Note: In Figures 1.1 through 1.4, "issues" are considered to be part of candidate "image." The direction of the arrows indicates "pressure" or "initiative" of impact upon the other elements.)

The Preprimary Phase

During the preprimary phase, candidates must achieve visibility, establish credibility or "fitness," and begin to build a viable organization (Trent and Friedenberg, 1991). According to Judith Trent (1978; Trent and Friedenberg, 1991), this period is important because the public begins to establish expectations of the candidates, the important issues begin to emerge, and the front-runners begin to be determined. All of these stress beginnings—images are being framed, altered, and reframed; much discussion centers on who will or will not be running; and the debate is characterized by uncertainty.

The dominant elements of this stage of the campaign are finance, polls, and organization (see Figure 1.1). Fund-raising and organizational development are critical and time-consuming at this point of the campaign. Key donors provide the necessary funding to identify early staff members and to pay for modest travel. Potential large-sum contributors are personally contacted, consulted, and courted. The campaign identifies and begins "to work" sympathetic or supportive political action committees to obtain immediate money needed and build the structure for future fund-raising efforts.

From an organizational perspective, state coordinators and congressional district supporters are identified. A campaign organization is needed in every state. Nomination politics affect the duties and behind-

Figure 1.1
Preprimary Campaign Phase

Dominant Elements

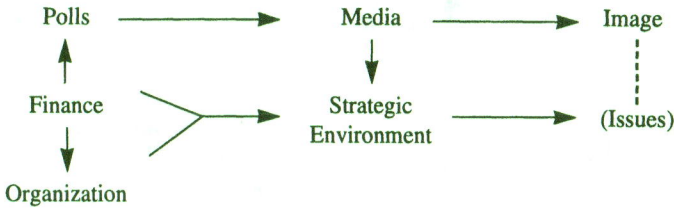

Polls ⟶	Media ⟶	Image
↑	↓	⋮
Finance ⟶	Strategic Environment ⟶	(Issues)
↓		
Organization		

the-scene activities of grass-roots supporters. Candidates must "wheel and deal" with party bosses. Although the actual number of supporters may be low, the structure must be established at this phase of the campaign. Campaigns need a small but highly skilled and professional staff. By the primary season, it's too late to hire important, high-level staff members.

Political opinion polls are always critical to candidates, but they serve a dual function in the preprimary period. Straw polls provide legitimacy for the candidacy to the media as well as to potential key donors. For the media, early polls create candidate performance expectations, front-runner status, and initial candidate image and issue positions. Early campaign polls aid candidates in surveying issues and developing positions.

The strategic environment is characterized by a lack of formal rules, emphasis on many candidates, and talk of various factions needing appeasement within the political parties. This lack of a clear context means that the media have an important role: the media, or "Great Mentioner," provide predictions of candidate viability and/or potential weaknesses. The importance of labels cannot be underestimated. Few candidates have well-defined images in the preprimary period. They are in the process of defining and shaping their image portrayal.

Recently, Robert Savage identified five areas essential for the creation and maintenance of a "presidential" image (1986, 5–9). The task in the preprimary period focuses on emerging and announcing the candidacy. There is always the risk of entering the race too soon or too late. In the former case, public apathy may result; in the latter case, there may be too little time to raise funds and generate adequate support.

The collective media set the agenda for the preprimary period and may help or hurt a candidate's early image. The reputation of a candidate will dictate the frequency, slant, and tone of coverage.

In creating a rhetorical vision, the candidate must develop and articulate the campaign theme. This theme extends beyond specific issues and allows the candidate to share his or her vision of the American Dream. The rhetorical agenda, which is part of the rhetorical vision, consists of key issues that the candidate will emphasize during the campaign. These issues are based on poll results, and in the early campaign they are localized to maximize impact.

Of course, unexpected events outside the campaign may suddenly affect the strategic environment. National or international events may dominate the headlines and force candidates to respond.

Campaign rituals during this period include fund-raising, speaking engagements, and countless parties and dinners. These events create media attention, introduce the candidate to the voters, build group support, and help the candidate to sharpen skills for the primary period that follows.

Finally, perhaps the most difficult element of building candidate image in the preprimary phase is the need to demonstrate that the candidate is "presidential timber." It is essential that the candidate be perceived as a "statesman." Candidates attempt to convey credibility by exhibiting knowledge and expertise as well as by taking trips abroad or introducing legislation. Image building in the preprimary period is a task of creation, definition, and demonstration rather than reinforcement or expansion. The media play a major role in the definition of early candidate image.

The keys to the preprimary period are finance, organization, and both candidate and public opinion polls. Strength in these areas will propel the candidate into the next phase—the primary campaign.0

The Primary Phase

This phase of the presidential election process has changed the most over time. Until the twentieth century, primaries were not a part of the presidential campaign. By 1916, twenty-six states were holding primaries as part of the presidential election process. However, it was not until the 1970s and 1980s that primaries played an important role in the nomination process. Before 1968, party bosses controlled delegate selection. Candidates were forced to "lobby" party leaders to win the nomination. Winning primaries was not necessary, and entering them was often a sign of weakness rather than strength. Delegate selection was not necessarily connected to electoral strength and was not representative of the overall population (Keeter and Zukin, 1983, 6). Women and minorities in particular were largely excluded from the process.

Network televised news coverage of the Vietnam War and the civil rights demonstrations in 1968 brought about a new "informed" public.

Everyone saw the same news. Candidates soon realized that they could reach the public via the network news. The nomination system became nationalized (Keeter and Zukin, 1983, 7). Party leaders were soon seen as out of touch with their constituency and were less able to influence that constituency's behavior. The lack of representativeness in the nomination process and the new "informed" public led the Democratic party to reform its delegate selection process.

In 1971 the McGovern/Fraser Commission of the Democratic party implemented many changes in delegate selection. There were two important changes: first, a new quota system for delegate selection required a certain percentage of minorities, women, and young people; and second, uniform rules were published for all delegate selection (Keeter and Zukin, 1983, 8). These changes attempted to take away the power of party bosses and make the process more representative. Primaries were the easiest way for states to comply with the new rules.

In 1976, the Democrats implemented a percentage rule calling for the elimination of "winner-take-all" primaries. Candidates who received some percentage of the vote would earn a proportional number of delegates to the national convention. This rule further stressed the importance of running in the primaries and caucuses. "By 1976 the nominating system was based almost entirely on elections, with most of the convention delegates selected in primaries and bound by those results" (Keeter and Zukin, 1983, 9).

As the Democrats made their reforms, the Republicans were swept into the new system. Most of the Democratic election reforms were passed into law, which required Republican compliance as well. All these changes during the early 1970s helped to create and magnify the importance of primary and caucus elections as a means of determining delegate selection. Candidates could no longer win the nomination, as John F. Kennedy or Hubert Humphrey had done. Primaries and caucuses were the only way to win a nomination.

These changes have not occurred without controversy. Delegate selection rules are not neutral, and there is evidence that they are "biased against lesser-known minority candidates" (Edwards and Wayne, 1990, 28). The strategic environment is conditioned by these rules and how they affect candidate image and fund-raising efforts.

The dominant elements of this phase of the campaign are media, the strategic environment, and campaign organization (see Figure 1.2). The key tasks a candidate faces during the primary include the identification of a solid vote, the persuasion of the uncommitted vote, and maintenance of preferred image across parties.

Figure 1.2
Primary Campaign Phase

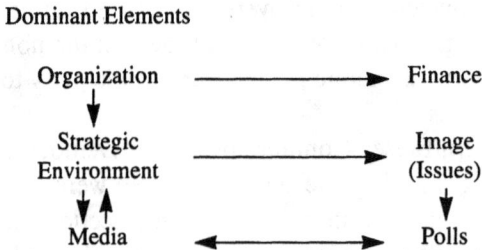

Dominant Elements

Organization ──────────▶ Finance
 │
 ▼
Strategic ──────────▶ Image
Environment   (Issues)
 ▼▲   ▼
Media ◀──────────▶ Polls

Media become the gatekeepers of access to the public as well as the judge and jury of electoral performance. Campaigns are simplified, dichotomies are created, winners and losers are labeled. As a result, front-runners emerge more quickly from media analyses and labels than from actual votes. Media expectations often determine the magnitude of candidate success or failure.

Media reports can greatly affect poll results, which in turn affect future primary elections and caucuses. Poll results justify media labels and become the mainstay of most primary period coverage. Michael Traugott (1992) argued that polls have the greatest influence during this phase of the campaign (131). Polls are used by the public to assess candidate viability and electability. They can also enhance candidate name recognition and even provide momentum for candidacies. From the candidate perspective, targeted media such as radio and direct mail are particularly valuable, since the relevant electorate is small and it is relatively easy to tailor candidate appeals directly to them.

A strong organization is vital to primary success. The strategy team must decide which contests to enter and develop an appropriate strategy for each. These strategies must be designed specifically for each state or region; yet because of the nationalization of the election process, they must also be consistent across states and regions. A sound strategy will reinforce specific images in every contest, help avoid direct contradictions, and focus on relatively few themes. The result is often "mush" that sounds grand—potentially effective on television, but relatively free of policy content.

During the primary, specific state campaigns require early money. Availability of funds will dictate primary strategies. In many ways beyond advertising and day-to-day operations, finance has less impact on candidate image. The media have greater influence in determining elements such as win-ability and amount of news coverage.

External organization is also central, for these are the people who wear the buttons, listen to the speeches, place the yard signs, and carry the placards. They are instrumental in getting out the vote—which is critical in a primary where voter turnout is low.

The strategic environment is fully energized at this point. In a contested nomination, candidate organizations must be ready to respond to new issues, charges, or allegations. The contest feeds the media, which affects candidate polling numbers, issue positions, and candidate image. In many ways, candidates are more concerned with image, leadership, and personality qualities than issues—especially in terms of media coverage.

Thus, the strategic environment and the media influence the other elements, whereas the organization's operational support should be one of routine implementation.

The Convention Phase

Today, political nominating conventions are simply media events. They no longer serve as decision makers but as ratifiers of the party's nominees. Larry David Smith and Dan Nimmo (1991) characterized conventions as "a week-long hyped, publicized, televised spectacle that recognizes politics for what it is as currently practiced. . . . Teleconventions . . . showcase what is normally a concealed side of the contemporary conciliation of interests" (218).

But conventions do provide drama and follow a pattern (Smith and Nimmo, 1991). First, there is some conflict over either the nomination or various platform positions. Second, party leaders generate compromise among the various factions. Then comes the big celebration with the focus on the candidate and the pending campaign. Finally, the media passes judgment and begins forecasting the race.

Conventions serve several functions (Trent and Friedenberg, 1991, 41–45). They provide legitimation of the nomination process and the party's nominees. They also provide an opportunity for the party to show unity and showcase party principles. Finally, conventions provide the opportunity for candidates to share their social agenda and issue positions. Thus, party conventions are highly orchestrated events resulting from the "process of give-and-take among party members, the news media, and various governmental institutions" (Smith and Nimmo, 1991, xiv–xv).

The dominant elements of the convention phase of the campaign are organization and media (see Figure 1.3). The candidate's campaign organization plans the convention. Maximum control of all events is the operative goal of convention management. The length and tone of media coverage become strategic concerns. Prime time becomes the place for

Figure 1.3
Convention Phase

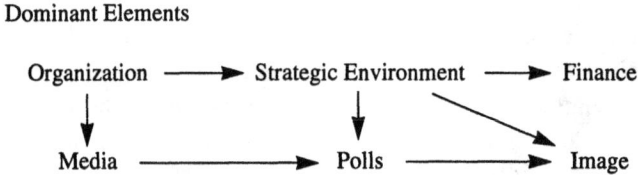

Dominant Elements

Organization ⟶ Strategic Environment ⟶ Finance

Media ⟶ Polls ⟶ Image

noted speakers, rallies, and events to ensure a large audience and positive reception of party message. Media judgment and interpretation influence tracking polls and projections of nominee viability long after the convention. The nominee's organization attempts to maximize the traditional "convention lift" in polls and positive reporting, and thereby frame the political agenda and environment for the fall campaign. A successful convention will lead to increased fund-raising support. By this time, candidate image and issue positions are set in the public's mind. In fact, many voters have already made up their mind on who they will support. Entering the final phase of the campaign generates a drastic shift in the elements.

The General Election Phase

This is the shortest and most intense phase of the entire election cycle. The political parties are mobilized, the electorate is finally interested or becoming so, and the context is national rather than state or regional.

In this final phase of presidential campaigns, the dominant elements are strategic environment, media, and organization (see Figure 1.4). The strategic environment is critical to all decision making. It is dominated by the peculiar calculus of the electoral college. Candidates write off some states as irretrievable, minimize the attention given to others, and focus on building the largest coalition possible given the requirements of securing 270 electoral votes. Issue positions and image maintenance are also concerns of the strategic environment. If behind in the race, corrective positions and strategies must be developed.

The media reach the voters through paid advertising and news coverage. How campaigns are covered affects public perceptions of the status of the candidates and the race. The coverage and general consensus in reports of "how the race is shaping up" affects the strategic environment and candidate standing in the polls. Above all, there is a sense that time is running out—this is heightened and "reinforced by polls that repeatedly

Figure 1.4
General Election Phase

Dominant Elements

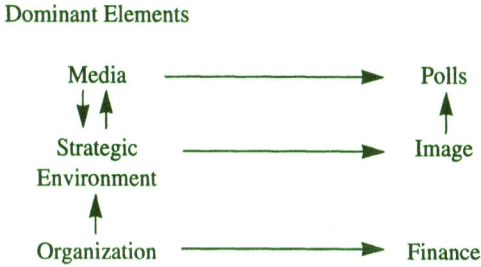

announce the candidates' standings; these serve as reminders that only so many weeks remain until the election" (Kessel, 1988, 81).

Much of the campaign money is earmarked for television. Media usage during the later stages of the campaign is concentrated on reinforcing existing images and motivating the potential electorate.

By the time of the general election phase, candidate images are established. Voters know who the candidates are and what they stand for. Candidates, in Richard Fenno's terms, stress empathy above identification, for voters must be motivated at all costs (1978). Advertisements become more emotional, less issue-based than before.

The organization is running at full speed. Day-to-day operational concerns are primarily event planning and coordination, but finances are also important—when to spend, what to spend on, and where to spend are the big questions, made increasingly difficult as the laws governing spending limits and disclosure become more complex. Candidates increasingly rely on soft money to allow them to save funds for the final days of the campaign, when massive spending can make the difference between victory and defeat (Caddell and Wirthlin, 1981, 8).

In summary, although it is useful to describe and analyze the rhetorical functions of the six elements common to all campaigns within each phase of a campaign, it fails to capture the dynamic aspects of presidential campaigns. A presidential campaign is not separated into tidy phases, each separately and individually packaged. It is a process, and it must be understood as a process.

By using a model we attempt to recognize the dynamic elements of a campaign, but the model also allows for the stable elements to be separately analyzed within the context of each phase. Thus, we can achieve a more solid understanding of both the separate elements that form the process as well as the process as a whole.

THE 1992 PRESIDENTIAL CAMPAIGN: AN OVERVIEW

The model for the 1992 presidential campaign is the focus of subsequent chapters in this volume. Our analysis in this chapter provides more of an overview of the campaign, and a brief discussion of the phases will illustrate the major considerations and influences of the elements within each phase.

The Preprimary Phase

Although 1992 was a unique preprimary season for the Democrats in many ways, the elements of organization, fund-raising, and public opinion polls were crucial for the candidates in gaining viability to enter and to survive the primary season. (In the next chapter, Judith Trent provides a detailed analysis of the early campaign period.)

Since the 1980s, there has been a distinct pattern: the acknowledged front-runner at the beginning of the primary season would most likely be the candidate nominated at the convention. This certainly was the case for all incumbents, even though Carter had a somewhat more difficult renomination than Reagan or Bush. According to Ross Baker, in 1992 if one was "to consult the list of hopefuls in January, look for the names mentioned most commonly by experts as the front-runners, and then in July tally the delegate votes, you would have found George Bush and Bill Clinton at the top of both lists" (1993, 40).

The *Hotline* (1992, vol. 5, no. 73), a daily political news summary, identifies "six rules of front-runner status" (17). Front-runners are the focus of summary news stories. They get preferred positioning, listing, and pictures in news stories; get mentioned when only one of the candidates gets mentioned; get attacked regularly in news stories; get examined more closely and in greater detail in stories; and benefit from exclusive analyses of how they obtained the front-runner status. By mid-January, Bill Clinton met all six "rules" of front-runner status and had the best organization and the most money compared to the other Democratic opponents.

The unique preprimary phase of the 1992 presidential campaign was cut short by the Persian Gulf War, which provided not only the most important event of the Bush presidency but what many analysts thought would virtually guarantee his renomination and easy reelection. Indeed, in the afterglow of the war Bush enjoyed some of the highest approval ratings of any president. In March 1991, Bush topped 86 percent (Baker,

1993, 41–42). He had presided over the end of the Cold War and won a major military victory.

Another notable element of this period in terms of the Democrats were the number of "leftovers" from the 1988 presidential contest who declined to enter the 1992 race. Late announcements in general and the absence of many well-known Democrats were directly related to the Persian Gulf War. Bush simply seemed unbeatable. One by one, presumed front-runners for the Democrats declined to enter the race: Gary Hart, Jesse Jackson, Albert Gore, Joseph Biden, Richard Gephardt, Bruce Babbitt, Lloyd Bentsen, and Bill Bradley. Throughout the summer of 1991 there were daily stories and updates on Democratic candidates deciding to run or not to run. Very early in the year, Lloyd Bentsen, the vice-presidential nominee in 1988, was the most frequently mentioned choice among party activists and leaders. The situation was so bad that in late August 1991, former vice-president and the party's 1984 presidential nominee Walter Mondale wrote in an editorial for the *New York Times* that "when many of our best leaders decline to run, the Democrats lose credibility as a national party. . . . we should be embarrassed by our own shortage of candidates. The public is cheated—and our nation is weaker" (*Hotline,* August 28, 1991, vol. 4, no. 231: 8).

Another element of the strategic environment, though less important at the time, was the fact that in June 1990, Bush "reluctantly" agreed to a tax increase as part of a budget reduction plan that broke his most resounding pledge of the 1988 campaign: "read my lips—no new taxes!" Reagan loyalists thought Bush had sold out and had retreated from the basic philosophy of Reaganomics. This created opposition within the Republican ranks.

Money allows a candidate to hire a staff to work on issue definition, strategy, and the ability to get the message out to influence early polls and to attract media attention. Although the Democrats started late, their ability to attract funds, staff an organization, and gain media attention played an important role in getting to the primary season.

While the media were focusing on well-known Democrats who were declining to run, the first Democrat to officially announce his candidacy was former U.S. senator Paul Tsongas of Massachusetts. He did this in early March 1991 at the very height of Bush's public popularity. Because of his lack of name recognition, fund-raising and staffing an organization were very difficult for Tsongas. He had to rely on free media to circulate his message.

Senator Tom Harkin of Iowa was the most successful in early fund-raising and campaign organization. Prior to his mid-September 1991 announcement, Harkin launched a direct mail fund-raising campaign that resulted in his qualification for matching public funds. In early September, Jerry Brown sent a letter to 5,000 supporters requesting campaign contributions. Brown promised he would not take more than $100 from any contributor. Campaign finance reform became a centerpiece of his early nomination bid. In August 1991, the announcement that Bob Farmer, former treasurer of the Democratic National Committee, was joining the fund-raising efforts of the Clinton campaign increased the credibility of the Clinton candidacy. The *Washington Times* reported that the hire "sent a signal that the party's big-money contributors saw the governor as one of the few remaining Democratic contenders who can mount a credible national campaign against President Bush" (*Hotline*, August 29, 1991, vol. 4, no. 232: 3).

Fund-raising for incumbents is much easier. Bush did not really begin his efforts until mid-October 1991, when he established his reelection committee. In early November, Bush raised $1 million at a fund-raiser in Houston, Texas. In fact, in less than one week Bush and Quayle raised more than all the Democratic candidates to date with over $2.4 million. The Bush campaign employed eleven workers in a small office in Virginia. There were very important strategic implications to the Bush campaign fund-raising efforts. The campaign wanted to raise as much money as possible before the end of the year in order to avoid competition with state and local fund-raising efforts. In addition, the Bush campaign wanted to take advantage of the late start of the Democratic opponents by raising as much money as possible to lock up the available federal matching dollars—leaving less for the eventual Democratic nominee (*Hotline*, November 1, 1991, vol. 5, no. 34: 4). In fact, by January 1992, Bush had easily qualified for the most federal matching funds—exceeding $3.5 million to Clinton's $1.4 million (*Hotline*, January 3, 1992, vol. 5, no. 67: 3).

Throughout the summer, Bush virtually ignored the pending campaign. In late September 1991, Bush still enjoyed an overall favorable rating of 71 percent (*Hotline*, September 26, 1991, vol. 4, no. 9: 7). Within a matter of weeks, however, Bush's public popularity began to decline, and a majority of citizens (59%) thought he was spending too much time on foreign policy issues and not enough on domestic issues (*Hotline*, October 11, 1991, vol. 5, no. 20).

By mid-November there was serious talk of Pat Buchanan challenging Bush for the nomination. Because of public pressure and the possible challenge for the nomination, members of the White House staff decided to speed up the timetable for assembling Bush's reelection team and organization (*Hotline*, November 20, 1991, vol. 5, no. 46: 8). Bush's problems provided new excitement for the media and resulted in more challenging and negative stories for the White House. In mid-January 1992, *USA*

Today's headline of "Bush Appears Vulnerable" was the first to challenge the assumption of Bush's automatic reelection (*Hotline,* January 13, 1992, vol. 5, no. 73: 17).

It was late January, less than two months before the New Hampshire primary, when Bush finished hiring his initial campaign staff. As the model implies, the early strong poll numbers provided positive media coverage and enhanced fund-raising potential. However, as the poll numbers changed, so did the tone and content of media coverage. The strategic environment changed quickly for George Bush. So quickly, in fact, that he was not ready (from an organizational perspective) to run an active primary campaign, and this lack of organization hurt his New Hampshire primary campaign.

When Buchanan entered the race in December 1991, he had neither organization nor money. He did have, however, a national reputation as a media pundit with some name recognition. Because of his strong verbal challenges to the president, Buchanan enjoyed a great deal of media coverage. His only hope was to run a 90-day campaign to win New Hampshire. A victory in New Hampshire would provide enough momentum to enhance his credibility, his fund-raising efforts, and perhaps attract professionals to join his campaign. In reality it was too late to mount an adequate challenge to President Bush. Buchanan lost virtually all of the preprimary period to build funds, establish a campaign organization, and refine a "presidential" image.

Candidate standing in the polls influences media coverage, candidate image, and strategic environment. All the Democrats except Harkin were trying to be "more conservative" and "mainstream" than past Democratic nominees. Each candidate had to overcome his own "image/media" problem. Tsongas had to prove he was fit to run and govern. Clinton was unknown, too regional, and too conservative. Clinton also knew he would have to face personal questions. Bob Kerrey was too sheepish and lacked clear program alternatives. Harkin was too liberal, too angry, and too "hot" for television. Doug Wilder was too vague, and race dominated his coverage. Before Brown's announcement, a headline in the *Sacramento Bee* asked "Moonbeam for Pres?" The article concluded, "Despite his own assurances that he's grown up, Brown is as flaky as ever. If anything, his attention span seems to have shortened" (*Hotline,* August 26, 1991, vol. 4, no. 229: 6). The "Governor Moonbeam" tag stayed with Brown throughout the race, as did jokes about his 1-800 campaign phone number.

Among the announced candidates, Bob Kerrey became the media's early favorite. He had received the nation's highest military decoration, the Congressional Medal of Honor, for his service in Vietnam. This fact was not only good for his image but also countered some of the more traditional Republican complaints about Democrats being soft on military support (Baker, 1993, 43). In addition, Kerrey was a handsome, charismatic, "generational candidate" who could challenge Bush in the West, a region of traditional Republican strength. Kerrey started with high expectations and became the party's leading contender. However, when he announced his candidacy, Kerrey had neither staff, organization, nor funds. He simply wasn't ready. In public speeches, he appeared to ramble and did not have a set campaign speech or platform. He did not play to his strengths as a veteran. He had a chance to hire both George Stephanopoulos and James Carville but lost them to Clinton. As late as mid-October 1991, Kerrey was favored by Democrats 21 percent to Clinton's 15 percent (*Hotline*, October 15, 1991, vol. 5, no. 21: 9).

However, organizational and staffing problems plagued his campaign. In January, just one month before the New Hampshire primary, Kerrey hired a new campaign manager and media consultants. But three weeks after the New Hampshire primary, Kerrey had to get out of the race because his campaign was broke. Kerrey started too late and did not use the preprimary period to his advantage.

Bill Clinton was not going to run for the nomination if Al Gore was going to run. When Gore declined to run, Clinton gave serious consideration to entering the race. In early 1991, assuming Bush's victory, Clinton was getting ready for the 1996 presidential contest. Political consultant Frank Greer and pollster Stan Greenberg decided to present Clinton as the agent of change. The problem was how to come to terms with rumors of marital problems between the Clintons. The lesson from Gary Hart in 1988 was to somehow acknowledge the past without confessing to a specific act. In late August 1991, columnist Sandy Grady of the *Miami Herald* wrote, "Will we make Bill Clinton the Gary Hart of 1992? . . . How long will it take another reporter, after he announces his candidacy, to ask the 'big A' question? . . . No doubt, Clinton's 'no comment' about his sexual past will start a feeding frenzy in Sharkland" (*Hotline*, August 22, 1991, vol. 4, no. 227: 7). It was only a matter of time.

Throughout the summer and fall of 1991, the media pursued New York governor Mario Cuomo. Ever since his notable keynote address to the Democratic Convention in 1984, he had been highly regarded as a potential nominee. Despite his numerous denials about entering the race, he was the focus of much media speculation and encouragement. In late September, polls still showed that most Democrats favored Cuomo as their nominee over the other announced candidates (*Hotline*, September 27, 1991, vol. 5, no. 10: 15).

In early October, Cuomo announced that he would reconsider his position. The "big tease" from Cuomo continued through the month of October. He appeared on numerous talk shows and gave public speeches fueling speculation about his potential candidacy. Political analysts and pundits began talking about the "dream ticket" of Cuomo and Kerrey. All this attention literally froze the other campaigns. Cuomo's activities decreased the other candidates' fund-raising efforts as well as free media exposure. The situation got so bad that party chairperson Ron Brown publicly urged Cuomo to decide "within 10 days whether he wants to enter the presidential fray" (*Hotline,* October 29, 1991, vol. 5, no. 31: 3). By mid-November, even candidate Harkin wrote an op-ed piece for the *Washington Post* that attacked the media and Cuomo. He was "fed up with the recent media deification" of and infatuation with Cuomo. In terms of his decision to run or not, "to elevate a personal decision into a national debate is a disservice to the other candidates who have been trying to get their message out to the American people. . . . This is one Democrat who's had enough" (*Hotline,* November 15, 1991, vol. 5, no. 43: 5). Ultimately, Cuomo declined to run, stating he needed to attend to the problems of New York as a full-time governor and that there were plenty of qualified and good Democratic candidates already in the race. As predicted by the model, his strong showing in the polls sustained media interest throughout the period and influenced the strategic environment.

Although Clinton did not receive a great deal of media coverage throughout the summer, he used the preprimary season well. He hired a staff, established a national organization, and developed his position as well as strategies for the months ahead. The candidate with the most money and the best organization who has completed the essential groundwork can make up for weaknesses or unexpected events. After several candidate forums, Clinton began to gain public support, media attention, and momentum. He stormed Florida in December 1991 to position himself for the straw poll. The beauty contest had no value other than subsequent publicity and media coverage. He won the contest because of superior organization and personal effort. Within two months, Clinton went from fourth place in the polls in New Hampshire (behind "undecided") to first place in preference among the Democrats in the state (*Hotline,* January 13, 1992, vol. 5, no. 73).

In the preprimary phase, the dominant elements are campaign organization, finance, and public opinion polls. Initially, name recognition and favorable standings in the polls helped the campaigns of Bush and Cuomo. Lack of a good campaign organization hurt the efforts of Wilder, Kerrey, Harkin, Buchanan, and Bush. Harkin failed to maximize his early fund-raising success. No amount of money could salvage his nomination efforts. The media, of course, had their own stars: Kerrey, Cuomo, and

Clinton. Among the Democratic candidates, Clinton was most successful in managing the elements of the preprimary campaign phase.

The preprimary period of the 1992 presidential campaign illustrates the importance of campaign organization, money, and standings in public opinion polls. The media become pivotal in constructing the strategic environment for the candidates.

The Primary Phase

Convention rules for delegate selection affect primary contest strategies. For Democrats, there is more participation of women and minorities. Also, with proportional representation of state or primary delegations, minor candidates can last longer and carry their campaigns to the convention, receiving valuable television coverage. Republicans, in contrast, prefer "winner-take-all" primaries to help avoid the likelihood of a split convention.

Both Democrats and Republicans front-load the primary process. The first few events are critical for standings in the polls, fund-raising, media coverage, and image definition. It is essential for candidates to have adequate funds and well-developed organizations to mount serious challenges in the early primary states.

The dominant elements of this phase of the campaign are organization, the strategic environment, and the media. The media focus most of their attention on the early primaries. In 1988, for example, one-third of all media coverage during the primary season was devoted to stories about the Iowa caucus and the New Hampshire primary (Baker, 1993, 45). In 1992, New Hampshire was the first real primary because Democratic candidate Tom Harkin was from the caucus state of Iowa.

By the time of the New Hampshire primary, the Persian Gulf War was ancient history in the minds of the public. Only 7 percent of the voters in New Hampshire indicated that the war victory influenced their vote (Baker, 1993, 46). Factors that did influence voter decisions were the recession, near-record unemployment, and the national debt and deficit.

Interestingly, campaign organization played a critical role for all of the candidates, but for very different reasons. Both Democratic and Republican candidates entered the presidential primary season late and somewhat unprepared. Bush and Clinton survived the primaries for many reasons, not the least of which was their ability to adequately staff and fund a national campaign organization.

The media, of course, played a pivotal role in the primary season. Television continues to dominate as the primary source of candidate and issue information. Everette Dennis (1992, 57) and his colleagues found that television was the primary source of information about the campaign for 83 percent of the public, up from approximately 64 percent in 1988. Of those, 49 percent received most of their information from the networks, followed by 39 percent from local coverage and 36 percent from the news network CNN.

Alan Brinkley, a professor of history at Columbia University, believes that "the press plays a larger role in the primary process than in the general election" (Dennis, 1992, 73). Journalist Susan Tifft concurs, arguing that there is some connection between the press's portrayals and voters' perceptions of the candidates. For Everette Dennis, media portrayals of candidates result in the "invisible" nominating process that affects public opinion in very powerful ways (Dennis, 1992, 48).

One unique feature about this election was the expansion of news outlets that served as gatekeeper during the primary campaigns. In the past, major news and press outlets such as the *New York Times, Washington Post,* various news magazines, and television news programs were the primary sources of candidate and campaign information. In 1992, such shows as *Donahue,* CNN's *Larry King,* and such tabloids as the *Star* played an important role in disseminating candidate information to the general public.

This campaign was unique in the direct involvement of local television stations. Nearly half of all local television stations used special satellite feeds for live interviews with the major candidates for office. This clearly favors the candidates: they can avoid the "challenging" and "difficult" national press corps, play to localities, and enjoy longer interviews rather than short sound bites used by the networks.

Another reason the media were so important in the primary campaigns is that the public simply did not know the Democratic candidates. As late as December 1991, less than a majority of the public could identify the announced Democratic candidates (Dennis, 1992, 83–84).

The traditional news organizations wanted to avoid the mistakes made during the 1988 presidential campaign by providing less coverage of the "horse-race" nature of campaigns; avoiding meaningless photo opportunities, empty sound bites, and private details of the candidates; and providing more attention to issues, voter profiles, and political advertising analyses (Dennis, 1992, 23–28). For example, news organizations attempted many more candidate profiles. They went out of their way to avoid covering scandal. Despite rumors of Clinton's affair with Gennifer Flowers, the traditional media did not want to be the first to carry the story. They took a wait-and-see attitude. It was the tabloids that broke the story. Many polls focused on voter anger and frustration—how they feel and what they think about issues—rather than simply reflecting candidate preferences.

Thus, the media generally focused less on the horse-race aspects of the primaries, provided more in-depth candidate profiles, and used more complex public opinion polling to understand voter attitudes and behavior. The media's "rules and guidelines" for coverage naturally influence the strategic environment.

George Bush did not enjoy campaigning and thought it was somewhat belittling for an incumbent president to devote time and effort on the campaign trail. He was also sensitive to characterizations of the 1988 presidential campaign as one of the "nastiest" in American history. There were even rumors that Bush was seriously considering not running for another term. As a result, he delayed important and major organizational decisions. Bush originally planned to field an organization in January 1992 and to announce his candidacy the following month. In contrast, Reagan began his 1984 reelection efforts a year and a half in advance of November's election.

In addition to a late start and much hesitancy, Bush's campaign organization was in disarray—which contributed to an image of a presidency in disarray. Sam Skinner and Bob Teeter were having difficulty getting decisions made. Bush was finally forced to ask longtime friend and then Secretary of State Jim Baker to come back as his chief of staff. It was, according to many insiders, simply too late ("Rocky Road to Houston," 1992, 68).

When Pat Buchanan announced his challenge for the Republican nomination, he had no staff, no polls, and no money except his own $50,000 loan to the campaign ("Assault on the Monarchy," 1992, 63). He arrived in New Hampshire just eleven weeks before the primary. When he opened his campaign headquarters, Buchanan had two chairs and a table.

Buchanan challenged Bush for the "Reagan Democrats" and the conservative right of the Republican party. Buchanan's inflammatory and fiery rhetoric helped him to receive a great deal of "free" media attention and publicity, but it also labeled him very early in the contest as primarily a "protest vote" to send a message to Bush. Early on, the Bush campaign largely ignored Buchanan until it became clear that Buchanan could indeed embarrass the president. Bush found himself on the defensive and fighting to reestablish his "conservative" credentials for party regulars.

Buchanan's 37 percent to Bush's 53 percent New Hampshire Republican primary vote was portrayed by the media as an astonishing victory for Buchanan. In newspapers across the nation there were headlines like: "A Blow for Bush," "Bush in Real Trouble," "Very Bad News for the President" (*Hotline*, February 19, 1992, vol. 5, no. 99: 10).

The media certainly provided enough momentum for Buchanan to contest the southern primary states on Super Tuesday. However,

Buchanan could not challenge Bush in every state without adequate funding and organization. He lost all eight states and was out of money. He broke 30 percent in only two states, Florida and Rhode Island. Buchanan's campaign never fully recovered. Toward the end of the primary season, Buchanan toned down his sharp rhetoric and personal attacks against Bush.

It was not surprising that the Democratic primary races received the most media attention. The unrepresentative state of New Hampshire received more coverage than any other single primary (Dennis, 1992, 84). Clinton enjoyed favorable media coverage and was portrayed as the frontrunner a month before the New Hampshire primary.

Right before the New Hampshire primary, Clinton was hit with two very big stories. A woman, Gennifer Flowers, claimed that she had had a twelve-year affair with him. Ironically, his appearance along with his wife to address the issue on CBS's *60 Minutes* immediately following the Super Bowl provided Clinton with the largest national audience thus far in the race. Overnight, his name recognition increased and his favorable ratings rose to 67 percent (Baker, 1993, 48). Then, a week before the primary, Clinton was charged with being a Vietnam draft evader. During the ordeals, he went from 15 points as winner of the primary in polls to trailing Tsongas by 11 points. The Clinton campaign had plenty of money and bought two 30-minute segments on local television for his electronic town meetings using a question-and-answer format with the audience. Tsongas won the primary with 33 percent of the vote, followed by Clinton with 25 percent. Clinton's second-place finish (as was the case for Republican Pat Buchanan) was portrayed as a moral victory for the Clinton campaign. His strong showing in Tsongas's backyard, his national exposure, and his handling of personal adversity actually strengthened his position in the public opinion polls. Clinton survived the New Hampshire campaign to challenge Tsongas in the more friendly territory of the southern primaries on Super Tuesday.

Kerrey's third-place finish in New Hampshire severely hurt his efforts at fund-raising and staffing state campaign organizations. Kerrey simply did not have enough money to wage a campaign in the Super Tuesday southern primaries, so he withdrew from the race.

The lack of funds also ended Harkin's campaign. Just two days before Super Tuesday, he withdrew from the race for the Democratic nomination, telling Clinton that "the bad news is when you're out of bucks, you're out of gas." Harkin withdrew because he became ineligible for federal matching funds after failing to capture at least 10 percent of the primary vote (he was already $300,000 in debt). He was hoping to survive the southern primaries and go forward in Michigan and Illinois, states that would be strong with traditional Democrats among labor and blue-collar workers (*Hotline*, vol. 5, no. 112: 5).

After the New Hampshire primary, each campaign focused its efforts on states where it thought it would do well and had a strong organization. Jerry Brown focused on Maine and South Dakota; Clinton on Georgia, a state in his own backyard and one that voted just a week before the Super Tuesday primaries.

By the March 10, 1992, Super Tuesday primaries, Clinton was the solid front-runner. The theory behind the southern primaries was for the region to have an impact on the selection process and hopefully force the party to nominate a more moderate to conservative candidate. Clinton won seven out of twelve primaries that day. He came out of the primaries with momentum and the label as front-runner in the media.

Despite Tsongas's victory in New Hampshire, fund-raising became very important and increasingly difficult. Only in Florida, a state with many Northerners, did Tsongas think he could defeat Clinton. Tsongas received the editorial endorsements, but Clinton had the superior grass-roots organization. Just a week before the primary, many analysts, such as Robert Barnes and Robert Novak, predicted a Tsongas victory. Tsongas wanted to demonstrate that he was not a regional candidate. Tsongas lost Florida 51 percent to 34 percent.

Hindsight suggests that Tsongas's campaign organization made two strategic mistakes in planning for Super Tuesday. First, he turned down opportunities to appear on the network television morning programs, thereby losing an opportunity to address the nation and tell Southerners why they should vote for him. Second, perhaps the valuable resources spent in Florida, Tennessee, and Texas should have been saved for the upcoming Michigan and Illinois primaries, where he had a better chance of defeating Clinton ("The Gospel of Saint Paul," 1992, 39).

The media portrayed the Michigan and Illinois primaries as "do or die" for the Tsongas candidacy. Clinton won the primaries two to one over Tsongas. The media began identifying Clinton as the party's nominee. Tsongas was out of money and "suspended" his campaign. He had won six primaries and three caucuses in the West, but his strength was too regional.

New York was the next big primary challenge between Clinton and Brown in early April. By the end of March, Clinton shifted his strategy. His campaign no longer focused on Brown but began to focus on Bush. He attempted broader appeals and was more aware of his image. He also began to shore up the traditional Democratic base with direct appeals to gays, minorities, and blue-collar workers. Clinton also wanted to challenge Ross Perot for the votes of the "Reagan Democrats" (Baker, 1993, 58).

Clinton appeared on *Donahue* a week before the New York primary. Despite the generally favorable treatment by the press, Clinton acknowledged that he accepted the show's invitation to "bypass a hostile New York press corps that had pounded him for two weeks" (*Hotline,* vol. 5, no. 130: 6). Clinton easily won the primary, but not by a large margin.

The strategic environment was energized by several events: the Gennifer Flowers affair, the Los Angeles riots, record unemployment, and the candidacy of Ross Perot. Two days after the New Hampshire primary, Ross Perot, a Texas billionaire, revealed on the *Larry King Show* that he would consider running for president if supporters got his name on the ballot in all fifty states. He never entered a primary, but he enjoyed great popularity and free media. Throughout the primary season, exit polls showed that Perot was favored over Bush and Clinton. Soon the media began focusing on Perot's lack of specifics and past styles of management. On July 16, 1992, Perot got out of the race on the grounds that the Democratic party had finally "revitalized itself."

Bush ran in 39 primaries and won all of them. Clinton ran in 36 primaries and won 30 of them. Clinton won the most populous states and did well across all demographic groups. However, turnout was low for the primaries. Only about 19 percent of the voting age population participated in the nomination process. In addition, there was constant talk about voters preferring other people as options to support (Baker, 1993, 59–60).

The lack of campaign organization and adequate funding hurt Bush and ended the campaigns of Buchanan, Wilder, Kerrey, Harkin, and Tsongas. In many ways the media played the most crucial role in the primary period. Everette Dennis (1992) refers to their role as the "invisible nominating" process that impacts public opinion (48). Media descriptions, interpretations, and labels influenced not only the strategic environment but also candidate standings in the polls.

By late March and throughout the spring, Clinton and Bush were in a virtual tie in public opinion polls (*Hotline,* vol. 5, no. 122: 24). The media began to focus on the eventual contest. Clinton was the "presumptive" nominee, the "come-back kid." Bush was in a "fight for his political life."

Who would have thought that someone called an adulterer, a draft dodger, and a marijuana user could be nominated for the office of President of the United States? Initially, the press liked Clinton, then did not like him, and finally liked him again. He was characterized as "slick Willie" because of his lack of specifics on issues and his careful use of language. However, all the candidates had image problems: Kerrey was too wooden and unemotional, Harkin too liberal and strident, Brown too erratic and unconventional, and Tsongas too solemn (Baker, 1993, 68–69).

Clinton's survival in the New Hampshire primary and southern wins on Super Tuesday propelled him toward the eventual nomination. For the first time, the southern cluster of primaries actually succeeded in allowing the region to nominate not only a self-proclaimed moderate but also one of their own. At least through the primaries, Clinton was successful in using the media, keeping support of the traditional Democratic base, and appealing to defected moderates and so-called Reagan Democrats.

After the primaries, Clinton advisors found that people still did not know Clinton. His "negatives" were higher than his "positives." Few knew his family or personal background. Thus, in early June, advisors encouraged Clinton to tell his story, recollections of his youth, friendships, and lessons learned. The campaign began making his biographical film detailing his past and portraying him as husband, father, and a poor child of an alcoholic and abusive father.

The campaign also sought media opportunities where he could engage in conversation about himself. He appeared on such shows as *Arsenio Hall* and *MTV*. For example, the infamous appearance on Arsenio Hall's program where Clinton played the saxophone in dark sunglasses was carefully planned ("The Long Road," 1992, 37). He practiced the sax for several days in preparation for the appearance. The result was front-page headlines, two days of showing the clip, and the resulting image of a common, nice, perhaps even "hip" kind of guy running for president. The campaign wanted as much exposure as possible after the primaries leading up to the convention.

The Convention Phase

The parties' conventions were surprising and in stark contrast to each other. For one party, the convention was well orchestrated and resulted in a positive jump for the candidate in the opinion polls. For the other party, the convention was in disarray and generated an impression that haunted the nominee throughout the general election. The surprise was that the Democrats were the well-organized group and the Republicans were the more fractious group. The Republican convention helped to reinforce Clinton's image as a different kind of Democrat, a competent, moderate Democrat.

As noted earlier, the key elements to the convention phase of a campaign are organization and media. The candidate now controls the party and stages the convention. As primarily a media event, the party hopes to champion the "right" issues, showcase the candidate and party, convey a positive image, and generate a "bounce" in the public opinion polls.

The Democratic convention was held first in early July. Clinton not only had to make peace with challengers Tsongas and Brown, but he also had to appease various interest groups with an acceptable platform. Clinton's campaign organization was simply superb. The staff exerted "iron control," and every single event was carefully planned ("The Long Road," 1992, 37). One convention "rule" was that every speaker at the convention must endorse Clinton formally and in advance of the convention. In short, "no endorsement, no speech." Anyone who could possibly embarrass the candidate or the party was not allowed to speak and was kept out of view of the prime-time television audience. Every convention delegate was given cards with "talking points" to be used during media interviews so everyone was echoing the same themes and "the party line."

Such detailed planning resulted in a novel Democratic convention with no major fights over the platform or among candidates or delegates. The media were quick to note the historical change. The press characterized the Democrats as united and in good spirits. The front-page headline for the *Philadelphia Inquirer* read, "Democrats got their act together: Instead of squabbling, they tried something different" (*Hotline,* July 20, 1992, vol. 5, no. 204: 16).

Although Tsongas endorsed Clinton, he also expressed some concern that the platform was not stern enough in budget matters and that Clinton made too many promises to special interest groups. Brown's support, however, was more problematic. Prior to the convention, he threatened to wage a floor fight on several issues. But both candidates were given little opportunity to voice their concerns to delegates at the convention.

Clinton's most difficult challenge was Jesse Jackson. Although Clinton won the vast majority of African-American votes in the primaries, their turnout was lower than in 1988 and Clinton did not want to jeopardize support of southern Reagan Democrats. The campaign developed a strategy that was most successful. At a meeting of Jesse Jackson's Rainbow Coalition, Clinton publicly criticized the rap singer Sister Souljah for song lyrics that encouraged blacks to stop killing each other and to start killing cops. Although Jackson felt he was "set up," the press and the public praised Clinton's remarks. Jackson had less than a starring role at the convention. The party placed more focus on party chairperson Ron Brown.

Kathleen Frankovic (1993) has argued that the Democratic convention came at the time of opinion movement for many voters. In the week before the convention and the week of the convention, the public did indeed reassess the Clinton candidacy. Events that affected voters' attitudes included Jackson's endorsement of the ticket, Gore's selection as the vice-presidential nominee, and general positive media portrayal of the candidates and the convention (117).

Of course, Clinton's nomination acceptance speech was the highlight of the convention and the subject of media speculation and analysis. In preparation for the address, Clinton reviewed videotapes of past acceptance speeches, including Reagan's speeches of 1980 and 1984, and Bush's 1988 convention address. In addition, he reviewed various speeches by Abraham Lincoln, Franklin Roosevelt, and John Kennedy (*Hotline,* July 16, 1992, vol. 5, no. 202: 10).

Clinton's address received good reviews by the press. To the largest single audience thus far, Clinton provided very personal accounts about his past and what he hoped to do in the future. He identified with change and new ideas while painting Bush as a caretaker of the status quo. Clinton attacked Bush's weakest points: his character, his judgment, and his leadership potential. The media reported that he exceeded his own expectations and was successful in ensuring the party's base, energizing party members, reaching out to independents and Perot supporters, and presenting a compelling story of personal experiences and values.

The selection of Tennessee senator Al Gore as the vice-presidential nominee was also well received in the media and among party members. He too gave a personal, emotional, and passionate acceptance address.

The Democrats emerged from the convention united, in good spirits, and ready for the fall campaign. In just one week, Clinton gained 30 points in public opinion polls. More important, he now enjoyed a 20-point lead over Bush. Clinton's "favorable" rating went from 41 percent before the convention to 63 percent after the convention; his "unfavorable" rating dropped by half from 50 percent to 25 percent (*Hotline,* July 20, 1992, vol. 5, no. 204: 1). In addition, the ticket was successful in getting people to believe the message. Forty percent of the public thought Clinton and Gore were a "different kind of Democrat," and the majority felt they could understand the problems of the "common voter" (Frankovic, 1993, 118).

On the Monday after the convention, *Newsweek* magazine asked the question, "Regardless of your vote, who will win the election?" The response favored Clinton 48 percent to Bush's 36 percent. Just ten days earlier, Bush was favored 50 percent to Clinton's 22 percent. Another postconvention poll showed that 78 percent of Clinton voters were certain of their vote compared to only 67 percent of Bush voters (*Hotline,* July 20, 1992, vol. 5, no. 204: 24).

The Republican convention was a very different story. Bush faced little opposition during the primaries. Certainly after the Democratic convention, it was clear that Bush needed a positive convention and a lift in the polls. Bush needed to do several things: reassure the conservative base of the party, avoid a fight over the abortion issue, articulate a domestic agenda, and demonstrate that he is a leader with vision. Bush only accomplished the first objective.

The Republican convention was mismanaged from the very beginning. Bush's team lost control of the podium and platform discussions. For some reason, the Bush organization thought it had to appease Buchanan and allowed him to speak. If that had not been bad enough, Buchanan was an early speaker in the prime time that served as the de facto keynote address. The nation's first real look at the convention was Buchanan's very negative and vicious speech in which he equated the fall election to a "religious and cultural holy war" for the values and the very soul of the nation. It was the first of several speeches that portrayed a party of narrow-minded intolerance. It appeared that the conservative wing of the party took over the convention. The party's platform and speeches by Buchanan, Pat Robertson, and Marilyn Quayle presented a picture of a harsh, angry, and combative party more concerned with Christian theology than with public policy. In the end, party regulars were not as committed to Bush as they had been to Reagan.

The poor handling of the convention put more pressure on Bush to give "the speech of his life." The Bush staff was having trouble preparing the speech. The president arrived in Houston without even a working draft ("Rocky Road to Houston," 1992, 69). He ended up with a "cut-and-paste" speech sandwiched together by many writers.

The news media were quick to note the contrasts between the two conventions. For example, the *New York Daily News* wrote, "these people are so disorganized, why, you might even think they were Democrats" (*Hotline,* August 17, 1992, vol. 5, no. 224: 7). Media descriptions of Bush were generally very negative. He seemed passive and almost disengaged from convention activities. Michael Kramer of *Time* magazine characterized an interview with Bush as "too little defense and only a halfhearted offense . . . the president seemed intellectually spent" (*Hotline,* August 24, 1992, vol. 5, no. 231: 25).

Defying tradition, the Clinton campaign did not disappear during the Republican convention. They held press briefings every day across the street. In addition, they had their own monitors to isolate every charge made during the convention, and they were ready for immediate response. They did not make the mistakes of the 1988 campaign by doing nothing in August while holding a double-digit lead. In addition, the bus tours of Clinton and Gore were very successful for the Democrats.

The Republican convention provided only a temporary bounce in the polls of 5 percent. In essence, voters disliked the Republican convention, thinking that Bush and others spent more time attacking Clinton than explaining what they would do if Bush were to be reelected. Within one week, Clinton was back to a 20-point lead in the polls.

The campaign organizations made all the difference in media interpretation and representation of the conventions to the public. In a change from recent history, the Democrats were harmonious and the Republicans were in disarray. The Democratic platform was moderate; the Republican platform was very conservative. The Democrats were united; the Republicans were fractious. The Democrats talked about the future; the Republicans talked about having won the Cold War. Bush seemed out of touch with voters; Clinton connected with the public. The fall campaigns were, in many ways, a mirror of the conventions.

The General Election Phase

Although it is the shortest period of the campaign, the general election phase is the most important. It culminates in a winner and a loser for the highest elected office in the nation (and some would argue even the world). The general public becomes attuned to the election. A single mistake can change the course or outcome of a campaign. Campaign organization, strategic environment, and media are the critical elements in this phase of the election.

The campaign organization must execute the electoral strategy of targeting some states and ignoring others, while targeting specific voting blocks or groups of citizens. The organization must maintain the base of supporters and maximize the vote of undecideds, independents, and defectors from the opposition. In addition, the campaign must use polling to design advertising appeals and to orchestrate favorable news coverage for the candidate.

The overall strategy of the campaigns was reflected in the very different goals of the conventions. As already noted, the Republicans wanted to shore up the conservative base of the party and use the general campaign period to go after undecided or uncommitted votes. The Democrats, in contrast, used the convention to appeal to moderates and undecideds and actually deemphasized the traditional party base of more liberal voters and members of special interest groups. The general campaign of the Democrats was to maintain the postconvention level of support, especially in key states, whereas Perot appealed to the most angry and frustrated voters.

Clinton's campaign theme was reflected on the now famous sign of campaign staff member George Stephanopoulos, "It's the economy, stupid!" The campaign wanted the election to be a referendum on the condition of the U.S. economy. Perot's campaign was a crusade against Washington and "business as usual." Only someone with business experience who was "outside the mess" (i.e., the Washington Beltway) could clean it up. Bush's essential campaign message was simply that his opponents were worse than he had been. He was left to defend the state of the economy in response to Clinton and his competency of job performance in response to Perot.

Although it is nearly impossible to calculate the actual cost of a campaign, Bush clearly outspent his opponents. The Bush campaign spent nearly $180 million to Clinton's $156 million. Both candidates received over $55 million from the public campaign fund. Perot spent $69 million, all of which were private and unrestricted funds (Arterton, 1993, 84).

As was the case with the convention phase, Bush's campaign organization lacked adequate preparation for the fall campaign. Laurence Barrett (1992) of *Time* magazine argued that Bush wasted all of August attempting to organize his campaign with the appointment of James Baker as chief of staff and other key players, as well as conducting research on various themes and potential campaign issues. He asserted that Bush was "a good three months behind on almost everything" (43). Throughout the campaign, the Bush staff was too indecisive on ads and strategy. "There was no organization, no direction, the pros complained. Nothing was getting done" ("A Silver Bullet," 1992, 84). As an example, the result of one six-hour meeting was nothing more than a concept for a single negative ad ("A Silver Bullet," 1992, 84). A study by Everette Dennis and his colleagues at the Freedom Forum Media Studies Center concluded that "the Bush campaign's disorganization, particularly in its late organization of a political consulting team, hurt the president's chances of a second term in the White House and helped Bill Clinton win his bid for the presidency" (1993, 15).

In stark contrast to the Republican campaign effort was the Clinton campaign organization. They learned many lessons from the 1988 campaign—F. Christopher Arterton (1993) has argued that the Clinton campaign was tactically superior to the Bush campaign. They used a "sophisticated data-mapping operation" to identify and rank key markets every week. The analysis would dictate where the campaign would go next. Ultimately, the Clinton campaign focused on 32 states with the potential of 376 electoral votes (87).

Clinton's staff was ready for virtually any Republican maneuver or tactic. First, they had a response team whose sole job was to answer immediately any charge or allegation made by the Bush campaign. After searching a computerized data bank, the staff would compose an immediate rebuttal and provide the response to the press before the story deadlines of the print journalists. The goal was to get their side of the question or issue in the story and prevent two days of potentially negative coverage. In addition, the quick response would not only discredit Bush's campaign efforts but would also result in a more skeptical press looking for distortions from the Bush organization. If necessary, Clinton or Gore would personally respond to a story or Republican allegation.

When Perot reentered the race in October, he *was* the campaign organization. He had no handlers, no image-makers, no consultants, and he surrounded himself with only "yes-people" and volunteers. He favored an organizational staff that was "compliant, united, and quiet" ("The Second Coming," 1992, 86). Perot did not travel or campaign in the traditional way; he relied more on television appearances and paid media to get his message to the voters. He actively avoided the traditional, established news media. Perot did not want journalists to serve as the conduit for his campaign activities or to have his message reduced to mere sound bites on the evening news.

The strategic environment played an important role in the presidential campaign of 1992. The electorate was angry, frustrated, cynical, and distrustful of politicians in general. Many thought that the government was in a state of perpetual gridlock, unable or unwilling to attempt to solve the nation's problems. Many thought they were witnessing the end of the American Dream. However, the electorate was also tuned in to the contest. By election day, 70 percent of the voters indicated that they were "paying a lot of attention to the campaign," and the nation experienced the first increase in voter turnout since the presidential election of 1960 (Frankovic, 1993, 127). The ratings of talk shows went up when candidates were on, and more people watched Perot's first "infomercial" than a baseball playoff game that aired at the same time. The debates also enjoyed the largest television audience in American history. Because of this intense voter interest, the candidates provided very detailed plans for their various programs. The public was not interested in business and politics as usual.

There are some factors that a campaign can control and anticipate in the strategic environment and others that lie outside its control. In the 1992 presidential campaign, such factors included the economic turndown, the demise of the Soviet Union, and the candidacy of Ross Perot.

The Bush campaign never felt that the economy would be the key issue of the election. When they realized the significance of the issue, Bush tried very short-term strategies to address voter concerns. First, he said there were genuine signs of improvement and the nation needed patience to weather the temporary economic storm. Next, Bush blamed the gridlock in Congress for not fully passing his earlier budget measures.

Finally, Bush argued that the whole world was experiencing economic difficulties and we were in no worse shape than any other country.

Bush's primary strategy was to destroy the opposition. The campaign attacked Clinton's policies to no avail. He then directed voter attention to Clinton's character. First the issue was framed in the context of traditional family values, then within the context of trust, and finally within the context of competence, citing Arkansas's national rankings in areas such as education, pollution, and civil rights (Arterton, 1993, 79). Bush never gave the public positive reasons to vote for him, just reasons not to vote for Clinton.

Toward the end of the campaign, Bush's message began to resonate with voters. With just two weeks left in the campaign, Clinton's support eroded somewhat—especially in terms of his perceived honesty and trustworthiness. In some polls, Bush was as close as 5 percent to Clinton ("To the Wire," 1992, 93). Bush was viewed as the best leader, the most "presidential," the most trustworthy, the best able to deal with problems, but he was not viewed as an agent of change or as the candidate best able to take care of the economy (Frankovic, 1993, 120–24). But issues of trust and character work both ways. There was public concern over Bush's vicious attacks on his opponents, calling the Democratic candidates "bozos" and labeling Gore as the "ozone man." Also in the final days of the campaign, there were stories reporting that Bush knew and supported the policy of "arms for hostages" in the Iran-Contra affair. Such stories questioned Bush's credibility and character, and they resulted not only in stopping the erosion of support for Clinton but also in refocusing the campaign on Bush and his poor performance.

By the end of September, however, the campaign was virtually over. Nothing seemed to work. Bush's support hovered around 40 percent for the entire campaign. The only "electoral math" that made sense was to lose the popular vote but win the electoral college vote. The campaign focused on 29 critical states, with Bush trailing in 23 of them ("A Silver Bullet," 1992, 82, 85).

The Clinton campaign conducted a great deal of research throughout the spring, summer, and early fall to develop issue and message strategies. There were four variations on the basic message: people first (i.e., invest in people for a secure economic future), opportunity with responsibility (i.e., no more something for nothing), the middle class as primary target (i.e., populism of the center), and reinventing government ("Manhattan Project," 1992, 42). The campaign also used focus groups to isolate strategies and messages to counter potentially negative attacks. The research identified the best strategy for all attacks: to claim that the charge was "politics as usual" and in keeping with the "Willie Horton" style of attack politics ("War Room Drill," 1992, 79). The campaign especially wanted Clinton to shift from discussing policy to discussing people, and to focus on the middle class.

In addition to holding media attention, the postconvention bus trip allowed Clinton to perfect his basic stump speech of "people first." Soon polling results showed that the message was beginning to work. Clinton was perceived as an average guy who could understand the problems of middle America. He spent little time, money, or energy going after the traditional Democratic base. To do so might have alienated voters and hurt his appeals to independents and other marginal voters.

Clinton's avoidance of military service during the Vietnam conflict was more important as an issue to voters than marital fidelity. Twenty percent of the voters indicated that the lack of military service influenced their vote compared to only 12 percent citing marital infidelity (Frankovic, 1993, 122). However, by midsummer Clinton held a solid lead in the polls showing him ahead of Bush and Perot on every issue, even on the issue of family values ("War Room Drill," 1992, 78).

The Perot candidacy certainly influenced the strategic environment. It is still not clear, however, which candidate the Perot campaign affected the most. The Bush campaign hoped it would cause voters to reconsider Bush and help win several states. At the very least, the Perot candidacy helped Clinton by holding attention and focus on the economy and budget issues.

According to Frankovic (1993), the main impact of the presidential debates was in validating the candidacy of Ross Perot (120). Voters generally thought that Perot "won" the first debate and Clinton the second and third debates. After the first debate, the news media portrayed Bush as the clear loser, behind the other two candidates. Everette Dennis and his colleagues (1993) found that "the news analyses often amounted to little more than a summary of debate highlights, merely using stronger adjectives than the lead stories to describe aspects of the debates" (35). In essence, media coverage of the debates contributed very little information or insight beyond what the audience had learned from watching the events themselves. By the end of the third debate, voters thought Clinton was the best candidate to deal with the economy, but 56 percent still questioned his trustworthiness (Frankovic, 1993, 120, 124). (Robert Friedenberg provides a detailed analysis of the debates in Chapter 4.)

Many observers think the media did a better job covering this presidential election than the one in 1988. However, there is also general consensus that there was a lack of equity and fairness in the coverage of the Republican convention and the campaign of George Bush in general (Dennis, 1993, 10, 14, 155–74).

One major innovation of the election was the continual use of "non-news programming" by the campaigns to reach voters. The candidates wanted more lengthy interaction, less interpretation of their message, and avoidance of "gotcha" journalism. Generally, the candidates stayed away from network news interview programs. Instead, they appeared on the morning shows, and evening news magazine and talk shows. This strategy worked best for Clinton by providing an opportunity for him to talk about himself, build trust with voters, and attempt to demonstrate that he was "not just another politician" (Arterton, 1993, 90–91). Bush was reluctant to follow this strategy, but he was forced to do so. From January to election day, the candidates appeared on various television talk shows a total of 96 times: Clinton was the clear leader with 47 TV appearances, Perot 33, and Bush 16. It is interesting to note that Clinton appeared on *Donahue* 3 times, Perot only once, and Bush not at all. However, Perot appeared on the *Larry King Live* show 6 times compared to Clinton's 4 and Bush's 3 times (Dennis, 1993, 16).

Perot's campaign was conducted primarily through paid media. He spent $24 million in the first two weeks of the fall campaign. Perot relied on his 30-minute "infomercials" as his campaign message and his 60-second television spots to frame the public debate on the economy. His commercials were among the best of the campaign and most remembered by the public ("The Second Coming," 1992, 87). However, it was Perot's appearance on *60 Minutes* nine days before the election that not only stopped his rise in the polls but resulted in a sharp decline of public support. During the interview he got irritated, threatened to leave, and detailed rumors of a plan to disrupt his daughter's wedding as reasons why he originally got out of the race, raising doubts about his fitness for the presidency.

The Clinton campaign made the best use of paid and "free" media exposure, and it actively nurtured local news coverage as well as national news coverage. Of course, every event and candidate appearance was designed with national coverage in mind, but the campaign also valued securing local exposure in important states and media markets. The campaign noted that providing the candidates access to the local media resulted in a 2 or 3 point overnight climb in the polls (Arterton, 1993, 87). In addition, the Clinton campaign produced videos and encouraged video-conferences and satellite feeds for local news operations.

Although Clinton prevailed, half of the record number of voters were not satisfied with their choice of available candidates (Frankovic, 1993, 126). This gave Clinton a coalition cohesive enough to win the election, but fragile enough to raise serious concerns about his ability to govern.

CONCLUSION

This chapter has presented a model of six stable elements within the evolving process of presidential campaigns. Our argument is that there are a finite number of elements involved in the communication-oriented aspects of a presidential campaign. However, the role and function of these elements are dependent upon the specific phase of the campaign. At the very least, the model attempts to capture the dynamism of the elements and hence the campaign by exploring the interaction among the elements in the various phases. The model also provides a way to begin a macro-analysis of campaigns from a communication perspective.

In the preprimary phase of the campaign, name recognition helped the campaigns of Bush and noncandidate Cuomo. Lack of a campaign organization hurt the candidacies of Wilder, Kerrey, Harkin, Buchanan, and to some extent even Bush. The news media had their favorites: first Kerrey, then Cuomo, and finally Clinton. Among the Democrats, Clinton was the best prepared to enter the primary phase of the campaign.

Again, Clinton's organization was far superior to that of his opponents, and his use of media virtually saved his candidacy. For the first time, the southern primaries on Super Tuesday propelled a candidate (in this case, Clinton) toward the eventual nomination. Although Bush easily won the Republican nomination, Buchanan's challenge demonstrated that Bush was vulnerable.

The contrasting conventions played an important role in the campaign. For the Democrats, the convention was well orchestrated and resulted in a permanent jump in the polls for Clinton. For the Republicans, the convention conveyed a message of anger and intolerance. The Democrats talked about change and the Republicans talked about the past. Perhaps not since the Democratic convention of 1968 have conventions played such a critical role in a presidential campaign.

Bush's campaign organization never found the correct message or strategy to seriously challenge Clinton. The Clinton campaign used the media well, both in terms of paid broadcasts and free exposure. Bush simply did not present a good case for his continued governance. His focus was on Clinton, not on America's future. In the end, the incompetence of the Bush campaign was inversely matched by the brilliance of the Clinton campaign.

Finally, it is important to note that this model is designed as a heuristic device, a tool to facilitate our understanding of the communication aspects of presidential campaigns. It is not immutable. Like all forms of communication, it too is a process. We expect the model to evolve, while retaining its overall structure, as the process of presidential campaigning also evolves.

REFERENCES

Arterton, F. Christopher. 1978. "Campaign Organizations Confront the Media-Political Environment." In *Race for the Presidency*, James D. Barber, ed., 3–24. New York: Prentice-Hall.

———. 1993. "Campaign '92: Strategies and Tactics of the Candidates." In *The Election of 1992*, Gerald Pomper et al., eds., 74–109. Chatham, NJ: Chatham House.

Asher, Herbert. 1980. *Presidential Elections and American Politics*, rev. ed. Homewood, IL: Dorsey Press.

"Assault on the Monarchy." 1992. *Newsweek*, Nov./Dec., vol. 120, no. 27: 62–64.

Baker, Ross. 1993. "Sorting Out and Suiting Up: The Presidential Nominations." In *The Election of 1992*, Gerald Pomper et al., eds. Chatham, NJ: Chatham House.

Barrett, Laurence. 1992. "The Fat Lady Hasn't Quite Sung." *Time*, Nov. 2, vol. 140, no. 18: 24–43.

Blumenthal, Sidney. 1980. *The Permanent Campaign*. New York: Touchstone Books.

Burnham, Walter. 1993. "The Legacy of George Bush: Travails of an Understudy." In *The Election of 1992*, Gerald Pomper et al., eds. Chatham, NJ: Chatham House.

Caddell, Patrick, and Richard Wirthlin. 1981. "Face Off: A Conversation with the Presidents' Pollsters." *Public Opinion*, Dec./Jan., 2–12.

Chagall, David. 1981. *The New Kingmakers*. New York: Harcourt, Brace, Jovanovich.

Dennis, Everette. 1992. *Covering the Presidential Primaries*. New York: Freedom Forum Media Studies Center.

Dennis, Everette, et al., eds. 1993. *The Finish Line: Covering the Campaign's Final Days*. New York: Freedom Forum Media Studies Center.

Denton, Robert E. 1988. *The Primetime Presidency of Ronald Reagan*. New York: Praeger.

Denton, Robert E., and Gary Woodward. 1990. *Political Communication in America*, 2d ed. Westport, CT: Praeger.

DiClerico, Robert E., and Eric Uslaner. 1984. *Few Are Chosen: Problems in Presidential Selection*. New York: McGraw-Hill.

Edwards, George C., and Stephen Wayne. 1990. *Presidential Leadership: Politics and Policy Making*, 2d ed. New York: St. Martin's Press.

Fenno, Richard. 1978. *Home Style: House Members in Their Districts*. Boston: Little, Brown.

Fineman, Howard. 1992. "The Torch Passes." *Newsweek*, Nov./Dec., vol. 120, no. 27: 4–10.

Foley, John, et al., eds. 1980. *Nominating a President: The Process and the Press*. New York: Praeger.

Frankovic, Kathleen. 1993. "Public Opinion in the 1992 Campaign." In *The Election of 1992*, Gerald Pomper et al., eds., 110–31. Chatham, NJ: Chatham House.

Germond, Jack, and Jules Witcover. 1988. *Whose Broad Stripes and Bright Stars: The Trivial Pursuit of the Presidency 1988*. New York: Warner Books.

"The Gospel of Saint Paul." 1992. *Newsweek*, Nov./Dec., vol. 120, no. 27: 37–39.

Hotline. 1991–1992. Vol. 4, no. 224–vol. 6, no. 68.

Keeter, Scott, and Cliff Zukin. 1983. *Uninformed Choice*. New York: Praeger.

Kernell, Samuel. 1986. *Going Public: New Strategies of Presidential Leadership.* Washington, DC: Congressional Quarterly Press.

Kessel, John. 1988. *Presidential Campaign Politics: Coalition Strategies and Citizen Response.* Chicago: Dorsey.

Ladd, Everett, and John Benson. 1992. "The Growth of News Polls in American Politics." In *Media Polls in American Politics,* Thomas Mann and Gary Orren, eds., 19–31. Washington, DC: Brookings Institution.

Lichter, S. Robert, et al., eds. 1988. *The Video Campaign: Network Coverage of the 1988 Primaries.* Lanham, MD: American Enterprise Institute.

"The Long Road." 1992. *Time,* Nov. 2, vol. 140, no. 18: 29–43.

"Manhattan Project." 1992. *Newsweek,* Nov./Dec., vol. 120, no. 27: 40–56.

Owen, Diana. 1991. *Media Messages in American Presidential Campaigns.* Westport, CT: Greenwood.

Polsby, Nelson, and Aaron Wildavsky. 1980. *Presidential Elections: Contemporary Strategies of American Electoral Politics,* 7th ed. New York: Free Press.

Ratzan, Scott. 1989. "The Real Agenda Setters." *American Behavioral Scientist,* 451–63.

"Rocky Road to Houston." 1992. *Newsweek,* Nov./Dec., vol. 120, no. 27: 65–69.

Sabato, Larry. 1981. *The Rise of the Political Consultants.* New York: Basic Books.

Savage, Robert. 1986. "Statesmanship, Surfacing, and Sometimes Stumbling: Constructing Candidate Images During the Early Campaign in America's New Political Era." *Political Communication Review* 11, 5–9.

"The Second Coming." 1992. *Newsweek,* Nov./Dec., vol. 120, no. 27: 86–87.

Selnow, Gary. 1991. "Polls and Computer Technologies: Ethical Considerations." In *Ethical Dimensions of Political Communication,* Robert E. Denton, Jr., ed., 171–98. New York: Praeger.

"A Silver Bullet." 1992. *Newsweek,* Nov./Dec., vol. 120, no. 27: 82–85.

Smith, Larry David, and Dan Nimmo. 1991. *Cordial Concurrence: Orchestrating National Party Conventions in the Telepolitical Age.* Westport, CT: Praeger.

"To the Wire." 1992. *Newsweek,* Nov./Dec., vol. 120, no. 27: 92–95.

Traugott, Michael. 1992. "The Impact of Media Polls on the Public." In *Media Polls in American Politics,* Thomas Mann and Gary Orren, eds., 125–49. Washington, DC: Brookings Institution.

Trent, Judith. 1978. "Presidential Surfacing: The Ritualistic and Crucial First Act." *Communication Monographs* 45, 281–92.

Trent, Judith S., and Robert V. Friedenberg. 1991. *Political Campaign Communication,* 2d ed. Westport, CT: Praeger.

Walsh, Edward. 1992. "The More Seed Money, the Better the Harvest." In *The Quest for National Office,* Stephen Wayne and Clyde Wilcox, eds., 50–56. New York: St. Martin's Press.

"The War Room Drill." 1992. *Newsweek,* Nov./Dec., vol. 120, no. 27: 78–81.

Wayne, Stephen. 1992. *The Road to the White House 1992.* New York: St. Martin's Press.

Wayne, Stephen, and Clyde Wilcox, eds. 1992. *The Quest for National Office.* New York: St. Martin's Press.

2

The Early Campaign

Judith S. Trent

By the time votes had been counted on the evening of November 3, it was generally conceded that the 1992 presidential campaign had been one of the most bizarre in recent memory. Not only was it "the first presidential election of the post–Cold War era and the first appearance of a baby boom candidate" (Von Drehle, 1992, 10), it was also the first time in twenty years that reapportionment and redistricting of the House of Representatives coincided with a presidential election. Even two of the principals, George Bush and Bill Clinton, were heard to observe on more than one occasion that 1992 was a strange year for politics.

From the outset, it was clear that Campaign '92 would be anything but ordinary. For example, two years before the general election some of the most likely Democratic presidential contenders called press conferences, not to announce that they would be candidates for president but to explain that they would not be entering the race. Fifteen months later, during the New Hampshire primary, the man the media had decided was the Democratic front-runner sidestepped allegations of marital infidelity, pot-smoking, and draft-dodging—and remained solidly in the race. A well-known Republican journalist waged a short-lived but surprisingly powerful challenge to the incumbent president of his own party. Technologies such as toll-free numbers, electronic databases and bulletin boards, satellite television, and cable television (C-SPAN, CNN, Discovery Channel, MTV, and Public Access) became primary rather than auxiliary channels for candidates' messages. A smooth-talking Texas billionaire made his entry into elective politics by running for president and stole the spotlight from the professional politicians. And the sitting president of the United States, emulating a strategy pioneered by his challengers, fielded questions on MTV two days before the election. It was, in short, a campaign unlikely to be forgotten.

But one of the most unusual departures in 1992 was that the campaign started so late—later than any presidential contest since 1972. In fact, by

March 1991, or twenty months before the general election, when there were "no candidate footprints in the pristine snows of New Hampshire" and the "Iowa cornfields" were "untrampled," a writer for the *Washington Post* speculated about what would happen "if they gave an election and no Democrats showed up" (Williams, 1991, 25).

The problem was not that Democrats had little desire to win back the White House, it was just that the incumbent's unprecedented popularity with the American people intimidated even the most obvious contenders for the nomination. For example, at various times throughout 1990 and 1991, well-known Democrats such as House Majority Leader Richard Gephardt; Senate Majority Leader George Mitchell; senators Bill Bradley, Sam Nunn, Albert Gore, Jr., John (Jay) Rockefeller IV; and New York governor Mario Cuomo publicly decided against running, even after having given earlier signals that they might be interested. Bill Bradley, for example, used much of 1989 to take public-speaking lessons and build a national fund-raising base. Sam Nunn resigned from a golf club that does not allow women to be members or even guests. And by the first week in January 1991, Lloyd Bentsen had put together a brain trust to map out his campaign strategy (Clift, 1990, 35; "Bentsen's Time of Decision," 1991, 4; Taylor, 1990, 12).

Nothing, however, developed from any of these early forays because in January 1991, thirteen months before the Iowa caucus and the New Hampshire primary, George Bush was in an extraordinarily strong political position. He was commander-in-chief and, as such, one of the heroes of Desert Storm, the Persian Gulf War that had been played out on American television. And most public opinion polls showed his approval rating at 91 percent, the highest ever recorded for any sitting president. In addition, the Democrats were in some disarray. In the aftermath of Reagan's administration and three successive defeats in presidential elections, there appeared to be little ideological consensus and polls showed significantly reduced support for even veteran senators who had voted against the president's war policy (Yepsen, 1991, A10). Moreover, at least one Democrat argued that there was really no hurry to begin the 1992 contest. As Senator Albert Gore, Jr., said,

those involved last time share the common view that the race was too long. The eventual nominee gets drained of the stamina needed to finish strong. So there's an unspoken agreement to hold off for a while . . . and there is a Catch-22 at work too. Since nobody is out there, nobody feels the need to head them off at this point. (Williams, 1991, 25)

Despite its late start, the early stages of Campaign '92 unfolded. Once they did, the importance of the surfacing and primary periods, in terms of the communication functions performed, were at least as important to the results as they had been in previous elections. It is the purpose of this chapter to explore how and why.

THE SURFACING STAGE

For a number of years, I have argued the wisdom of studying the early campaign, the surfacing and primary periods, not only because it sets the scene for all that follows but because it frequently determines what will happen in later stages. With no exceptions since 1972, presidential contenders who have become viable candidates are those who surfaced earlier than their competition. Issues discussed during the general election stage are those that are debated by presidential hopefuls in New Hampshire and Iowa. And media-inspired labels for candidates appear at the beginning of the contest and seldom disappear.

The phenomenon known as surfacing, or the preprimary stage of the campaign, had its first real debut in 1976 when fourteen politicians traversed the early primary states as much as two years in advance of the presidential election, trying to create for themselves enough of a national identity to be considered viable candidates. Since that time, and with very little deviation in either form or content, surfacing has played a major role in presidential politics and accounts for what has become known as the seasonless or permanent campaign (Trent and Friedenberg, 1991, 11; Blumenthal, 1982, 23).

Surfacing was originally defined as "the series of predictable and specifically timed rhetorical transactions which serve consummatory and instrumental functions during the preprimary phase of the campaign" (Trent, 1978, 282). No precise timetable exists for this initial stage except that it concludes before the first state delegate caucus or the first primary election takes place. When it begins is solely dependent on candidates' perceptions of their national visibility and credibility, financial backing, and organizational strength. In other words, hopefuls must determine how long it will take to create a presidential image and interest for themselves in the public imagination and what rhetorical transactions will be most helpful in achieving that identity. These are not easy decisions, and in every presidential season there are examples of would-be candidates who have seriously overestimated their assets or underestimated the rigor of the challenge the surfacing stage presents. The 1992 hopefuls were no exception. In fact, their failure to understand the amount of time it would take to do all that was necessary to create a national persona or a sense of excitement about their candidacies was one of their biggest mistakes.[1]

On December 10, 1991, when Patrick J. Buchanan announced his intention to oppose George Bush for the Republican nomination, he did so without having first constructed a solid organizational or financial base upon which to mount a presidential campaign. Although he had national exposure as a writer/commentator and was familiar to viewers of CNN's *Crossfire* and to readers of his nationally syndicated newspaper column, he had never before run for political office. Perhaps because of his lack of personal experience in elective politics, he failed to use the time either before or after the announcement of candidacy to engage in the rhetorical transactions typical of and necessary to successful surfacing. He was competing against a political establishment (the Republican party) that was controlled by the sitting president, yet he did not construct any parallel organization or structure in the primary states. Certainly no early blueprint existed for the way in which his campaign would unfold in each state or region. In fact, even in the heat of the New Hampshire primary—the last ten days—Buchanan was his own strategist, speechwriter, direct-mail writer, and fund-raiser (Buchanan, 1992). As the candidate himself said in early January,

As for money, I'm our biggest contributor. We just sent out the direct mail. We need between one and two million dollars by New Hampshire. It's a very tough time—the recession and Christmas. We started early enough to make the case but we didn't start early enough to raise money. (Weymouth, 1991, 23)

In a similar vein, Senator Bob Kerrey, who announced his candidacy on September 15, 1991, did not take the time necessary to put together either an adequate campaign staff or a fund-raising operation. The problems created by his failure to do so became readily apparent when, during the New Hampshire campaign, he had to take the time to reorganize his staff, replacing key people. Three weeks after New Hampshire, on March 5, he was forced to withdraw from the race because his campaign was broke—so broke that he was effectively shut out of the group of primaries held on March 3 ("Junior Tuesday"). He did not have the money for direct mail, television, or even to allow members of his staff to have separate hotel rooms ("The Gospel of Saint Paul," 1992, 39).

Although on April 30, 1991, Paul Tsongas was the first to announce his intention to seek the nomination of the Democratic party, he, like many other hopefuls, failed to understand the time it would take to fulfill the demands of the surfacing stage. Tsongas, who retired from the U.S. Senate in 1984, was hardly a household name. In fact, even among the other fairly obscure Democrats who announced a few months later, Tsongas was the least well known. He had served for four years in the U.S. House of Representatives and one term in the U.S. Senate, and had left public life six years earlier to battle a deadly form of cancer. Yet at the time he announced his candidacy, only nine months before the first primary, Tsongas had but a three-person campaign staff, little money, and no detailed plan to raise the funds necessary to carry his campaign to the primaries that closely followed New Hampshire (Toner, 1991, C19). In fact, his first campaign trip to primary states such as Colorado, California, and Florida was only after he declared his presidential intentions. With little doubt, his campaign spokesperson did not overestimate the senator's problems when she said that Mr. Tsongas will "obviously not be the 'Democratic Party establishment candidate'" (Toner, 1991, C19). In spite of having had almost five months as the only announced Democratic contender, the senator was ultimately unable to sustain the momentum that can be garnered from a New Hampshire primary victory because of his failure to "prepare the ground" during the surfacing stage. In other words, he had not used the preprimary period to establish the kind of organizational and financial base that would see him through the rapid series of primaries that began five days after New Hampshire and concluded four months later.[2]

Timing played an important role for Virginia governor L. Douglas Wilder as well. The governor had taken office in January 1990 and spent much of the year traveling to seventeen states criticizing the president's economic policies, forming his own political action group, and courting the national press. Yet when Wilder formally announced his candidacy on September 13, 1991, he generated little enthusiasm among Democratic voters and only marginal attention from the media (Clift, 1990, 35; "Governor Takes on President," 1990, A4). One of Wilder's problems was that he was so unknown outside of Virginia that significantly more time than had been allowed would have been necessary for him to develop a national identity. Not too surprisingly, on January 13, 1992, exactly four months after the governor entered the race and a month before the Iowa caucus and New Hampshire primary, he withdrew (Balz and Dionne, 1992, 15).[3]

Thus, timing plays a critical role in the surfacing period. In 1992, as in every presidential election since 1976, the only contenders able to do well in the primary stage were those who understood the importance of timing to the surfacing period. In addition, because the first stage began so much later in 1992 than it had in other years, the Democratic hopefuls had yet another disadvantage. Most had done little to prepare for the primaries in advance of their formal entrance into the race. So for all except Tsongas, there was little time to work any potential kinks out of campaign messages without fear of what a single blunder might do to their candidacies. It proved to be a problem for at least one candidate. Senator Kerrey planned to use health care as the issue that would set him apart from the other Democratic hopefuls. However, he had not taken the time to work out the details of his health plan before announcing his candidacy. During his first postannouncement campaign swing, he appeared confused not only about the way in which he would finance the plan but even about its essential features. In fact, he told his audiences that if they wanted more than a broad outline he would send them a copy of the legislation (Germond and Witcover, 1991b, A15; "The Gospel of Saint Paul," 1992, 39).

Not only can the first stage be analyzed in terms of its timing demands on the candidates, it can also be understood with regard to the characteristic functions served by specific acts of communication. In 1992, regardless of a shortened first stage, four such functions appear to have been of particular importance.

The first function for Campaign '92 was that it provided information regarding the "caliber" of those who would be president—their fitness for office. During the early portion of a campaign, the public image of each candidate begins to be formed as voters draw inferences from campaign actions about how a candidate may perform as president. During early 1992, for example, the electorate could view the missionary-like zeal of Paul Tsongas, the out-of-the-mainstream rhetoric of Jerry Brown, the all-American appeal of Bill Clinton, or the too hot rhetoric of Tom Harkin and make judgments regarding their presidential qualities. Paul Tsongas, with his bright blue Speedo bathing suit (for swimming laps daily at the nearest YMCA to prove that he was physically fit) and his 83-page position paper ("A Call to Economic Arms"), may have been perceived as courageous and sincere but he was also viewed as naive (Pearlstein, 1991, 8). His campaign theme was "change and rebirth" (a self-proclaimed metaphor for his own life), suggesting an economic renaissance in which he was David who would slay Goliath (Fallon, 1992, 8). The problem was that he was an out-of-office, one-term senator, with unassuming physical stature, a monotone speaking voice, and little or no national political presence, so it was not believable that he could topple a president with record-setting political popularity (Pearlstein, 1991, 8).

To a large extent, the credibility factor that plagued Tsongas also dogged former California governor Edmund G. (Jerry) Brown. Years earlier Brown had been tagged "Governor Moonbeam" and was the object of comedians' one-liners because of his campaign themes to "protect the earth," "serve the people," and "explore the universe" (Trent and Friedenberg, 1991, 20). Although he entered the 1992 surfacing period with the advantage of national public recognition, what voters knew about him frequently drew laughter rather than respect. Part of Brown's problem during the surfacing period was living down his earlier reputation so that he could present himself as a credible presidential candidate. Perhaps this was the reason that in announcing his candidacy on October 21, 1991, he said, "I am only one person with faults and flaws. And in my fifty years I have made many mistakes. But I commit to each of you that I will strive to my utmost to continually change within myself" (Germond and Witcover, 1991a, A14).

Iowa senator Tom Harkin was another Democratic hopeful who seemed unable to convince voters outside of his home state that he possessed the stature of a president. After announcing his candidacy on September 15, 1991, the senator quickly emerged as the leader in attacking the president. During a November 1991 meeting of Illinois Democratic party leaders, Harkin said, "I don't mean to hold George Bush's feet to the fire, I mean to stick them in there" ("Oval Office Door," 1991, A6). He also argued that liberalism remained the right message—the right way for Democrats to define themselves. However, Harkin's rhetoric was viewed as "too hot" ("Six Men and a Donkey," 1992, 28), "too abrasive" (Balz, 1991, 14), and even too opportunistic—the idea being that he would say anything or do anything to win (Marcus, 1992, 13). At a time when the other Democratic contenders were perceived by New Hampshire voters to be listening to their economic problems and offering a change from the liberal theology that had been the party's prescription for years, Harkin's strident message of liberalism appeared not only out of sync, but unpresidential.

On the other hand, Arkansas governor Bill Clinton was widely praised—at least by Democratic party leaders in campaign appearances following his announcement of candidacy on October 3, 1991. He was variously referred to as "the man with a plan" (Clift, 1992, 36), "the most engaging extemporaneous speaker in American politics" (Yoder, 1991, A10), an agent for change ("Six Men and a Donkey," 1992, 30), and substantive (Yoder, 1991, A10). The media reported, for example, that speeches before such groups as the AFL-CIO (American Federation of Labor and Congress of Industrial Organizations) and the Association of State Democratic Chairs in Illinois brought "rave reviews" and "clearly eclipsed the presentation of his five rivals" ("Oval Office Door," 1991, A6).

Thus, in 1992, as in other presidential campaign years, the actions of the contenders during the earliest portion of the contest could be seen as representative of their behavior if elected. Potential presidents are not supposed to be mean or nasty, or even naive. Nor should any reference to them provoke laughter. Whatever voters ultimately decide, it seems clear that one function of the surfacing stage is to provide at least some indication of the "caliber" of the individual—the fitness for office. In other words, a candidate's behavior during the surfacing stage gives voters a first impression, one that is frequently difficult and sometimes impossible to change.

The functions performed by the 1992 preprimary period were not limited to symbolism. There were three contributions related to the pragmatic or "instrumental" aspects of the campaign, and each proved important to the success or failure of individual candidates in subsequent stages.

The first instrumental function was that the electorate began to have some information about the candidates' goals, potential programs, and their initial stands on issues. As the presidential hopefuls campaigned in the early primary states, they were able to determine what issues appeared to resonate with voters and then formulate specific responses. Thus, voters began to gather information about how Paul Tsongas would revitalize the economy, why Jerry Brown would change the political process, how Bill Clinton would reform education, what Pat Buchanan meant by his slogan "America First," how Bob Kerrey would reform health care, and why Tom Harkin believed that the Free Trade Agreement with Mexico was wrong. Although such information gathering is important to the surfacing stage in every presidential election, in 1992 its significance was emphasized because of the failure of one of the candidates to involve himself directly in the process. The contrast with those who did was profound.

Even the sitting president of the United States has to surface as a candidate for reelection. And George Bush did. But he was too late, and he was personally uninvolved for too long. He waited until October 11, 1991, less than four months before the New Hampshire primary, to file his papers with the Federal Election Commission. Even then he did not formally announce his reelection bid until February 12, 1992, just six days before the New Hampshire primary. Moreover, although surrogates for the president campaigned in New Hampshire, Bush himself made no visits to the state until January 15, 1992, a month before the primary—and then he made only three others. The problem was not only that he was being challenged from within his own political party but that he was so distanced from the concerns of New Hampshire voters during the surfacing period. In short, Bush failed to engage himself in the unique blend of interpersonal and technological politics that New Hampshire voters demand of presidential candidates (Kendall and Trent, 1989, 3). Although he used the days just before the primary to make appearances with his wife and Arnold Schwarzenegger at several shopping centers and high school gymnasiums, the president's challengers used the surfacing period to campaign throughout the state, listening to the problems of ordinary voters, formulating responses to frequently expressed concerns, and solidifying their positions on specific issues. While his challengers gave every appearance of sympathizing with the economic problems of New Hampshire citizens, Bush gave every appearance of being totally disengaged. For example, on one of his visits a woman handed the president her unemployment-insurance identification booklet as evidence of her misery. He autographed it and handed it back ("Assault on the Monarchy," 1992, 64).

A second and closely related instrumental function of the preprimary period in Campaign '92 was that voters began to develop expectations about the candidates' administrative and personal styles. For example, by December 1991, Bill Clinton had already put together a campaign staff organized and financed well enough to totally overwhelm the other Democratic hopefuls and "win" for him the Florida straw poll ("Six Men and a Donkey," 1992, 30); this demonstrated the kind of administration he might have if elected. On the other hand, Bob Kerrey's failure to raise money, develop a campaign speech, put together a staff, or organize his campaign for the Florida straw poll also sent voters a message about the kind of administration a President Kerrey might have ("Six Men and a Donkey," 1992, 28).

The personal style of the candidates was also revealed during the early days of the 1992 campaign. Paul Tsongas, for example, had a penchant for self-deprecating humor, for drawing an analogy between his presumed recovery from cancer and rebuilding America's economy, and for overlaying a moralistic tone on all that he said. The idea conveyed by this was that he was a candidate who always told the truth—no matter how painful; a candidate who, as an underdog, was in the race not for personal benefit but to give something back. Tsongas introduced his economic plan by warning that it would not be popular because reversing the downward cycle of the American economy would mean sacrifice for all. He labeled himself a "non–Santa Claus" because of his "tough" prescription for economic recovery; but the self-righteousness evident in many of his public statements caused others to label him "Saint Paul" ("The Gospel of Saint Paul," 1992, 37). A few examples from his speeches help provide the flavor of the senator's personal style.

Shortly after he announced his candidacy, Tsongas offered an explanation for the attention he was getting from the media by saying: "It's like Economics 101. There's an enormous demand for a candidate out there and at the moment, I am the only supply" (Barrett, 1991, 27). Throughout the surfacing period he talked about his bout with cancer, correlating it with why he was running for president and how he would solve the problems of the country. When asked why, after all he had been through with his illness, he would put up with the stress of a year-long campaign, he said: "I guess my answer is kind of syrupy. I survived, and there is an obligation that goes with that. I know what the country has to do, and I don't hear anyone else saying it. So what am I supposed to do—say that the rest of you are on your own? I have an obligation to give something back" (Pearlstein, 1991, 8). He offered, he said, a different path: "harder but more hopeful, longer but more compelling, steeper but more worthy" (Toner, 1991, C19).

The personal style of another Democratic hopeful was revealed during the surfacing period. And it was vastly different.

When the governor of Arkansas decided to enter the 1992 presidential race, he was unknown nationally, except, perhaps, for having given a widely criticized, rambling nomination speech for Michael Dukakis at the 1988 Democratic convention. Within a few months, however, Clinton was able to position himself as a "different kind of Democrat." With the help of a finely crafted message of limited change and a well-organized and well-financed campaign, he began to move himself to the front of the line of those Democrats with announced presidential ambitions. During that time, a somewhat contradictory portrait of the governor emerged—largely because of two characteristics of his personal style. On one hand, Clinton could be seen as the "all-American": both the captain of the football team and the student government president ("Six Men and a Donkey," 1992, 28). Yet over the years he had been labeled "Slick Willie," in part because of his ease and skill in communicating with people—a smoothness that some found difficult to believe could be true; but also because of his habit of trying to please everyone and thus appearing to argue for opposing sides of an issue—portraying himself as the ultimate politician (Klein, 1992, 15). The dual image may well have sent contradictory messages during the surfacing period. But the single most important information voters received from Clinton's personal style was that he took time to talk with them and hear their personal stories. He appeared to care. At almost every rally during his New Hampshire campaign, the governor stayed until he answered all the questions people gave him, shook every hand extended to him, and frequently put his arms around people who shared their problems with him. He was, in fact, interpersonally involved with the people who came to see and hear him—no matter how many there were. When they cried, he cried; when they asked a question, he responded with the next question; when they indicated pain, he appeared to understand and experience the same pain; and "to an extent unprecedented in any recent election" was able to "assuage their fear"

(Klein, 1992, 15). Thus, in the preprimary period voters began to form expectations about Clinton's administrative and personal style.

The final instrumental function evident in Campaign '92 was clearly the most important in that it not only dominated subsequent stages of the election, but it had much to do with electoral outcome.

To some extent, the first stage of Campaign '92 was remarkably like previous campaigns in that as the candidates traveled the early primary/ caucus states they began to "come to grips with the issues on people's minds," began to "formulate 'solutions' to problems that seem to be compatible with popular perception" (Trent and Friedenberg, 1991, 23). In other words, the rhetorical agenda for the 1992 campaign was established during the surfacing stage. Once set, it never changed, forcing each contender to either adhere to it or adjust his message enough to appear to be adhering to it. The problem was that the dominant theme was negative— not only was everything bad but it was going to get a lot worse. It was as if a "virus of pessimism" had swept across the country, replacing the hope and faith long part of the American Dream with a sense of fear and worry that America was in decline and that the "country was seriously off on the wrong track" (Goldman and Mathews, 1992, 23). Thus, by the time the surfacing stage of the 1992 race finally began to pick up some steam, "America was in a sour mood" (Ifill, 1991, 4-1). Unemployment was rising, the national debt had quadrupled to $4 trillion since 1980, corporations were "downsizing," the savings and loan industry was in ruins, real estate values were crumbling, blue- and white-collar jobs were disappearing, and banks were shaking under backlogs of bad debt. In the Midwest, farmers who had worked hard and saved their money for years were uneasy about the future, frightened that everything they had gained could slip away at any moment. In New Hampshire, workers were striking at the paper mills and knitwear factories, and the Federal Deposit Insurance Corporation had seized five failing banks (Ifill, 1991, 4-1). One American in ten was on food stamps, and one in eight was living below the national poverty line (Goldman and Mathews, 1992, 23).

Although Tsongas may have been the first 1992 contender to focus his campaign message on America's economic woes, he was soon joined by the others as they traveled New Hampshire, talking with voters, listening to stories of financial distress, sympathizing with them and assuring them that if elected they would begin solving the problems that were being ignored by the incumbent and his administration. Even a candidate as ideologically rigid as Buchanan, after his first postannouncement swing through New Hampshire, began developing a populist message that allowed him to respond to people who asked him what he would do to get them jobs ("Assault on the Monarchy," 1992, 63). But one of the candidates spent very little time listening to voters' issues or formulating his response to their concerns. It was not only that he was seldom in New Hampshire; when he was, his time was spent speaking at big rallies or shaking hands at shopping malls. There was little or no effort expended in the surfacing stage to come to an understanding of what Americans were thinking and feeling. Had he listened, he might have come to some understanding of the issues that mattered to voters, and ultimately he might have saved his presidency—for the issues dominant during the surfacing period remained important in later stages.

THE PRIMARY STAGE

Primaries, the second stage of the early presidential campaign, have become one of the most controversial election events. That's not surprising since the primary elections, not the national nominating conventions, have determined the identity of the Democratic party's nominee since 1972 and the Republican party's nominee since 1980.

Although primaries have been referred to as "America's most original contribution to the art of democracy" (Miller, Wattenberg, and Malanchuk, 1986, 533), there is no universal agreement that they represent the *best* way to select presidential candidates. In fact, the 1992 presidential primaries were criticized for some of the same reasons previous ones had been: there were too many of them, they took too long, cost too much, and at least during the first month of the season followed each other too closely. There is some truth to each charge. For example, in 1992 as in 1988, there were thirty-six primaries and twenty caucuses beginning early in February and concluding in the second week of June. In addition, just as in 1988, the primary season continued to be expensive. In 1988, those contenders who received federal matching funds were allowed to spend $3 million more than they had been in 1984 ($27 million each), and the total amount spent by the Democratic and Republican presidential candidates in the 1992 primaries and caucuses was approximately $153 million.[4] Finally, the 1992 primaries and caucuses continued to be heavily loaded toward the beginning of the season so that twenty-seven of them fell within three weeks of each other—much the same schedule that had occurred in 1988. "Front loading" the primary schedule is always a problem for presidential hopefuls who have failed to use the surfacing period to their advantage, and this was especially true in 1992 because of the extraordinarily late start of the campaign. Most contenders simply did not have time to reorganize or regroup between primary campaigns or even to do the fund-raising necessary to sustain their candidacies. As a result, two of the Democratic contenders, Tom Harkin and Bob Kerrey, withdrew within a three-week period after the February 18 New Hampshire primary and before Super Tuesday on March 10, 1992. As Harkin said four days before withdrawing, "The problem right now is money. What we've got to do is get individuals to start sending in some dough" (Berke, 1992, A11).

Although many of the criticisms of the second stage of Campaign '92 paralleled those from previous elections, there were some traditions that were not upheld. For the first time in recent presidential campaigns, the tradition of the Iowa caucus as the first real test of candidate strength was broken. Although Iowa had failed to catapult the winner of either the Republican or Democratic caucus to their respective party nominations in 1988, in three earlier elections (1976, 1980, and 1984) it had exerted far more influence in selecting the eventual nominees than other states, even those that were larger. The Iowa caucus was influential because it was the first real test of electoral appeal and strength. The theory was that if a hopeful could be victorious in Iowa, the win would focus national attention on the campaign and build a momentum that virtually guaranteed front-runner status from the national media. In other words, the surge of publicity would provide a "bounce" toward the nomination—a bounce substantial enough so that before late spring (when states with large numbers of delegates go to the polls) the race would essentially be over. Thus, Republican and Democratic presidential hopefuls would "set up their tents" early in Iowa; seeking delegates, first to county, then to state, and finally to the national nominating conventions. However, in 1992 an Iowa campaign never really occurred. The Democratic contenders essentially ignored the caucus because it was clear that state party members would stick by their senator, Tom Harkin; and the Republican challenger, Pat Buchanan, chose New Hampshire, not Iowa, as the site for his initial battle against President Bush.

If Iowa broke tradition of the early campaign, the New Hampshire primary put to rest a notion that had taken on an almost mystical quality over the years. Beginning with the first preferential presidential primary in 1952, New Hampshire citizens have boasted that they always vote for the candidate who eventually becomes president. Thus, on February 18, 1992, when New Hampshire Democrats selected Paul Tsongas and Republicans selected George Bush, they did more than vote for losing candidates. They may well have ended at least part of the "mystique" of the New Hampshire primary or what has been called "the most cherished of American political rites" (Gold and Trent, 1980, 5).

In spite of problems created and traditions destroyed during the primary stage of the 1992 presidential campaign, the communication acts and symbols of the period provided four functions that were important to the entire electoral process.

The first function served by the second stage is that the primaries and caucuses (especially those that occurred in the first two months) became a source of information for the political parties (at least to the Democratic party) before they bestowed their nominations on a single individual (Broder, 1992, 4). Through the primary campaigns, the Democratic party learned which contenders could craft a message for voters and deliver it effectively in a variety of formats. They were also able to distinguish among those who could organize a campaign staff and those who could not, those who could raise money from constituencies broader than the ones to whom they normally appealed and those who could not, and those who could sustain the emotional and physical stress of a prolonged campaign and those who could not. It was useful information; indeed it was critical for the Democratic party to know that it was Bill Clinton and not Bob Kerrey, Tom Harkin, Jerry Brown, or Paul Tsongas who had the ability—as well as the emotional and physical stamina—to rebound from mistakes, organize a staff that could operate on a national scale, raise sufficient money to allow a full-fledged campaign in each of the early primary states, and have a "plan" from which he could speak knowingly on a wide variety of issues. And as the primaries showed, in almost "all those respects" Bill Clinton was better—"something that could not have been discerned simply from inspecting their resumes or credentials" (Broder, 1992, 4).

The 1992 primaries might have also provided more early information to the Republican party about its major candidate and the issues, had anyone been listening. Months before the primaries began, at least one national survey indicated that a vast majority of Americans (83%) wanted presidential candidates to concentrate on domestic issues, not foreign affairs, and that they disapproved of the president's handling of the economy (Nelson, 1991, A26). An exit poll during the Georgia primary on March 3, 1992, found that the economy was the potent issue in producing a sizeable anti-Bush vote ("Blacks, Economy Play Key Roles," 1992, C7). But the president had been slow in acknowledging that a campaign was even occurring. He seldom campaigned personally in the nation's first primary state, and he appeared to have little understanding of the disaffection and pessimism of growing numbers of Americans, not only about current economic conditions but about the likelihood that anything would improve (Goldman and Mathews, 1992, 21). The Republican challenger, Pat Buchanan, who had no firsthand electoral experience, no formal credentials for the presidency, and a "fly by the wire" organization ("Assault on the Monarchy," 1992, 64), won 37 percent of the Republican vote in

New Hampshire, 36 percent in Georgia, and 30 percent in Maryland and Colorado (two states in which he had never campaigned) while running against the sitting president of his own party. This demonstrates that the Republican party and its major candidate were not listening to all the messages sent by the early primaries.

Not only do presidential primaries provide valuable information to the political parties about the viability of their contenders, they are also a source of valuable feedback to the candidates about the campaign they are conducting. Thus, a second important function of the primary season is that the candidates begin to learn from the voters about their campaigns, the organization they have put together, the competence of their staffs, the fund-raising efforts, their own physical and emotional stamina—in other words, their strengths and weaknesses as campaigners (Trent and Friedenberg, 1991, 29). During the surfacing period, the only way candidates can measure how they are doing is via the media, an occasional straw poll of party leaders, or, in some cases, the results of media polls. But the primaries provide direct feedback from the voters and, thus, an opportunity to reposition stands on issues, themes, images, and overall campaign strategies.

For example, feedback from New Hampshire indicated that Bob Kerrey frequently seemed remote, vague, unfocused on the campaign, and spoke a kind of "senatese," reciting subsections of amendments (Goldman and Mathews, 1992, 34–35). However, in his first campaign appearance in Georgia immediately after the New Hampshire primary, the senator, clearly trying to reposition himself as focused and aggressively in command, made a number of harsh and concrete attacks on Clinton and concluded a press conference by asserting that Clinton could not win the general election and would "get opened up like a soft peanut in November" (Goldman and Mathews, 1992, 38).

One of the most interesting 1992 repositioning efforts was the attempt of Jerry Brown to change his fairly long-standing image as a "flake" to a credible presidential contender (Goldman and Mathews, 1992, 28). Although he was clearly able to tap into the anti-insider mood of voters in a number of primaries and caucuses to eventually win 608 delegates, there was no indication that his image had undergone any significant change. In fact, after almost six months of campaigning, Brown was still referred to as "a nut," "a flake," "a little cuckoo," and "too much on the fringes to be president" by Democrats during the New York primary (Schmalz, 1992a, A8).

However, Campaign '92 was not without successful attempts to reposition. In fact, it may well be that the repositioning attempts done by the governor of Arkansas, between the March 3 primaries (Junior Tuesday) and the March 10 primaries (Super Tuesday), and then again after the April primaries in preparation for the Democratic nominating convention and general election, can be considered among the most successful examples in recent presidential campaigning.

Clinton's first major turnaround followed his defeat in all but two of the six primaries/caucuses held on March 3. Believing that their campaign had "hit the bottom," that Tsongas was gaining ground with his economic plan, and that the governor was still suffering from the "ton of mud dropped on him" during the New Hampshire primary, Clinton and his staff retooled his economic message (Goldman and Mathews, 1992, 38–39). The governor began attacking Tsongas as a "Reagan retread," redefining the major difference between their economic plans. He argued that the senator offered only pain (no tax cut for the middle class, a cut in social security, and a gasoline tax), while he offered both fairness and growth—opportunity with responsibility. He focused attention on the differences between them, maintaining that his plan was "people-based economics." He thereby repositioned himself as the candidate under whom the economy would grow but not at the expense of segments of America such as the middle class or social security recipients. At one campaign stop after another, Clinton said, "We cannot put off fairness under the guise of promoting growth" (Goldman and Mathews, 1992, 39). On Super Tuesday, the governor won eight of the eleven primaries (mostly the South and the border states), and four days later Tsongas suspended his campaign.

The second successful effort was focused on repositioning Clinton's image—not reinventing but recasting. It was called "The Manhattan Project," and it was born in part to solve the governor's "trust" or "character" problem and in part to enable him to reach a national audience. Although he had won the April primaries (New York, Kansas, Wisconsin, and Pennsylvania) and was assured of the nomination, a number of polls indicated that his negative rating had increased to 41 percent, that he was perceived as less honest and trustworthy than President Bush, and that there was little understanding of who he was and why he wanted to be president (Goldman and Mathews, 1992, 40–41).

He had, in fact, continued to have "character" problems even during the April primaries. For example, during the New York campaign, Jerry Brown, his last remaining competitor, had portrayed Clinton as unelectable, "an abuser of the public trust, and fiscally and perhaps morally irresponsible" (Schmalz, 1992b, A1). Brown further accused the governor of being a hypocrite who sought black support but played golf at a whites-only club in Arkansas and referred to him as "the prince of sleaze" (Ifill, 1992, A1). It was also during the New York primary that

Clinton admitted having smoked (but not having inhaled) marijuana as a student in England, and an interview with Hillary Clinton was published in which she talked about a rumor, "apparently well-known in Washington," that President Bush had had an extramarital affair (Sontag, 1992, A14). Although Clinton won the primary, he had been forced to spend much of the campaign defending himself against personal accusations, trying to relieve doubts and reservations about his character as opposed to talking about his policies and what he wanted to do as president (Toner, 1992, A9; Ifill, 1992, A1).

Thus, after the April primaries, when the Clinton campaign staff sought to reposition his image, they knew it was necessary to tell Americans about the man: his disadvantaged childhood, his values, his work in Arkansas against special interest groups, and what he stood for. Consequently, they revised and made more specific the ideas in his basic stump speech and extended the campaign's media reach to include not only the morning and evening television talk shows but MTV, where Clinton could advance his own themes in response to "soft" questions and directly answer viewers' questions. Although doubts about Clinton's character remained throughout the general election, the repositioning of the governor's image in the final months of the primary period was successful: polls showed that Clinton's negative rating began to drop and that he was running ahead of both President Bush and Ross Perot (Goldman and Mathews, 1992, 56).

Also important are the functions provided to the electorate. Just as the primary campaign is valuable in giving contenders the feedback necessary for repositioning, so too can it offer voters the information necessary for cognitive adjustment or readjustment—a chance to reevaluate (Trent and Friedenberg, 1991, 31).

As the presidential hopefuls campaign across the state, meeting and speaking with people at all manner of public events or private fund-raisers, voters have the opportunity to see and hear a potential president and witness for themselves the candidate's habitual patterns of thinking and acting. They need no longer rely on earlier, sometimes inaccurate, descriptions by the media or by others. Jerry Brown does look a little "out on the fringe" as he campaigns in his L.L. Bean togs, white turtleneck, and a bulky plaid jacket that make him look rather like a cross between a priest and a lumberjack. Paul Tsongas is very witty and tells a lot of funny stories as he meets and talks with small groups of people. Bob Kerrey never seems to look people directly in the eye when he greets them or shakes their hand. Pat Buchanan, on the other hand, never takes his eyes off the person with whom he is talking; he is very intense.

In other words, as the contenders seek all possible campaign outlets during the primary stage of the campaign, voters are able to witness how the candidates handle themselves verbally and nonverbally. Voters can then form their own initial opinions or readjust their prior ideas about a candidate. From listening to speeches, informal conversations, and answers to questions, "voters begin to have some information regarding the candidate's beliefs, attitudes, and value orientations" (Trent and Friedenberg, 1991, 32). If Paul Tsongas can only talk about the sacrifices that must be incurred to "right" the economy, how will he ever understand the pain already felt by countless Americans who are out of work? If Pat Buchanan is really the Washington "outsider" he claims to be, how will he be able to "make government work"? If Tom Harkin is the champion of the poor, the ethnics, the handicapped, and the laborers, why is he so mean to people around him, especially those who wait on him? Answers to questions such as these provide information about the contenders that enable voters to create a "mosaic model of communication," discovering bits or pieces of information and then arranging the pieces into a new or reinforced cognitive pattern (Becker, 1971, 33).

The final function served by the communication acts and symbols is closely related to each of the others in the second stage in 1992; it gives both candidates and voters time to frame questions and evaluate responses to the questions asked. Because of the primary campaigns, contenders have a chance to answer voter doubts about their candidacy and voters have the opportunity to evaluate the responses. For example, the primary period gave Paul Tsongas time to hit his stride and let voters respond to what he was saying rather than his noncharismatic image. It gave Bill Clinton the chance to present himself, problems and all, and see whether or not he could overcome voter doubts. And it gave Pat Buchanan the opportunity to test the amount or degree of unhappiness among conservative Republicans for their incumbent president. Regardless of the outcome, the fact is that the primary period gives candidates the time to answer questions or address doubts and gives voters the time to reflect on those responses.

These were the communication functions of the primary stage of the 1992 campaign. As in other years of contemporary presidential elections, they were important because they allowed the *people*—not the political parties, not the media—to determine who the candidates would be.

A POSTSCRIPT

Although the electoral adventures of Ross Perot must be woven into the fabric of any account of the general election stage of Campaign '92, no analysis of his candidacy has been included in this chapter. Perot did not directly campaign, nor was his name on the ballot in any of the state primaries.[5] It can reasonably be argued that the second stage of the campaign (beginning February 10, 1992, with the Iowa caucus and concluding with the North Dakota primary on June 9, 1992) was the period in which Perot was surfacing for his first—although officially undeclared—run for the presidency.

Two days after the New Hampshire primary, Perot announced in an interview with Larry King on CNN that he would run for president if supporters placed him on the ballot in all fifty states. His announcement was not preceded by any of the rhetorical transactions that typically define surfacing.

During the almost five-month period of his undeclared candidacy, Perot surfaced by establishing a state-of-the-art voice-mail phone system with 100 lines that automatically routed calls to volunteers overseeing ballot-petition efforts in individual states (Fineman, 1992, 32). He encouraged the organization of a massive volunteer effort and occasionally held a rally in those states where enough petition signatures were obtained to put his name on the ballot. Although he hired two experienced political strategists six weeks before he withdrew, most of Perot's surfacing was conducted on television talk shows and by telephone.

His strategies were neither traditional nor timely, but they were effective. By the time he withdrew on July 16, 1992, at least one public opinion poll found that Perot could have received as much as 30 percent of the vote (Apple, 1992, A13).

NOTES

1. The candidates who announced (and if applicable, withdrew) during the first or second stages included the following:

DEMOCRATIC CANDIDATES

	Announced	*Withdrew*
Paul Tsongas	April 30, 1991	April 7, 1992
Larry Agran	August 22, 1991	—
Douglas Wilder	September 13, 1991	January 13, 1992
Bob Kerrey	September 15, 1991	March 5, 1992
Tom Harkin	September 15, 1991	March 9, 1992
Bill Clinton	October 3, 1991	—
Tom Laughlin	October 18, 1991	—
Jerry Brown	October 21, 1991	—

REPUBLICAN CANDIDATES

	Announced	*Withdrew*
David Duke	December 2, 1991	April 22, 1992
Pat Buchanan	December 10, 1991	—
George Bush	February 12, 1992	—

2. The 1992 presidential primary and caucus schedule was as follows:

Feb. 10, 1992	Iowa Caucus	Mar. 17, 1992	Illinois Primary
Feb. 18, 1992	New Hampshire Primary	Mar. 17, 1992	Michigan Primary
Feb. 23, 1992	Maine Caucus	Mar. 24, 1992	Connecticut Primary
Feb. 25, 1992	South Dakota Primary	Mar. 28, 1992	Virgin Islands Caucus
Mar. 3, 1992	Colorado Primary	Mar. 31, 1992	Vermont Caucus
Mar. 3, 1992	Georgia Primary	Apr. 2, 1992	Alaska Caucus
Mar. 3, 1992	Maryland Primary	Apr. 5, 1992	Puerto Rico Primary
Mar. 3, 1992	Minnesota Primary	Apr. 7, 1992	Kansas Primary
Mar. 3, 1992	Idaho Caucus	Apr. 7, 1992	New York Primary
Mar. 3, 1992	Utah Primary	Apr. 7, 1992	Wisconsin Primary
Mar. 3, 1992	Washington Caucus	Apr. 11–13, 1992	Virginia Caucus
Mar. 5–19, 1992	North Dakota Caucus	Apr. 28, 1992	Pennsylvania Primary
Mar. 7–9, 1992	Democrats Abroad Caucus	May 3, 1992	Guam Caucus
Mar. 7, 1992	Arizona Caucus	May 5, 1992	DC Primary
Mar. 7, 1992	South Carolina Primary	May 5, 1992	Indiana Primary
Mar. 7, 1992	Wyoming Caucus	May 5, 1992	North Carolina Primary
Mar. 8, 1992	Nevada Caucus	May 12, 1992	Nebraska Primary
Mar. 10, 1992	Delaware Caucus	May 12, 1992	West Virginia Primary
Mar. 10, 1992	Florida Primary	May 19, 1992	Oregon Primary
Mar. 10, 1992	Hawaii Caucus	May 26, 1992	Kentucky Primary
Mar. 10, 1992	Louisiana Primary	May 26, 1992	Arkansas Primary
Mar. 10, 1992	Massachusetts Primary	June 2, 1992	Ohio Primary
Mar. 10, 1992	Missouri Primary	June 2, 1992	Alabama Primary
Mar. 10, 1992	Mississippi Primary	June 2, 1992	California Primary
Mar. 10, 1992	Oklahoma Primary	June 2, 1992	New Jersey Primary
Mar. 10, 1992	Rhode Island Primary	June 2, 1992	New Mexico Primary
Mar. 10, 1992	Tennessee Primary	June 2, 1992	Montana Primary
Mar. 10, 1992	Texas Primary	June 9, 1992	North Dakota Primary

3. Although Wilder's brief campaign to be the Democratic nominee floundered on many fronts, there is little question that the governor's race was a factor. Because he had been successful in rising above the politics of race in Virginia, he hoped to do the same nationally. But in an early effort to see how the governor might do against the other Democratic contenders in New Hampshire, his staff learned that group members liked the accomplishments and positions on issues attributed to the governor more than they did the other candidates, until they learned that he was African-American. When they saw a picture of him, all the focus group members changed their idea of which candidate they preferred ("Six Men and a Donkey," 1992, 29).

4. The 1992 Federal Election Commission reported each Democratic and Republican candidate's financial disclosures for primary campaign spending (excluding spending by PACs) through June as follows:

Larry Agran	$ 372,287
Jerry Brown	7,974,486
Pat Buchanan	9,663,130
George Bush	55,703,722
Bill Clinton	56,336,841
David Duke	283,613
Tom Harkin	5,444,570
Bob Kerrey	7,367,401
Paul Tsongas	9,027,226
Douglas Wilder	802,969
TOTAL	$152,976,245

5. Although Perot was not on the ballots and did not officially campaign in the 1992 primaries, he actively encouraged his supporters to cast a vote of "undecided" in lieu of his opponents.

REFERENCES

Apple, R. W. 1992. "Governor Finds an Edge." *New York Times,* June 30, A13.

"Assault on the Monarchy." 1992. *Newsweek,* Nov./Dec., 63, 64.

Balz, D. 1991. "Tom Harkin: A Democrat and Proud of It." *Washington Post,* July 1–7, 14.

Balz, D., and E. J. Dionne, Jr. 1992. "Kerrey Takes a Swing behind Clinton." *Washington Post,* Jan. 13–19, 15.

Barrett, L. 1991. "The Underground Primary Begins." *Time,* Apr. 8, 27.

Becker, Samuel L. 1971. "Rhetorical Studies for the Contemporary World." In *The Prospect of Rhetoric,* Lloyd F. Bitzer and Edwin Black, eds., 21–43. Englewood Cliffs, NJ: Prentice-Hall.

"Bentsen's Time of Decision." 1991. *Newsweek,* Jan. 14, 4.

Berke, R. 1992. "Harkin Is Struggling to Stay in Race." *New York Times,* Mar. 5, A11.

"Blacks, Economy Play Key Roles in Outcome." 1992. *Journal-News,* Mar. 4, C7.

Blumenthal, S. 1982. *The Permanent Campaign.* New York: Simon and Schuster.

Broder, D. S. 1992. "No Way to Pick a President." *Washington Post,* Apr. 27–May 3, 4.

Buchanan, Pat. 1992. Face-to-face interview. Feb. 17.

Clift, E. 1990. "Slow Out of the Gate." *Newsweek,* Nov. 12, 35.

———. 1992. "Bold Plans and Trims on the Edges." *Newsweek,* Jan. 20, 36.

Fallon, P. 1992. "Paul Tsongas' Journey." Unpublished paper.

Fineman, H. 1992. "People's Politics." *Newsweek,* Apr. 20, 30–33.

Germond, Jack, and Jules Witcover. 1991a. "Brown Is Challenging Politics." *Cincinnati Enquirer,* Oct. 22, A14.

———. 1991b. "Kerrey Strategy Is Surfacing." *Cincinnati Enquirer,* Oct. 11, A15.

———. 1992. "The Real Campaign under Way." *Cincinnati Enquirer,* Jan. 17, A15.

Gold, E. R., and J. S. Trent. 1980. "Campaigning for President in New Hampshire: 1980." *Exetasis* 6, 3–22.

Goldman, P., and T. Mathews. 1992. "America Changes the Guard." *Newsweek,* Nov./Dec., 23.

"The Gospel of Saint Paul." 1992. *Newsweek,* Nov./Dec., 37, 39.

"Governor Takes on President." 1990. *Cincinnati Enquirer,* Nov. 14, A4.

Ifill, G. 1991. "Facing a Tide of Voter Anger, Politicians Look to Channel It." *New York Times,* Nov. 3, 4-1.

———. 1992. "Bruised Clinton Tries to Regain New York Poise." *New York Times,* Apr. 5, A1.

Kendall, Kathy, and Judith Trent. 1989. "Presidential Surfacing in the New Hampshire Primary." *Political Communication Review* 14, 3.

Klein, J. 1992. "The Year of the Voter." *Newsweek,* Nov./Dec., 15.

Marcus, R. 1992. "Tom Harkin: Fighter for the Underdog or Rank Opportunist?" *Washington Post,* Mar. 2–8, 13, 14.

Miller, A. H., M. P. Wattenberg, and O. Malanchuk. 1986. "Schematic Assessments of Presidential Candidates." *American Political Science Review* 80, 521–40.

Nelson, J. 1991. "83% Say Domestic Issues Are Key for 1992 Race." *Los Angeles Times,* Oct. 13, A1, A26.

"Oval Office Door Is Cracked, and Democrats Line Up to Get In." 1991. *Cincinnati Enquirer,* Nov. 24, A6.

Pearlstein, S. 1991. "Piecing Together the Puzzle of Paul Tsongas." *Washington Post,* Apr. 29–May 5, 8.

Schmalz, J. 1992a. "After Scanning Ballot, New York Rolls Its Eyes." *New York Times,* Apr. 6, A8.

———. 1992b. "Brown in New York, Assails Clinton with a New Ferocity." *New York Times,* Mar. 23, A1.

"Six Men and a Donkey." 1992. *Newsweek,* Nov./Dec., 28, 29, 30.

Sontag, D. 1992. "Hillary Clinton: Speaking about Rumors." *New York Times,* Apr. 5, A14.

Taylor, P. 1990. "Democrats, Start Your Engines." *Washington Post,* Nov. 5–11, 12.

Toner, R. 1991. "It Is Official. Tsongas Is First to Enter '92 Race." *New York Times,* May 1, C19.

———. 1992. "Uneasy New York." *New York Times,* Apr. 6, A9.

Trent, J. S. 1978. "Presidential Surfacing: The Ritualistic and Crucial First Act." *Communication Monographs* 45, Nov., 282.

———. 1986. "They Keep Running and the Rules Keep Changing: An Overview of the Early Campaign from 1972 to 1988." *Political Communication Review* 2, 7–18.

Trent, Judith S., and Robert V. Friedenberg. 1991. *Political Campaign Communication,* 2d ed. New York: Praeger.

Von Drehle, D. 1992. "Election '92: The Year of the Truly Weird." *Washington Post,* Nov. 9–15, 10.

Weymouth, Lally. 1991. "Buchanan's Right Hook to Bush." *Washington Post,* Dec. 30–Jan. 5, 1992, 23.

Williams, J. 1991. "What If They Gave an Election and No Democrats Showed Up?" *Washington Post,* Mar. 18–24, 25.

Yepsen, D. 1991. "Another Casualty of War: Democrats' 1992 Chances." *Cincinnati Enquirer,* Mar. 10, A10.

Yoder, E. M., Jr. 1991. "Clinton as a Prime Candidate." *Cincinnati Enquirer,* Sept. 15, A10.

3

The 1992 Presidential Nominating Conventions: Cordial Concurrence Revisited

David M. Timmerman and Larry David Smith

The 1992 presidential campaign reversed long-held stereotypes for the Democratic and the Republican national conventions: the Democrats were unified and polished; the Republicans were fragmented and raw. *Time* magazine's description of the Democrats' assembly reflects that assessment: "It was like a Republican convention. Everything worked. The words were good. The television was good. The propaganda, especially, was good" (Kramer, 1992, 28). Still, there is little news in the strategic manipulation of "words, television, and propaganda" in a national convention context; to be sure, a contemporary "telepolitical convention" (Smith and Nimmo, 1991) is a product of carefully contrived scripts enacted on professionally designed stages. As we shall see, what was newsworthy in 1992 was the striking contrast in the content and style of the two conventions.

Although professional orchestration of convention content and delivery may have evolved over the years, the convention's institutional function remains constant. From the outset, the title "nominating convention" was a misnomer. Presidential conventions rarely make nominating decisions—rather, they endorse conclusions rendered elsewhere. Thus, Smith and Nimmo (1991) describe the convention's principal purpose as the orchestration of "cordial concurrence"—a notion that first appeared in the 1832 Democratic convention's platform. That platform contained one resolution:

The convention reposes the highest confidence in the purity, patriotism and talents of Andrew Jackson, and most cordially concurs in the repeated nominations which he has received in various parts of the Union as a candidate for reelection to the office he now fills with so much honor to himself and usefulness to this country. (Smith and Nimmo, 1991, 2)

The authors concluded:

Just as the first national convention of a major political party in 1832 did not "nominate" a candidate for president, but instead cordially concurred in repeated endorsements by various state legislatures, so too in 1988 neither major party convened to nominate, but instead to legitimate endorsements by voters in statewide presidential primaries. (2)

As Democrats and Republicans gathered in New York and Houston for their respective 1992 conventions, they too labored to orchestrate "cordial concurrence" in support of Arkansas governor Bill Clinton's and incumbent president George Bush's primary season victories.

That state primaries and caucuses foster intraparty debate over domestic, foreign, and personality matters is certain. Such debate is often acrimonious. The 1992 Republican contests featured a troublesome challenge to President Bush's leadership from the archconservative wing of his party. Governor Clinton also faced considerable opposition in the form of Jerry Brown's anti-establishment campaign as well as earlier challenges by Paul Tsongas, Tom Harkin, Bob Kerrey, and other often serious questions regarding his personal integrity. Traditionally, the convention brings a shift from these intraparty confrontations toward internal unity and, correspondingly, interparty conflict. These homecomings are not always filled with welcoming hugs and tears of joy. History indicates that a spirit of cordiality may not be taken for granted.

This chapter considers the orchestration of cordial concurrence within the convention context. We will use narrative principles to interpret the style and substance of the respective 1992 conventions' podium oratory, video presentations, and platforms. When considered in their totality, did these political hymnals direct the harmony indicative of cordial concurrence, or did they render a cacophony of conflicting partisan sounds? We will begin with a brief theoretical overview and follow with the specifics from 1992.

ORCHESTRATING CORDIAL CONCURRENCE:
A THEORETICAL PLAYBILL

Presidential nominating conventions perform institutional functions. Through the nomination, platform, campaign-rally, and governing-body functions, the parties attempt to solidify and occasionally expand their resources for the general election (David, Goldman, and Bain, 1960). Over the years these various activities have been allocated their own moments in the convention program: party business (e.g., seating delegations, selecting convention officers, organizing committees) is conducted early on Monday; platforms are discussed and ratified on Tuesday; demonstrations and entertainment (campaign-rally enactments) appear throughout; the nominating/voting activities take place on Wednesday; and the national committee members interact during the week and officially meet on Friday. These various institutional acts comprise what the 1988 Republican convention manager Bill Phillips termed the convention's "shell." Phillips's executive assistant, Merri Jo Cleair, explained that once the convention's order of business (the shell) is in place, convention programmers fill in "the entertainment or speeches and the special effects and the things you do for television" (Smith and Nimmo, 1991, 65). That is, the convention programmers build a show around the convention's shell that, if successful, introduces a keynote theme on Monday and maintains continuity throughout the four-day event.

To suggest that the conventions are "extended dramas" (Smith, 1987, 259) that lend themselves to narrative critique is not a bold inferential leap. Here we evaluate the narrative continuity of the 1992 conventions by way of the three-step technique Smith (1990, 1992b) calls "narrative synthesis." This method begins with a recognition of the narrative's function and, from that starting point, reduces the subject matter to its constituent parts: characters, values, and plots. Afterward, those raw materials are organized into a composite text to capture the story's theoretical implications. Smith has used this approach in critiques of the dialectical narrative (network television news) that attempts to separate fact from fiction for audiences (1988, 1992a); the rhetorical narrative (convention oratory and party platforms) that pursues persuasive goals (1987, 1989, 1990, 1992b); and the poetic narrative (Bruce Springsteen's lyrics) that involves artistic expression (Hemphill and Smith, 1990).

We take a convention's podium oratory, platform, and video presentations to be "rhetorical narratives that share three persuasive objectives: (1) to identify the combatants (the 'us' vs. 'them' characterizations central to a two-party system's rhetoric); (2) to establish party values; and (3) to generate the story lines that provide motives for the partisan action which shall be the campaign" (Smith, 1990, 21). We will interpret these narrative elements as they appear in approximately 300 speeches, two party platforms, and multiple video presentations.[1] We will show the extent to which the two parties successfully transformed the *individual* tales (i.e., candidate-based stories) of the primaries into the party narratives of the general election and, in doing so, orchestrated "cordial concurrence" and party unity.

CORDIAL CONCURRENCE REVISITED:
THE 1992 CONVENTIONS

Since the 1992 primary season yielded two clear-cut victors, the two parties once again assembled to endorse a foregone conclusion. Not only did the two political parties share this basic institutional objective, they also shared several tactical hurdles: how to reshape unpleasant histories, how to deal with minor actors seeking major roles in the four-day spectacle (Jerry Brown in New York and Pat Buchanan in Houston), and how to introduce—in the Republicans' case, recast—the show's leading characters. The 1992 New York Democratic National Convention (hereafter, DNC) and the Houston Republican National Convention (hereafter, RNC) faced major challenges with serious implications for the general election.

Essential to the successful orchestration of cordial concurrence is the management of the stage production itself. The New York convention turned to Hollywood-based producer Gary Smith, producer of the 1988 Atlanta DNC, to orchestrate his second consecutive convention. The Houston convention introduced a new player to the process in Hollywood-based David J. Nash, who replaced Mark Goode as the RNC's executive producer (Berke, 1992). The producers shared a "Hollywood" background, but the disparity in convention-related experience played a key role in the success of the two 1992 productions.

The Democrats had lost five of the last six presidential elections, and they gathered in New York armed with the traditional "time for a change" argument. Relying on the four-session approach that requires convention participants to endure six- and seven-hour sessions, the 1992 DNC used narrative tactics that managed to ease the pain that accompanies this marathon convention style. Monday's three-tier keynote and floor-based overview of female U.S. Senate candidates; Tuesday's reasonably smooth platform ratification and its now-traditional appearance by Jesse Jackson; Wednesday's nominating and voting rituals; and Thursday's acceptance speeches all unfolded in a slow but systematic fashion. Undeclared presidential candidate Ross Perot's announcement that he would not run for office further enhanced the Democrats' narrative tactics. After three days of arguments for "change," Thursday night's emphasis on the "agents of change" was boosted by Perot's departure, as the competing "agent of change" removed himself from the contest.

The GOP assembled in Houston and replayed its 1988 format via its six-session strategy (featuring two morning sessions on Monday and Tuesday, and four evening sessions throughout the week) as well as Ronald Reagan's opening night performance and the Tuesday night keynote address. There was one major deviation in the 1992 schedule: the party platform was discussed and ratified on Monday morning, not Tuesday (traditionally "Platform Day"). This procedural change suggests the controversial qualities of this particular Republican convention. The GOP endeavored to solidify its conservative base while simultaneously providing a much-needed "convention bounce" (i.e., improved polling numbers) for its nominee. Having it both ways—appealing to archconservatives and attracting mainstream voters—presented a formidable challenge for the Houston conclave.

The 1992 Conventions: The Master Plots

The New York Democrats told a story of change through the "New Covenant: People First" plot that unfolded in two parts. From Monday through Wednesday the Democrats argued for the need for change ("Part One") through traditional convention rhetoric based on the "us versus them" grammar of a two-party contest. Once that need had been established, the DNC followed with "Part Two" of the show and Thursday night's emphasis on the presidential ticket. Wednesday featured a transition from the "need for change" to the "agents of change" by way of a strategic appeal to party history. That is, the DNC used a segment honoring Robert F. Kennedy to establish its ticket's political heritage, to anchor its emphasis on "people first" via a romantic construction of Kennedy's philosophy, and to issue a direct appeal to the Reagan Democrats to return to their party. Whereas the 1988 Democrats labored to recast their party through an abridged platform and slogans such as "this is not your father's party," the 1992 Democrats took the opposite path. The New York Democrats directly embraced party history as they offered a "new argument," not a "new party." The "New Covenant" represented an attempt to unify traditional Democrats against a common foe (the evil elites that make up the GOP, personified in George Bush and Dan Quayle). Hence, they relished party history, described the evil qualities of Republican policies and personalities, and turned to a ticket that offered a new plan (the New Covenant) that featured values ("people first") predicated on a remodeled party history. DNC executive producer Gary Smith used a telegenic mixture of films, remote broadcasts, alternative forms of presentation (e.g., having the female Senate candidates address the assembly from the convention floor), and a coherent script to present the New Covenant theme. Smith's creative use of the "video wall" positioned behind the rostrum facilitated the production's thematic qualities. For instance, when speakers addressed the convention, the video wall featured the words "People First" softly displayed within the various murals (sketches of Clinton, scenes of Americana, etc.) and thereby constantly reinforced a single theme (the words "responsibility," "opportunity," and "community" also appeared). The 1992 DNC was a tightly packaged affair that reflected Smith's experience with party conventions.

The 1992 Houston Republicans followed a different approach. Billed "The American Spirit," the GOP convention enacted a disjointed "Return of the Evil Empire" script in which it stressed "what we're against" far more than any other topic. Although the party's evening sessions opened with videos that established "The American Spirit" themes, speakers did not reinforce those images from the rostrum. In 1992, the Party of Lincoln was a house divided. On the one hand, Americans witnessed the "party of inclusion" in which speakers such as Ronald Reagan, Jack Kemp, and Phil Gramm argued for individuality, compassion, and entrepreneurial freedom. On the other hand, Americans saw the "party of exclusion" in which speakers such as Pat Buchanan, Pat Robertson, and the party's platform presumed the GOP to be the "party of God" in direct conflict with the alternative lifestyles rendered by the Democrats' liberal philosophies. Each version of the Republican script opened with the proclamation "the end of the Cold War"; however, they quickly departed from that starting point as the various speeches unfolded. As a result, the two sets of values clashed, speeches contradicted one another (e.g., the placement of Buchanan just prior to Reagan on Monday evening), and Nash's inexperience with national political conventions showed repeatedly.

With disagreement over the nature of the "us" component of the convention's "us versus them" characterization, the Houston Republicans focused on "them." And "they" were evil. The "party of inclusion" saw an evil Congress: an Evil Empire of privilege, patronage, and procrastination. For the "party of inclusion," Harry Truman and his 1948 battle against the "do-nothing Congress" gradually assumed heroic status as the audience endured hours of Congress-bashing and a Republican version of the "time for a change" argument. This portion of the Houston rhetoric maintained that the nation's problems were a product of a highly partisan, ineffective Congress that had wreaked havoc on domestic problems while the president was hard at work ending the Cold War and policing the Persian Gulf.

The "party of God" also saw an Evil Empire in the Congress and dutifully harmonized the "time for a change" tune. But this facet of the Republican assembly stressed the evil qualities of "liberalism": abortion must be banned, alternative lifestyles rejected, liberalism ended, and threats to "God's party" defeated. Many of these threats were personified in direct attacks against Clinton, his wife Hillary, and Edward Kennedy (to name a few). An appeal to family values represented the crux of the story, yet the exact nature of family values differed substantially within the party.

Complementing the disjointed qualities of the GOP rhetoric was the show's uneven—and at times, bad—production qualities. The orchestra missed cues or began playing while speakers were still talking (e.g., Guy Vander Jagt, Marilyn Quayle), films rolled off cue and interrupted speakers (e.g., Vander Jagt, Robert Dole), balloon drops failed (the post-Reagan demonstration), and most important, the four nightly themes were anything but thematic (Monday, "world issues"; Tuesday, "the American agenda"; Wednesday, "family values"; Thursday, "the presidency"). When the disparities between the "party of inclusion" and the "party of exclusion" stories are coupled with these production problems, what emerges is a convention whose only common theme involved the evil qualities of the opposition—and the GOP had difficulty agreeing on that.

Thus, the 1992 conventions were very different affairs. One had a tightly scripted message and production values that facilitated the orchestration of cordial concurrence; the other was an uneven, disjointed show that stressed two Evil Empires and their threat to the Party of Lincoln's two offspring.

The 1992 Convention: The Characters

Smith (1990) maintains that convention rhetoric often features "broad appeals to widely admired values and stories" (24) that are given a sharp partisan edge through the characterization process. Through party characterizations, the 1992 "heroes and villains" are created in an effort to "generate conflict." As Smith reports, "In the absence of conflict, citizens and voters have few reasons for partisanship; as a result, party characterizations may be blunt, oversimplified, and insulting." The 1992 conventions most certainly subscribed to this narrative principle.

The DNC harmonized a "party of the past versus the party of the future" tune in which it lambasted the Reagan/Bush years and the economic recession Democrats attributed to those two administrations. Predictably, the Democrats blamed every conceivable problem on the GOP as they portrayed their party and candidate as the country's best hope. Texas governor Ann Richards proclaimed: "We're tired of hearing about the Eighties, they are over. We're tired of hearing about the Reagan era, it's over." Atlanta mayor Maynard Jackson quoted Ronald Reagan's 1984 campaign theme ("Morning in America") to his rhetorical advantage: "There's mourning in America all right. There's weeping and mourning." Jackson continued: "Let us tell Bush and Quayle 'if you fool us once, shame on you. But if you fool us twice, shame on us.'" Unlike the 1988 Atlanta convention and its reluctance to directly attack Ronald Reagan, the New York Democrats did not hesitate to attack the Reagan/Bush administration.

Many attacks focused more on Bush's leadership involving foreign and domestic issues. With regard to foreign policy, examples include Jesse Jackson's claim that it is "racist and wrong" for the Bush administration to "lock the Haitians out" and the party platform's concern for "national security" matters. Yet the bulk of the DNC's attack strategy blasted Bush's domestic policies and his leadership style. For instance, Party Chair Ron Brown labeled Bush's administration a "failed presidency," and Mario Cuomo described Bush's leadership style through a maritime metaphor. The New York governor lamented that "the ship of state is in trouble" and argued:

The crew knows it. The passengers know it. Only the captain of the ship, President Bush, appears not to know it. He seems to think that the ship will be saved by imperceptible undercurrents, directed by the invisible hand of some cyclical economic god, that will gradually move the ship so that at the last moment it will miraculously glide past the rocks to safer shores.

Clinton joined this attack by comparing the current situation to one faced by another Republican president. The Democratic nominee recalled the tale of Abraham Lincoln's frustrations with General George McClellan during the Civil War. Like Lincoln, who asked McClellan to loan him the army McClellan himself would not use, Clinton challenged Bush by saying "if you won't use your power to help America, step aside. I will."

According to Democrats the crux of Bush's leadership problem was the president's lack of political vision. Bill Bradley attempted to incite a cheerleading session by describing Bush's reaction to the deficit, rising health care costs, the Los Angeles riots, and the environment. The New Jersey senator said Bush "waffled and wiggled and wavered" on these crucial matters. Charleston (SC) mayor Joe Riley, Jr., described the Bush administration as "visionless" and "directionless." Louisville mayor Jerry Abramson announced that the country could no longer wait for Bush to "rediscover America" and "get it right the second time." Maxine Waters claimed "we can't wait around for George Bush to develop the 'vision thing,' we need Bush to get ready for the 'exit thing.'" And Ron Brown suggested that the president was helpless: "George Bush, the guy who's fallen and just can't get up."

Joining the DNC's portrayal of Bush's leadership style were relentless attacks on his economic policies and the perceived lack of compassion that inspired those decisions. Bronx Borough president Fernando Ferrer said Bush had "presided over the largest dismantling of the American economy since 1929" and renamed the president "George 'what recession?' Bush." Senator Harris Wofford (PA) concluded that Bush "must have pushed the snooze button" when the "economic alarm" sounded. "George Bush has driven the world's most powerful economy into the ditch," declared John Martin, chairman of the National Association of State Legislators. Paul Tsongas maintained: "The Bush legacy is clear. America has become the greatest debtor nation on earth, increasingly unable to compete in world trade markets as it sinks further into debt. He has taken the treasure of ten generations and sacrificed it to false happy days political rhetoric." Clinton described Bush as a president "caught in the grip of a failed economic theory"; Tom Harkin dubbed Bush "George Herbert Hoover Bush"; and—in one of the DNC's most colorful remarks—Representative Alan Wheat (MO) observed that "nobody can do that voodoo better than you do."

Accompanying these attacks on economic matters were negative portrayals of the Republicans' electoral strategy and political philosophy. Cuomo labeled the GOP tactics as a "cynical political arithmetic that says you can add by subtracting, you multiply by dividing." Joe Riley noted Republicans "divide us, to pit urban against rural, city against suburb, rich against poor." Hubert Price (president of the National Association of Democratic County Officials) harmonized that Bush and the Republicans responded to cries of suffering with "a constant stream of platitudinous el toro pooh pooh." Bob Kerrey offered a personal view by stating, "I'm a man who became a Democrat in 1978 because I do not believe the Republican party gives a damn about the American people." And, in an emotional speech that recounted how she and her two children had contracted the AIDS virus, Elizabeth Glaser recalled: "Exactly four years ago my daughter died of AIDS. She did not survive the Reagan administration. I am here because my son and I may not survive four more years of leaders who say they care, but do nothing."

Complementing the negative portrayals of Bush and the Republicans were predictable descriptions of the Democratic party and its nominee. The 1992 DNC portrayed itself as the party of inclusion, the party of change, and as a party that respects its political history. Throughout, DNC speakers depicted Clinton as the embodiment of these treasured principles. For example, Cuomo commended Clinton because he "believes, as we all here do, in the first principle of our commitment, the politics of inclusion"; and Ron Brown claimed Clinton brought "together under one great, vibrant tent people of all races, genders, sexual orientations, classes, ethnic groups, religions, and the disabled of America." Representative Jose Serrano (NY) said "Bill Clinton is the embodiment of the American dream" and that the Arkansas governor had "faced difficulties and obstacles to his progress that George Bush and Dan Quayle could never imagine, much less overcome." Last, Boston mayor Raymond Flynn identified Clinton as someone "who knows what it means to come from a family that lives from paycheck to paycheck," to which Governor Zell Miller (GA) added: Clinton "feels our pain, shares our hopes and will work his heart out to fulfill our dreams."

To anchor these characterizations in party tradition, the DNC revisited party history. Richard Gephardt noted that the 1992 convention had returned the party to its "historic role as agents of our enduring American revolution." Barbara Jordan recounted the party's historic role as "the instrument of change in policies which impact education, human rights, civil rights, economic and social opportunity, and the environment." Ron Brown forcefully affirmed, "We stand for the noble past of Roosevelt and Truman and Kennedy and Carter." A film on the DNC platform identified Democrats as the descendants of Thomas Jefferson. Moreover, the convention's tribute to Robert Kennedy (featuring a film and speeches by Joseph and Edward Kennedy) conveyed RFK's legendary idealism and compassion for the disadvantaged and oppressed. In that vein, Cuomo cast the Arkansas governor as a leader who "cherishes the ideals of justice, liberty, and opportunity and fairness and compassion that Robert Kennedy died for."

These coherent portrayals of party identities were quite a contrast to the 1992 Republican National Convention's characterizations. Confusion over the "us" characterization of the Houston convention's rhetoric produced an emphasis on "them," as the GOP said less about themselves and more about their perceived enemy. Consequently, Republicans briefly mentioned their "Party of Lincoln" heritage and, from there, focused on three levels of Democrat "Evil Empire" characterizations: the Evil Congress, the Evil Liberals, and the Evil Bill and Hillary.

The "Party of Lincoln" grammar provided the foundation for the 1992 rhetoric for the "party of inclusion." Allan Keyes (a Maryland U.S. Senate candidate) described the "spirit of Lincoln's republicanism" that made him "proud to be a Republican"; Ronald Reagan quoted Lincoln, labeled those sentiments as the party's foundation, and argued that until Democrats cite Lincoln as their guide their philosophy will remain unchanged; and Gerald Ford announced: "My fellow Republicans, don't you forget what this party is all about. This is the party of Abraham Lincoln, who lived and died for the proposition that all men are created equal." To be sure, this was the narrative of the party of inclusion: identify with Lincoln's image and, afterward, argue for individualism and equal opportunity. Jack Kemp's remarks typify this narrative strategy:

The purpose of a great party is not to defeat its opponents. The purpose of a great party is to provide superior leadership and greater cause. It's not to denounce the past, it's to inspire our nation to a better future. This great cause is the same today as it was when our party was founded. . . . Lincoln believed that in this country capitalism must grow from the bottom up, not the top down. It must begin on main street and extend to Wall Street, not the other way around.

Wisconsin governor Tommy Thompson turned to traditional convention campaign rally methods to compare the combatants. Thompson affirmed: "Republicans stand for change. Democrats stand in the way. They are the party of old thinking, we are the party of new ideas. They make things worse, we make things work. They cling to the status quo, we embrace change. They are the party of April 15th, and the Republicans are the party of July 4th." Thompson's remarks are particularly interesting in that they reflect the essence of the GOP's 1984/1988 narrative. In Dallas in 1984 and New Orleans in 1988 the RNC described the Democratic *leadership* as inefficient advocates of big government and tax-and-spend policies, and they contrasted that characterization with the innovative, patriotic Republicans. Thompson, Reagan, Kemp, and keynoter Phil Gramm were among the few to subscribe to this narrative tactic in 1992, as most Republicans focused on the various "Evil Empire" attacks.

"Evil Empire I" involved the Congress. Robert Michel of Illinois (the highest ranking Republican in the House) asserted that "this election is just as much about the Congress as it is about the presidency"; Bush lamented that the "gridlocked Democratic Congress [is] caught in a hopelessly tangled web of PACs, perks, privileges, partnership and paralysis"; and Guy Vander Jagt charged that "the Democrats have amply demonstrated in the House that they can't run a bank, a post office or a restaurant and they sure can't run the U.S. House either" and professed that it was time to change the "check bouncing, free lunching, ticket fixing, pay raising, tax increasing, budget busting, House of Representatives." There was no shortage of Congress-bashing in Houston; there were just different levels of intensity. Reagan introduced a "Clean House" slogan; Ford described the House as an institution "that knows all about checks but not one damn thing about balances"; and Robert Dole (KS) remarked "never before have so many done so little for so long." Phil Gramm issued the "party of inclusion" keynote with these remarks: "America's problem today is not that the president's plan to energize the economy has failed. Our problem is that it has not been tried. It is not that the president did not ask for change but that the Democrats who run the Congress killed those changes."

In contrast with the "party of inclusion's" emphasis on the battle between "America's party" and the Evil Empire on Capitol Hill, the "party of exclusion" attacked "liberalism." Televangelist and former presidential candidate Pat Robertson charged that an "insidious plague has fastened itself upon the families of America" and that "the carrier of this plague is the Democratic Party." Robertson used a strategic association to place his plague in a historical context: "Lyndon Johnson called it the Great Society. Bill Clinton calls it the New Covenant." William Bennett followed Robertson's lead with his line "America does not need false prophets bearing new covenants," and Vice President Quayle added, "The gap between us and our opponents is a cultural divide. It is not just a difference between conservative and liberal, it is a difference between fighting for what is right and refusing to see what's wrong." These negative characterizations traveled to such lengths as California attorney general Dan Lungren's "law-and-order" attack on "the liberals." After defending the use of the infamous 1988 "Willie Horton" television ad (calling the words "Willie Horton" a "liberal icon"), Lungren described how the "San Francisco Democrats" had "cloaked" themselves in "respectable Madison Square Garden colors" when, in fact, the New York Democrats were the same old party—a party that allowed criminals to harass the polity through its "legacy of leniency." Primary season runner-up Pat Buchanan extended this sartorial metaphor and established the scene for what would become an intensely personal attack on the Democratic nominee and his wife. Buchanan referred to the New York convention as a "giant masquerade ball" in which "20,000 liberals and radicals came dressed up as moderates and centrists in the greatest single exhibition of cross-dressing in American political history." This was Part One of the "party of exclusion's" characterization: identify the Democratic party as the home of liberals who are assaulting family values, willing to take "your money" to fund their proverbial "welfare state," and unwilling to toe the line on law and order. This was merely Part One—once the evil qualities of liberalism were established, direct attacks on individuals followed.

Virtually all GOP speakers attacked Clinton in one fashion or another. Reagan used humor through his "I knew Thomas Jefferson, and you're no Thomas Jefferson" jibe at Clinton; Kay Bailey Hutchinson joked about Clinton's economic program with the line "you know something? I think he really did inhale" (a reference to Clinton's public statements about his experience with marijuana); and Bush attacked Clinton for vacillating on the issues by stating "he's been spotted in more places than Elvis Presley." These types of negative characterizations are clearly the stuff of convention tradition, but the Houston conclave did not stop there. Buchanan asserted that "Bill Clinton and Al Gore represent the most pro-lesbian and pro-gay ticket in history" and charged that "when Bill Clinton's time came in Vietnam he sat up in a dormitory room in Oxford, England, and figured out how to dodge the draft." Buchanan also attacked the nominee's wife by saying, "Hillary believes that twelve-year-olds should have the right to sue their parents, and Hillary has compared marriage and the family, as institutions, to slavery and life on an Indian reservation." Labor secretary Lynn Martin pursued "the character issue" with this not-so-subtle remark: "No, you can't be one kind of man and another kind of president." Party Chair Rich Bond described Clinton as the "failed governor" of a small state; and Commerce Secretary Barbara Franklin maintained that when Clinton "looks at America's free enterprise system, he sees a chance to regulate, a chance to dictate, and a chance to tax, tax, tax. . . . [He] has nothing to offer but the same old liberal program repackaged in blow-dried rhetoric." After four days of negative characterizations that rotated between intensely personal attacks and philosophical debate, Bush described the situation in this fashion: "Who do you trust in this election? The candidate who raised taxes one time and regrets it, or the other candidate [who] raised taxes and fees 128 times, and enjoyed it every time?" According to the president, the nation faced a "dangerous combination" with Clinton's election, "a rubber check Congress and a rubber stamp president."

In complete contrast to the 1984/1988 GOP conventions and their emphasis on "Party of Lincoln," patriotic (i.e., inclusionary) characterizations, the Houston Republicans offered a less coherent construction of the "us versus them" narrative, as they vacillated between two sets of stories. As we shall see, the 1992 GOP offered incoherent characterizations of itself due to its apparent confusion over party values.

The 1992 Conventions: The Values

Along with the strategic construction of identities that establish the battle lines for the fall campaign is the articulation of party values that, in effect, provide the rationale for these "good" and/or "evil" characterizations. Speakers describe their commitment to "compassion," for "individual prosperity," and for the proverbial American Dream (to name but a few of these value-laden clichés). They explain the evil qualities of the opposition by noting their "permissiveness," their abuse of privilege, and their "insincerity." For the DNC, values such as compassion, hope (the nominee grew up in Hope, Arkansas), social responsibility, and tolerance battled Republican indifference, elitism, and irresponsibility. For the RNC, values such as faith in God, individual initiative, and a "limited government" battled the big-government, socially liberal, and morally corrupt tendencies of Democrats.

The most direct statements of party values are found in the respective platforms. Since these documents are the only institutionally approved statements of partisan resolve available, much debate surrounds their contents. The 1992 Democratic platform moved away from its 1988 edition (a seven-page "letter to the American people"—see Smith, 1992b) and returned to convention tradition with a 10,000-word document. The 1992 GOP platform belonged to the "Party of God." Although it followed a traditional format, the Houston platform took a decided turn to the conservative right on social matters.

The New York platform, entitled "A New Covenant," represented an attempt to recast the party's liberal history in more moderate terms. Thus, the *Chicago Tribune* described the document as a "self-help platform" that argued for a "new social contract" between the American people and its government ("Democrats Pass," 1992, 12). With phrases such as "governments don't raise children, people do" and with attacks on "big government theory that says we can hamstring business and tax-and-spend our way to prosperity," the DNC platform displayed "whole sections that would have been hooted down not too many years ago" (Rosenbaum, 1992a, A9). After describing "the last twelve years" of "Republican irresponsibility and neglect" that inspired "the anguish and the anger of the American people," the DNC platform called for "A REVOLUTION IN GOVERNMENT" ("Excerpts from the Platform," 1992, A10). The document's preamble captured the argument:

To make this revolution, we seek a NEW COVENANT to repair the damaged bond between the American people and their government, that will expand OPPORTUNITY, insist upon greater individual RESPONSIBILITY in return, restore COMMUNITY and insure NATIONAL SECURITY in a profoundly new era.

The DNC platform stressed virtues such as personal responsibility, strengthening the family, and the need for military might—all values that would find a positive reception in any GOP platform. The New York platform also endorsed government-paid abortions for the poor, higher taxes on the wealthy, and civil rights protection for homosexuals. This move toward the middle inspired Rosenbaum (1992b) to write: "The platform . . . puts new conservative words to an old liberal tune in an attempt to find a middle road between the unfettered capitalism espoused by Republicans and the welfare state economics of the Democrats' past" (A10).

This search for common ground represented a marked departure from the 1992 Republican platform. According to the *New York Times* editorial board, the Houston platform practiced the "politics of exclusion" ("The Politics," 1992, A18). The platform, entitled "The Vision Shared: Uniting Our Family, Our Country, Our World," featured scenes of Ellis Island on its cover that, in the *Times*'s view, were a distortion of its contents: "The Republican Party on display in Houston is far more exclusionist than these Ellis Island scenes would suggest. It's clear from the number of women and blacks present that the party has made strides. But on issue after issue—abortion, gay rights and race—the Republicans still have a long way to go before actions match their rhetoric." Indeed, the 1992 platform positioned the party as the "Party of Lincoln" (the platform's first two words are "Abraham Lincoln") in that it opened with Lincoln's preference for "individuality" over "government" ("Excerpts from the Republican Party's Platform," 1992, A8). From there, the platform described America's "rendezvous with destiny" in 1980 and how presidents "Reagan and Bush turned our nation away from the path of over-taxation, hyper-regulation, and mega-government." With the "shining city on a hill" restored, the GOP document argued that "Republicans believe government should strengthen families, not replace them" and that "we believe our laws should reflect what makes our nation prosperous and wholesome: faith in God, hard work, service to others, and limited government." From that preamble onward, the Party of Lincoln—1984 and 1988's "party of inclusion"—yielded to 1992's "Party of God" and its exclusionary rhetoric. A platform that initially endorsed "individuality" as a primary value quickly imposed restrictions on "individuality" with its pro-life, anti-homosexual, and anti–freedom of expression language (i.e., statements regarding the content of government-funded art). These traits, the narrative consistency of the Democrats' platform versus the inconsistency of the Republicans' platform, appeared from the rostrum as well.

The New York Democrats countered the "government-is-the-problem" theme used by the Republicans throughout the 1980s by portraying government, and the office of president, as powerful forces for "good." Subsequently, Senator Patrick Moynihan (NY) identified Democrats as people who believe that "government can embrace great causes, do great things," and Clinton defined the president's role "as a powerful force for progress." Yet the DNC tempered its view of government with a strong call to individual responsibility via an emphasis on individual initiative and responsibility (themes that would be welcome at any Republican convention in the 1980s). Clinton used Biblical imagery to label the concept: "I call this approach a New Covenant—a solemn agreement between the people and their government—based not simply on what each of us can take but on what all of us must give to our nation." Democrats consistently harmonized the "New Covenant" tune and the value of shared responsibility between government and the citizenry. For example, Senator John Breaux (LA) advocated "forg[ing] a New Covenant that asks all of our citizens to give something back in return for what this country gives them," and Representative Dave McCurdy (OK) maintained that "government is not some automatic teller machine drawing on someone else's account. Anyone who receives from government has an obligation to give something back."

To anchor its "New Covenant" rhetoric in Democratic history, the DNC turned to a widely shared value: "People First." The words frequently appeared on the video wall behind the speakers and served as the convention's dominant appeal. Ron Brown affirmed that Democrats know that government works best when it puts "people first." Bill Bradley challenged the party not only to win the presidential election but "to give American men and women control over their lives once again." Tom Harkin used the theme to draw a distinction between the two major presidential candidates' economic plans: "Governor Clinton's plan puts people first, George Bush's plan puts wealthy people first." After three days of "people first" graphics, films, and speeches, Clinton's acceptance speech issued the capstone call: "Our priorities must be clear: we will put people first again."

The "New Covenant: People First" story emphasized three issues that supported the value of shared responsibility: jobs, health care, and education. Many statements, such as the one given by Queens Borough president Claire Schulman, addressed all three issues. Schulman stated: "[Clinton] knows that the most critical issue facing us today is the creation of meaningful and important jobs for our citizens. He believes in a national health care plan that provides quality care for all Americans. And he will be an education president who provides equal and quality education for all our children." Still, "jobs" emerged as the principal concern. According to Clinton: "One sentence in the platform we built says it all: 'The most important family policy, urban policy, labor policy, minority policy, and foreign policy America can have is an expanding entrepreneurial economy of high-wage, high-skill jobs.'" Exploiting the Republican "family values" argument, Lena Guerrero harmonized "the most fundamental family value in America: a job." Lottie Schackelford (AR) reinforced the education issue by noting that Clinton "knows how important education can be in changing people's lives because it changed his." Jay Rockefeller used self-deprecating humor to talk about health care: "Americans deserve health care that you don't have to be a Rockefeller to afford." And once again, Clinton's acceptance speech summarized the argument:

"Jobs. Education. Health care. These are not just commitments from my lips. They are the work of my life."

The harmony in the New York convention's value orientations was quite a departure from its counterpart in Texas. The "party of inclusion" and the "party of exclusion" may have shared varying levels of identification with Abraham Lincoln, but they differed dramatically in expressions of party values. In fact, this was more often than not the thrust of the two GOP stories in that after either strong ("inclusion") or lame ("exclusion") identification with Lincoln, messages focused on values that were fundamentally incompatible. The Houston convention may have agreed that it faced a battle with an Evil Empire, but it did not concur on the exact nature of that conflict.

Condoleeza Rice articulated the "party of inclusion's" value orientation in a direct manner: "The Republican party, in the first platform in 1856, called upon this nation to abolish slavery and make 'we the people' an inclusive concept. That is the heritage that brings out the best of our party today." Joining this value orientation were Reagan, Kemp, Massachusetts governor William Weld, Senator John Seymour (CA), and keynoter Phil Gramm. Reagan described America as an "Empire of Ideals" and argued: "Whether we come from poverty or wealth, whether we are Afro-American or Irish-American, Christian or Jewish, from big cities or small towns, we are all equal in the eyes of God. As Americans, that's not enough. We must be equal in the eyes of each other." Kemp envisioned an "America that pursues . . . an equality that allows poor people—indeed all people—to become rich." Kemp wished not for a wealth predicated on "creature comforts," but for all Americans to achieve their "God-given potential." Again, he turned to Lincoln: "The party of Lincoln does not believe people are a drain on resources; we believe people are our resources."

William Weld extended that argument toward policy matters and advocated a political system with undying respect for the individual. The governor stated: "What brings us together as Republicans, indeed what defines our party, is an enduring faith in individual freedom. . . . I happen to think that individual freedom extends to a woman's right to choose. I want the government out of your pocketbook and your bedroom." Weld's direct attack on the GOP's pro-life platform and constituency was reinforced by John Seymour's announcement that he represents "pro-choice . . . pro-family . . . [and] pro-jobs." Finally, Gramm told a story attributed to Lincoln about a small boy who was frightened by a meteor shower. The boy's father offered these comforting words: "Son, don't look at the shooting stars, look at the fixed stars that have guided us in the past and will guide us in the future." Gramm continued, "As we look to the future tonight, let us be guided by the fixed stars of freedom and opportunity; of family and faith; of values and character."

Gramm's remarks not only anchored his construction of party values in Lincoln's image, but they also reached out to "party of exclusion" sentiments with its "family and faith" refrain. That portion of the Houston convention suffered the narrative liability that is an internally inconsistent story. Consider Dan Quayle's remarks: "Like so many Americans, for me, family comes first. When family values are undermined, our country suffers. . . . Americans try to raise their children to understand right and wrong, only to be told that every so-called 'lifestyle alternative' is morally equivalent. That is wrong." Platform chair Senator Don Nickles (OK) asserted that the party platform is about "the future"—a "future where our children and grandchildren can live on farms and in communities . . . instilled with the values of individual responsibility, respect for others, and—yes—belief in God, a word that does not appear in the Democrats' platform." Of course, Pat Buchanan and Pat Robertson extended that story line. And Buchanan's relentless attack, once again, focused on Hillary Clinton. The former TV commentator termed Mrs. Clinton's ideas "radical feminism" and declared that the Clintons advocate "abortion on demand, a litmus test for the Supreme Court, homosexual rights, discrimination against religious schools, [and] women in combat units." Buchanan asserted that the Democratic ticket stood for "change alright" but concluded that these types of innovations were bad for "God's Country." Robertson joined the call for change, yet the televangelist's idea of change was decidedly exclusive. Robertson announced: "The people of Eastern Europe got rid of their left wingers. It is time we in America got rid of our left wingers!" From there, Robertson attacked the Clintons' stance on "family values" and described their proposals as "a radical plan to destroy the traditional family and transfer its functions to the federal government." These direct attacks on alternative lifestyles, religious freedom, and—remarkably—political opposition are totally inconsistent with appeals for "individual freedom" and "limited government." Aside from "God" and occasional references to Lincoln, few heroes may be found in this story that culminates in value-based attacks on the Evil Enemy.

There were moments when Republicans engaged in more traditional attacks on Democratic values. Not every speech buried its head in the sands of exclusion. Robert Michel proclaimed that Democrats believe in "taxation without hesitation," and Allan Keyes attacked the Democrats' belief in "one power . . . the power of the federal government." Keyes artfully argued that the federal government "is their Great God, their Final Answer, their Ultimate Solution"; as he observed, "that's why . . . they have seen every problem as a national problem, demanding national solutions through ever-expanding national bureaucracies, feeding on more and more of our tax dollars." Perhaps Representative Newt Gingrich (GA) offered the best example of the GOP's disdain for the Democrats' philosophy: "If Thomas Edison had invented the electric light in the age of the welfare state, the Democrats would immediately introduce a bill to protect the candle-making industry [and] the Democratic ticket would propose a tax on electricity."

These more traditional attacks on Democratic policy, when joined with the GOP's "Party of Lincoln" self-characterization, have enjoyed a recent history of electoral success: that is, construct a reality in which the Democratic ticket is seen as extreme—usually extremely liberal—and invite mainstream Democrats to join "America's Party." A portion of the Houston convention followed this narrative strategy. Consider Bush's Thursday night statement: "We offer a philosophy that puts faith in the individual, not the bureaucracy. A philosophy that empowers people to do their best so America can be at its best. . . . This is how we will build an America that is stronger, safer, and more secure. We start with a simple fact: government is too big and spends too much." Had the RNC's script emphasized this argument across the four-day spectacle, these words would have been a capstone event on the level of other contemporary acceptance speeches. But this was not the case in 1992, and convention history clearly indicates that such narrative inconsistency is a prescription for electoral disaster in the fall.

CONCLUSION

The Democratic and Republican parties gathered in New York and Houston in conventions designed to do what over two-thirds of their predecessors have done: namely, orchestrate cordial concurrence behind a predetermined candidate. Both assemblies enjoyed state-of-the-art technological facilities. Both conventions received relatively equal amounts of network television exposure and used satellite technology to distribute their messages independently. Both conventions achieved varying degrees of the so-called convention bounce in the public opinion polls. (Clinton's poll numbers were enhanced by Ross Perot's departure from the race.) Consequently, it appears as if both parties successfully orchestrated some measure of cordial concurrence through their 1992 conventions.

From a narrative perspective, however, the key to convention orchestration rests with the production's continuity. In terms of the show's production qualities and thematic unity, the test of a convention's success or failure lies in its ability to articulate an internally consistent portrayal of party identities and values through master plots that establish the general election's strategy. The 1992 New York Democrats achieved this level of narrative continuity; the 1992 Houston Republicans did not. As a result, from a narrative point of view the Houston assembly represents the first failed convention of the telepolitical era.

The telepolitical age (1984–present) has seen the Democrats try very distinct approaches to presidential politics. In 1984, the party turned to a loyal partisan with direct ties to party history and a historic vice-presidential selection. In 1988, the party relied on a political technocrat unsure of his political heritage but committed to redefining the party as the "party of the future." The former took a stance (primarily on taxes) and was rejected; the latter avoided stances and was defeated by his functional equivalent. Where would the party go in 1992?

The 1992 Democrats gave the nation its first Baby Boomer ticket, positioned that team in the middle of the political spectrum, and used a traditional challenge—"it's time for a change." Columnist David Broder (1992) offers this assessment of that strategy:

This is a different kind of gamble the Democrats are taking this year—a gamble on a generation that has yet to produce a political leader who inspires national confidence. In nominating the Baby Boomer ticket of Bill Clinton, 45, and Albert Gore, Jr., 44, the Democrats have certainly broken with their past. Whether they have secured their future is another question altogether. (13)

The Democrats introduced their Baby Boomer ticket through a strategy that did not, as Broder suggests, break with "their past" but merely recast that "past." The New Covenant theme allowed the party to embrace—not reject—its history by asserting it had a new plan based on an old philosophy: people first. To place that theme in a historical context, the New York conclave evoked Robert Kennedy's image. The DNC established the need for change, introduced the type of change it proposed, placed that argument in a historical context, and presented a presidential ticket that personified the carefully crafted position.

The telepolitical era has seen the Republican party go undefeated in presidential contests. One of the many keys to this electoral success has been the GOP's ability to transcend partisanship through patriotic appeals. In 1984 and 1988, the Party of Lincoln argued for inclusion based on patriotism; a position that was expressed best in Katherine Ortega's 1984 keynote address when she proclaimed she supported Ronald Reagan "not because I am a woman. Not because I am of Hispanic heritage. But above all because I am an American." The story's internal consistency was its strength in that it focused on the positive, used party history as its foundation, and cast the negative in precise fashions. Throughout this winning streak the conventions played a pivotal role: convention films provided footage for fall television commercials, podium speeches introduced campaign and debate themes, and intraparty unity was achieved.

All this fell apart in 1992. A *New York Times* media critic described the situation in his discussion of the inconsistencies between the "party show" and the "television network program." He wrote: "Watching the Republican National Convention is a split-screen experience. It is like a concert with two orchestras whose conductors are not on speaking terms" (Goodman, 1992, B3). From our perspective, that split-screen experience featured the party of inclusion on one half and the party of exclusion on the other. Prior to the convention, Republican National Committee chair Richard Bond asserted that the 1992 election would be a "cultural war"; yet ironically, the first battle of that war was fought in Houston. That confrontation featured "conservatism with a snarl against conservatism with a smile" and, in so doing, revealed "a frustrated convention" (Apple, 1992a, A7).

Unsure of its identity, the Houston assembly focused on the enemy, embellished the negative qualities of the Evil Empire on Capitol Hill, and attacked the personalities of "liberal" Democrats. The godless tyrants that comprised Ronald Reagan's Evil Empire simply moved from the Kremlin to the Capitol and now aspired to the White House as well. Lewis's contention that the GOP became "merchants of hate" (1992, A19) is evident in Senator Richard Lugar's (IN) views on the "conservatism with a snarl" rhetoric: "You don't build majorities by excluding whole groups of people, and you don't have to be nasty to be conservative. I wish they'd cut it out. . . . I'm not comfortable with that at all" (Apple, 1992a, A7). That the Houston convention's story gradually moved from its Party of Lincoln foundation toward heroic images of a former Democratic president indicates the GOP's narrative confusion. As one reporter observed, "Harry S. [sic] Truman, the American President at the start of the cold war, has become the patron saint of George Bush, the President at the end" (Apple, 1992b, 1).

Exacerbating the RNC's problems was the unprecedented breakdown in the show's production standards. To that end, Berke (1992) states: "The political parties pulled off a striking role reversal at this year's national conventions: the Republicans stage-managed their show like Democrats and the Democrats put on theirs like Republicans. . . . When it came to production values, pacing and excitement, each side seemed to mimic the customs of its rival" (A8). As noted earlier, films rolled off cue, the orchestra interrupted speakers, and efforts to place prominent speakers in prime time either failed (e.g., Ronald Reagan) or caused complete schedule breakdowns (e.g., Barbara Bush). In short, the Houston convention was an ugly show, with an ugly message, and clearly set the scene for failure.

We fully realize that this is a harsh condemnation of the 1992 Republican convention; however, Smith and Nimmo (1991) demonstrate just how much the GOP is in touch with these tactical matters. The Grand Old Party introduced and refined many of the orchestral techniques that rendered the telepolitical era. Thematic speeches, stage theatrics, telegenic pacing, and inspirational films have been the hallmark of contemporary Republican conventions. Yet somehow the GOP ignored its own principles and produced an incoherent, mean-spirited show that culminated in George Bush comparing himself to Bill Clinton in terms of their physiques ("I am heartened by the polls—the ones that say I look better in my jogging shorts than the governor of Arkansas").

Such was the orchestration of cordial concurrence in 1992. The extent to which these assemblies successfully transformed the primary season's intraparty battles into the interparty war of the general election is the stuff of subsequent chapters in this volume. Our challenge has been to capture the results of the party's orchestration efforts and interpret that strategy as a rhetorical narrative. With luck, we have exposed the internal workings of these partisan constructions of reality and unveiled the strengths and weaknesses of those storytelling maneuvers.

NOTE

1. The remarks attributed to speakers appearing before the Democratic National Convention and the Republican National Convention are taken from the broadcasts of the conventions by the C-SPAN television network.

REFERENCES

Apple, R. W. 1992a. "G.O.P. Is Flirting with the Dangers of Negativism." *New York Times,* Aug. 19, A7.
———. 1992b. "Bush in a Truman Mode." *New York Times,* Aug. 20, 1, A8.
Berke, R. L. 1992. "Remarkable Role Reversals in the 2 Parties' Big Shows." *New York Times,* Aug. 21, A8.
Broder, D. 1992. "Can Clinton and Gore Generate Trust from Their Own Generation?" *Chicago Tribune,* July 16, 13.
David, P. T., R. M. Goldman, and R. C. Bain. 1960. *The Politics of National Party Conventions.* Washington, DC: Brookings Institution.
"Democrats Pass a Self-Help Platform." 1992. *Chicago Tribune,* July 13, 12.
"Excerpts from the Platform: A 'New Covenant' with Americans." 1992. *New York Times,* July 15, A10.
"Excerpts from the Republican Party's Platform: A New Call for Unity." 1992. *New York Times,* Aug. 18, A8.

Goodman, W. 1992. "Republicans Play a Dissonant Tune." *New York Times,* Aug. 19, B3.

Hemphill, M., and L. D. Smith. 1990. "The Working American's Elegy: The Rhetoric of Bruce Springsteen." In *Politics in Familiar Contexts: Projecting Politics through Popular Media,* Robert L. Savage and Dan Nimmo, eds., 199–213. Norwood, NJ: Ablex.

Kramer, M. 1992. "Front and Center: Clinton Surges into the Lead with a Flawless Performance as a Petulant Perot Bows Out and the President Goes Fishing." *Time,* July 27, 28–31.

Lewis, A. 1992. "Merchants of Hate." *New York Times,* Aug. 21, A19.

"The Politics of Exclusion." 1992. *New York Times,* Aug. 19, A18.

Rosenbaum, D. E. 1992a. "Democratic Platform Shows Shift in Party's Roots." *New York Times,* July 14, A9.

———. 1992b. "Party's Quest for a Middle Road: A Liberal Stance in Business Suits." *New York Times,* July 15, 1, A10.

Smith, L. D. 1987. "The Nominating Convention as Purveyor of Political Medicine: An Anecdotal Analysis of the Democrats and Republicans of 1984." *Central States Speech Journal* 38, 252–61.

———. 1988. "Narrative Styles in Network Coverage of the 1984 Nominating Conventions." *Western Journal of Speech Communication* 52, 63–74.

———. 1989. "A Narrative Analysis of the Party Platforms: The Democrats and Republicans of 1984." *Communication Quarterly* 37, 91–99.

———. 1990. "Convention Oratory as Institutional Discourse: A Narrative Synthesis of the Democrats and Republicans of 1988." *Communication Studies* 41, 19–34.

———. 1992a. "How the Dialectical Imperative Shapes Network News Content: The Case of CNN vs. the Entertainment Networks." *Communication Quarterly* 40, 338–49.

———. 1992b. "The Party Platforms as Institutional Discourse: The Democrats and Republicans of 1988." *Presidential Studies Quarterly* 22, 531–44.

Smith, Larry David, and Dan Nimmo. 1991. *Cordial Concurrence: Orchestrating National Party Conventions in the Telepolitical Age.* Westport, CT: Praeger.

"The Vision Thing." 1992. *New York Times,* July 12, 20.

4

The 1992 Presidential Debates

Robert V. Friedenberg

The 1992 election marked the fifth consecutive presidential election in which debates were held. Public opinion on holding debates has made them an institutionalized feature of our presidential elections. Though we were again reminded in 1992 that the ultimate decision rests with the candidates, the period leading up to the debates evidences the potent influence of public opinion.

DECISION TO DEBATE

Though early presidential debates were sponsored by the television networks and the League of Women Voters, in 1987 at the recommendation of a variety of experts, a nonprofit, nonpartisan corporation was established to sponsor presidential and vice-presidential debates. The Commission on Presidential Debates sponsored all of the 1988 debates. The Commission was designed as an ongoing body to foster the values of debate. In the years between 1988 and 1992, the Commission worked with a variety of organizations including the Speech Communication Association to promote and study political debates ("Commission on Presidential Debates," 1992).

The Commission was charged with developing a schedule and format for the debates and resolving the logistical problems involved in staging the debates. Well in advance of the fall campaign the bipartisan Commission on Presidential Debates proposed a series of three presidential and one vice-presidential debates for 1992. The commission proposal was for 90-minute debates to be conducted by a single moderator.

Democratic candidate Governor Bill Clinton accepted the Commission proposal, but incumbent Republican President George Bush did not. The Bush campaign was widely reported to object to the single moderator format, preferring instead a panel of questioners, as had been used in his 1988 debates with Governor Dukakis ("Debate Cancelled," 1992). The single moderator format had been offered by the Commission as the most conducive to follow-up questions and probing of the candidates. It was widely perceived as the format that would provide the voting public with the greatest amount of information.

Throughout early September 1992, the two campaigns exchanged barbs about debating ("Clinton: Bush Should Explain," 1992). By September 17, lacking the necessary lead time to make arrangements, the Commission was forced to cancel the first debate, which had been scheduled for September 22 ("Debates' Fate," 1992). However, representatives of both campaigns continued to claim that debates would take place, and Clinton intensified his attack on Bush's refusal to debate, particularly in the critical state of Michigan where the canceled debate was to have been held. Speaking repeatedly throughout Illinois and Michigan, Clinton attracted national coverage by scheduling a speech at the site of the canceled debate, East Lansing, Michigan, on September 22. "I showed up here to debate today," Clinton said to a large and appreciative audience. Clinton continued, mocking Bush's failure to debate by claiming that "I guess I can't blame him. If I had the worst record of any president in fifty years I wouldn't want to defend that record either" ("Bush, Clinton Take Taunting," 1992).

Meanwhile, with one debate canceled and the election only six weeks away, the Commission on Presidential Debates offered the candidates another proposal. This revised proposal called for two presidential debates and one vice-presidential debate. Again Clinton immediately accepted. The Bush campaign refused, claiming that it had sent a proposal for debates directly to the Clinton campaign and awaited a response. Robert Teeter, Bush campaign chairman, reiterated the Bush campaign's insistence that the format feature a panel of reporters to question the candidate, as opposed to a single moderator ("Debate Commission," 1992).

The Bush campaign no doubt favored the format in which a group of reporters rotated in asking questions for several reasons. First, it was the format in which Bush had excelled four years earlier. Second, it was likely to yield questions on a wide variety of topics. If the debate remained focused on one or a limited number of topics (as might happen with a single moderator asking follow-up questions), the dominant issue of the campaign, the Bush economic record, was almost certain to be discussed at length, with little discussion of Clinton or his policies. However, the use of a panel of reporters might facilitate questions about many of Clinton's often vague promises, as well as the controversial aspects of his life such as his reputed womanizing and draft dodging. If the debate were less focused, touching on a variety of different issues (as might happen with a panel of questioners who did not follow up and who had a variety of interests), Bush's campaign felt that Clinton would be disadvantaged by questions drawing attention to his shortcomings.

In light of Clinton's acceptance, his refusal to accept the offers of the nonpartisan Commission on Presidential Debates continued to cause Bush discomfort. By late September hecklers dressed in giant chicken costumes were showing up at the president's campaign stops. The giant chickens made a perfect visual for television news and on at least one occasion clearly irritated Bush (*CBS Morning News*).

Not only was his refusal to debate creating irritations on the campaign trail for Bush, it was also costing his campaign precious time in its efforts to catch Clinton. Clinton remained comfortably ahead as the question over the debates raged in the last ten days of September and the first days of October. Indeed, during this period, with the election less than a month away, most polls sponsored by national news organizations indicated that Clinton's lead appeared to be growing slightly ("Poll Watch," 1992). Moreover, NBC news reporter Andrea Mitchell claimed, shortly after the cancellation of the first scheduled debate, that Bush's own daily tracking polls made his campaign "aware of the negative position in which [his refusal to debate] put him." Moreover, Mitchell reported that "Clinton's tracking polls see the same thing. Attacks of Bush for not debating are resonating well" (Mitchell, 1992). Moreover, the candidate himself was getting fed up with the negative image his refusal to debate was creating, telling his staff "I'm tired of looking like a wimp" (Goldman and Mathews, 85).

With time running short, Bush challenged Clinton to a series of six debates, hoping to change growing negative public opinion about his refusal to debate. Bush suggested that they take place every Sunday evening from October 11 to the final Sunday of the campaign, November 1. The Bush challenge quickly resulted in direct negotiations between the two campaigns.

After extensive discussions, the campaign staffs announced their agreement. A series of four debates, three presidential and one vice-presidential, would be held. The sponsoring organization would be the Commission on Presidential Debates. Each debate would last for ninety minutes. The first would be held in St. Louis on October 11 and would utilize a panel of reporters, as Bush had wished. It would be followed by the vice-presidential debate in Atlanta on October 13. This debate would utilize the single moderator format. The second presidential debate would be held in Richmond on October 15. It would utilize a talk show format, allowing the audience to ask questions and the candidates to move about on the stage. Clinton strongly favored this format—one in which he had repeatedly excelled. The final debate would be held in East Lansing,

Michigan, on October 19. The first half of the debate would utilize the single moderator format while the last half would utilize a panel of reporters ("Details of Campaign Debates," 1992).

The overall package equitably settled the major format difference between the two campaigns. The format of the least important of the debates, that between the vice-presidential candidates, seems to reflect the Clinton-Gore campaign wishes. This no doubt reflects the fact that by early October (when the negotiations were held), the Clinton-Gore ticket could negotiate from a position of strength with a solid lead in virtually all the polls, and the public's sympathy over the evolving disagreement over debates.

The details of the format were worked out by negotiators representing President Bush and Governor Clinton, but days before their settlement wealthy businessman H. Ross Perot (candidate of the United We Stand, America movement) reentered the race. The two major candidates, no doubt fearful of offending Perot and his supporters, stated that they would not object if Perot were invited to participate in the debates. Perot had only reentered the race days earlier, but he seemed to be attracting the support of 7 to 10 percent of the public simply by entering the race; and during the spring, he had once actually been the front-runner when his support surged to about 30 percent. Recognizing that he would be waging an exceedingly well-financed campaign, the Commission on Presidential Debates determined that he warranted an invitation. It was extended and quickly accepted.

In large part because of the long-drawn-out delay over having the debates (unlike past years when the debates were held in prime time and carried by all the networks), in 1992 several debates had to be held early in the evening to avoid conflicts with the baseball playoffs and Monday night football. For the first time in history, a major network chose not to carry one of the debates live. CBS chose to show the American League Championship game between Oakland and Toronto rather than the first debate, contributing to the substantially lower audience that the debate drew (Paeth, 1992).

THE FIRST PRESIDENTIAL DEBATE

Characteristically, successful presidential and vice-presidential debaters have utilized a variety of rhetorical and image strategies in presenting to the public. The most successful debaters typically are those best able to:

1. direct their remarks at highly targeted audiences;

2. develop an overall theme throughout the debate;
3. debate not to lose by avoiding specifics and making use of proven safe responses;
4. present themselves as vigorous, active leaders;
5. foster identification of themselves with national aspirations;
6. foster identification of themselves with the dominant political party/philosophy;
7. personify themselves as exemplifying a desirable characteristic. (Friedenberg, 1990)

These practices provide us criteria with which to evaluate the 1992 debates. The first debate, held on Sunday evening, October 11, rotated questions between the three candidates. The candidate to respond first to a question was given two minutes, and the remaining two candidates each had one minute for refutation. Though the format did not provide an opening statement, it provided for two-minute closing addresses.

The responses generated by moderator Jim Lehrer's opening question typify the entire first 1992 presidential debate and much of what followed in the subsequent presidential debates. Lehrer directed his question to Ross Perot, who by lot had been determined to receive the first question.

Lehrer: The first topic tonight is what separates each of you from the others. Mr. Perot, what do you believe tonight is the single most important separating issue of this campaign?

Perot: The principle issue that separates me is that five and one-half million people came together on their own and put me on the ballot. I was not put on the ballot by either of the two parties, by any PAC money, by any foreign lobbyist money, by any special interest money. This is a movement that came from the people. This is the way the framers of the Constitution intended our government to be, a government that comes from the people. . . . The thing that separates my candidacy and makes it unique is that this came from millions of people in fifty states all over this country who wanted a candidate who worked and belonged to nobody but them. I go into this race as their servant. And I belong to them. So this comes from the people.

Clinton: The most important distinction in this campaign is that I represent real hope for change, a departure from trickle-down economics, a departure from tax-and-spend economics to invest and grow. But before I can do that I must challenge the American people to change, and they must decide. [Turning to face President Bush directly] Tonight I say to the president: Mr. Bush, for twelve years you've had your way, you've had your chance, and it didn't work. It's time to change. I want to bring that change to the American people. But we must all decide first: Do we have the courage to change for hope in a better tomorrow?

Bush: Well, I think the thing that distinguishes is experience. I think we've dramatically changed the world. I'll talk about that a little bit later, but the changes are mind-boggling for world peace. Kids go to bed at night without the same fear of nuclear war. And change for change's sake is not enough. We saw that message in the late 1970s when we heard a lot about change. And what happened? The misery index went right through the roof. But I've, my economic program is the kind of change we want. . . . But I'd say if you had to separate out, I think it's experience at this level.

As he did all evening, Perot immediately drew a sharp distinction between himself and the other two candidates while developing his overall theme. His was a campaign of the people, not of the parties, not of the PACs, not of the foreign interests, not of the special interests. Moments later, Jim Lehrer paraphrased Bush's claims to superior experience, and Perot responded by again returning to his theme, and then developing his second theme of the evening: that he was a man of action who would get things done.

Well, I don't have any experience in running up a four trillion dollar debt. I don't have any experience in gridlock government where nobody takes any responsibility for anything and everybody blames everybody else. I don't have any experience in creating the worst public school system in the industrialized world, the most violent crime-ridden society in the industrialized world. But I do have a lot of experience in getting things done. . . . I've got a lot of experience in not taking 10 years to solve a 10-minute problem. So if it's time for action, I think I have experience that counts.

Throughout the evening, Perot directed his remarks at voters who were undecided, those who sought change, and those who were disgruntled with the economy. Perot consistently sought to distinguish himself as the candidate who was not part of the current political system, as someone who could get things done. Repeatedly, he portrayed himself as an activist. For example, in response to a question about Medicare he responded by playing it safe. He provided no real details of what he would do, other than possibly copy good features from the programs of other nations, a suggestion that sounded safe enough. But he vigorously argued that he would be a man of action. "Now I'm back to square one. If you want to stop talking about it and do it then I'll be glad to go up there [Washington] and we'll get it done. . . . Talk is cheap, words are plentiful, deeds are precious. Let's get on with it."

Perot was highly effective, identifying himself with the national desire for action and the national frustration at the ineffectiveness of government under the two major parties. Finally (as he would do in later debates), in his concluding remarks, Perot combined his call for action with an attempt to identify himself as a selfless individual who ran for president to improve the lot of future generations of Americans. "When you go to bed tonight, look at your children. Think of their dreams, think of your dreams as a child, and ask yourself: 'Isn't it time to stop talking about it? Isn't it time to stop creating images? Isn't it time to do it?'"

Perot made use of several examples and stories to illustrate his points. He delivered his message forcefully. His use of humor softened his aggressiveness, while dramatizing the points he was making. In sum, Perot debated impressively. The least-known candidate in the field, he had presented a compelling overall theme: that he represented a dramatic change from the two major parties and that he would get things done. He avoided any major mistakes, and identified himself with the national aspirations for a more effective government.

From the very outset, Governor Bill Clinton also attempted to develop an overall theme. Clinton's overall theme of change was similar to Perot's, targeting much of the same audience that Perot targeted: the undecided voters, voters seeking change, and the economically disgruntled, as well as seeking to reinforce those already loyal to him. However, Clinton did distance himself from Perot by suggesting that Perot's economic policies might not work and were inferior to his own. Indeed, in light of Clinton's propensity to provide a myriad of detail in responding to questions, often confusing and boring listeners, the goal of his debate preparation had been to develop "an overarching theme with which to frame all his debate answers" (Shapiro, 1992). Clinton voiced his overarching theme with the first sentences out of his mouth. He represented "real hope for change." He confronted President Bush immediately, claiming that Bush was given his chance: "It didn't work. It's time for change." Clinton adhered to that theme all evening. He spoke of "having the courage to change," and needing to plan for changes caused by technology and the end of the Cold War. Even when the questions dealt with those areas thought to be Bush's strengths, foreign and military policy, Clinton argued for change. On two occasions Clinton granted that the principles of Bush's foreign and defense policy were sound, but that he would make major changes in the military, that he would produce a smaller but more mobile defense force and reduce our dependence on nuclear weapons.

When he did provide specifics, and he did a better job of it than either of his opponents, they were provided as part of stock responses that had been proven safe by repeated usage on the campaign trail. For example, his response to a question asking how he would reform the health care system included specific suggestions on two criteria (population growth and inflation) that insurance companies should make better use of in considering costs. Moreover, he cited three different health care proposals, two currently being used in Hawaii and Rochester, and a third proposed for Oregon, as potential models from which many of his ideas had been drawn. Additionally, he provided three specific figures to dramatize the savings his proposals would create over the existing Bush programs.

Though one might legitimately ask for more details on the critical question of implementation, the effect of this answer was to suggest to the viewer that Clinton was highly conversant with the health care issue, and had a specific plan to deal with the problem. It is important that those answers where Clinton did provide detail, like his response on reforming health care, were to questions that he had discussed repeatedly throughout the campaign using the same details that he provided in the debate. They were well-rehearsed answers that had repeatedly proven safe. Like Perot, Clinton presented himself as a vigorous leader, and identified himself with the national desire for action. However, unlike Perot he did not distance himself from the existing political system. Never speaking of his party by name, Clinton did repudiate past Democratic party policies, characterizing them as tax-and-spend. Rather, he offered himself as a leader who would provide for investment and growth.

Clinton's delivery was forceful. On several occasions, positioned as he was on the stage between his two foes, he turned to face Bush and addressed him directly, no doubt emphasizing the direct clash he was verbalizing at those moments. In sum, Governor Clinton had entered the debate as the leader. He did nothing that would dissuade those who supported him from continuing to support him. He presented himself as a strong and articulate advocate of change.

Lehrer's opening question allowed President George Bush to immediately respond by developing his major theme for the evening: that he was an experienced leader in foreign affairs. He argued that what distinguished him from the preceding two speakers was his experience. He claimed that "we've dramatically changed the world," characterizing those changes as "mind-boggling for world peace." Clearly Bush would have preferred to keep the debate centered on foreign affairs, but being the last respondent to the first question, he had little choice but to reply to Perot's and Clinton's repeated expressions of the need for changes in our economic policies.

Hence, in his opening statement Bush also launched his secondary theme. He argued that what was needed was not change for change's sake, but rather appropriate change such as what he now recommended. Bush reminded his audience of the misery index of the late 1970s to point out that change is not always desirable.

Bush's opening remarks suffered from several problems. First, unlike either Perot or Clinton, he was hesitant. The very first words out of his mouth in the debate, "Well, I think," are characteristic of powerless speech. He spoke of the "misery index," but never defined what that index was, no doubt causing his point to lose much of its impact, especially on younger voters who had little memory of the high inflation and high interest rates that created the misery index of the Carter administration.

Particularly in the early minutes of the debate, Bush sounded far less assured than either Perot or Clinton. He opened his second response, an opportunity to comment on additional differences between himself and the other candidates, by observing, "I just thought of another difference." While Perot and Clinton confidently spoke of the differences their candidacies represented, Bush sounded as though he was struggling to come up with differences between himself and his foes.

The weaknesses in Bush's responses in the early minutes of the debate illustrate a problem that he had trouble dealing with throughout the debates, and indeed the entire campaign. On one hand he was the incumbent president. As such, Congress notwithstanding, Bush was the most ready target for those who were dissatisfied with government policies. His incumbency required that Bush offer some defense of his four years of leadership. On the one hand, he acknowledged that as president he had made mistakes and that he was now ready to apply his years of experience to fashioning a stronger economic program. This role required that he offer a prescription for change. Running as an incumbent, but having to repudiate much of what he was held responsible for, made Bush's task extremely difficult throughout the campaign. That difficulty seems exemplified in Bush's diffident opening remarks.

Bush's difficulty in the opening ten minutes were compounded when, after the opening round of responses, the questioning turned to character. Bush used this as an opportunity to articulate his disagreement with Clinton's participation in anti–Vietnam War demonstrations while a student in Europe. Speaking of Clinton's participation in anti-war demonstrations, Bush observed that "I think it is wrong to demonstrate against your own country or organize demonstrations against your own country on foreign soil. I just think it's wrong." Bush went on to say that he was not questioning Clinton's patriotism, but rather "it's a question of character and judgment." Bush continued, admitting that he too had made mistakes. But unlike Clinton who failed to admit his mistakes, Bush claimed that he demonstrated his character by admitting his mistakes and attempting to correct them. As Bush attacked Clinton, viewers saw the two men turn and directly face one another. Clinton looked at Bush with a serious expression throughout the president's criticism.

After Bush's attack it was Ross Perot's turn to speak. Perot did not allow himself to get directly involved in the controversy over Clinton's past. However, he pointedly noted that it was "very important to measure where and when things occurred. Did they occur when you were a young person in your formative years? Or did they occur while you were a senior official in the federal government?"

When Clinton was given the opportunity to speak, he acknowledged Perot's answer but then immediately turned to speak to Bush directly. "I've got to respond to Mr. Bush," he began as he launched into a well-prepared response ("Debate Scorecard," 1992).

You have questioned my patriotism. . . . When Joe McCarthy went around attacking people's patriotism he was wrong. He was wrong and a senator from Connecticut stood up to him, [a senator] named Prescott Bush. Your father was right to stand up to Joe McCarthy. You were wrong to attack my patriotism. I was opposed to the war but I loved my country and we need a president who will bring this country together not divide it. We've had enough division.

As Clinton spoke, Bush dropped his head and looked, not at Clinton, but at his podium. This exchange was the most dramatic moment of the debate and was widely replayed. It also contributed to the early impression viewers might have had that Bush was not the vigorous, able leader that his foes appeared to be.

Although Bush did not come across well early in the debate, he improved. As the debate progressed, he offered cogent defenses for many of his policies, claiming that Clinton's military suggestions might weaken the nation to the point of risking peace, and that Perot's economic policies involved excessive taxes in contrast to his own policies that centered on limiting government spending. He defended his policies, observing that though there were problems we were still the military and economic "envy of the world."

Though Bush's image as a strong and active leader improved as the debate progressed, unlike Perot and Clinton he seemed unable to identify with any strong national aspirations, or any strong national philosophy. However, he made efforts to personify himself as the one candidate who could be trusted, particularly when it came to dealing with foreign and military policy. In his concluding remarks, he forcefully reminded his audience of his expertise and success in foreign policy, and called on viewers to trust him to finish the job.

Yet in concluding (as he had done in opening), Bush had to acknowledge his prior mistakes. He did so by claiming that "on the domestic side what we must do is to have change that empowers people, not tax and spend." He then itemized several areas that he would focus on in the coming term including education and job training. Though the remark was meant to contrast his own policies with those of Clinton, as the debate concluded it also served to remind viewers of the domestic shortcomings of his first four years in office.

The public response to the first debate centered around Ross Perot. The least known of the three candidates, Perot had targeted his message well, hammered home his intertwined themes that the two major parties were not governing effectively and that it was time for a change, avoided any serious errors, came across as an active and vigorous leader who recognized that the nation aspired to more effective government, and personified himself as the kind of can-do leader America needed. Virtually every evaluation of the first debate found Perot the big winner. ("Face to Face," 1992; "Round One," 1992; Van Sant, 1992; Broder, 1992; Rosenthal, 1992). The *New York Times* observed that "Mr. Perot probably made the biggest splash of the night," (Rosenthal, 1992) and a *Newsweek* poll found that 70 percent of the electorate took Perot more seriously as a presidential candidate after the first debate, and that 43 percent of the electorate felt he won the debate ("Face to Face," 1992).

Clinton seemed to finish second to Perot. Given his standing in the polls, second to Perot was a victory for Clinton. He had done what his handlers wanted. By hammering home his overarching theme that it was time for a change, by avoiding any big mistakes, and by appearing presidential and poised, particularly during those moments when he confronted Bush directly, Clinton had reinforced the plurality of voters who favored him at the outset of the debates.

President Bush, whose campaign needed a lift, did not get one from the first debate. Although he rallied as the debate progressed, he did poorly in the opening minutes of the debate as viewers first sized up and compared the three candidates. His message, diffused as it was between defending his record on foreign policy and acknowledging that he would change domestic policies, was a more awkward one to argue than those of Perot and Clinton. Moreover, in the most dramatic exchange of the evening, over his accusations about Clinton's character, Bush did not look or sound strong.

Traditionally, challenger candidates do well in debates. In this instance, with two challenger candidates on the platform, the incumbent was at a disadvantage never before seen in contemporary presidential debates. Although Clinton and Perot had not conspired in advance, and Perot often alluded to Clinton and the Democratic party he represented as part of the problem, Bush was nevertheless debating two candidates who were indicting his record. Moreover, he was unable to fully defend his own record, on occasion having to make a virtue out of admitting his mistakes. As the first debate illustrated, the debates placed Bush in an extremely difficult position.

THE SECOND PRESIDENTIAL DEBATE

On the morning of October 15, the *New York Times* reported that "President Bush heads into tonight's second Presidential debate with a still daunting challenge." The *Times* went on to report the results of their most recent poll, declaring that Governor Clinton was favored by 47 percent of registered voters, President Bush was favored by 34 percent, and Ross Perot was favored by 10 percent (Toner, 1992a). With less than three weeks remaining in the campaign, the remaining debates seemed to represent the president's best hope of catching Governor Clinton.

However, the second presidential debate followed the format that the Clinton campaign had wanted, in no small part because their candidate had excelled at it during the primaries. This talk show format allowed the 209 audience members who, according to moderator Carol Simpson of *ABC News,* were selected by an independent polling firm directed to recruit an audience of uncommitted voters, to ask questions of the candidates. Moderator Simpson was also allowed to ask questions, comment, and direct the questions to specific candidates. Each candidate was given time for a final statement. Most immediate reactions to the debate format focused on the use of voters as questioners and praised the format.

However, this format was seriously flawed in two major ways. First, the use of "uncommitted voters" proved to have disadvantages. Uncommitted voters, particularly late in a campaign, are not representative of the public. As the *New York Times* poll suggested, approximately 90 percent of the public was not uncommitted. Moreover, one could ask: what type of voter would be uncommitted late in the campaign? Though it is possible that such a voter is well informed and torn between two choices, it is more likely that such a voter is simply apathetic and uninformed.

The concept of using voters rather than the press has considerable merit. Presumably it was used to ensure that the questions asked would reflect public interests. But to allow undecided voters to ask questions does not seem to be the best way of reflecting public interests. It would have made more sense to have asked the independent polling firm to poll the public on a wide variety of public issues and then utilized the issues of uppermost concern to the public as the basis for questions. Or, perhaps the independent polling firm might have taken a list of well-constructed questions on public issues and asked the public to indicate those that were of greatest interest.

These and other procedures might have avoided the waste of time produced by such questions as the one directed to Clinton, asking if he would
"enter into a legally binding contract with the American people that if you
did not achieve these goals [significant yearly reductions of the deficit]
that you would not seek a second term." Similarly, what public interest
was served by hearing Bush respond to the question, "could we cross our
hearts; it sounds silly here, but could we make a commitment? You know,
we're not under oath at this point, but could you make a commitment to
the citizens of the United States to meet our needs and we have many, and
not yours? Again, I have to repeat that, it's a real need, I think, that we all
have." What public interest was served in asking each candidate "when do
you estimate your party will both nominate and elect an Afro-American
and female ticket to the presidency of the United States?" Clearly the time
spent on questions such as these detracted from the value the debate might
have served.

The second and potentially more serious flaw with this talk show format was that it did not treat each candidate equally. Like most talk shows,
it allowed the audience or moderator to direct questions, and allowed the
moderator to reword and interpret questions. This may be fine on a talk
show, especially if there is only one guest, but it creates fundamental
problems of fairness in presidential debates. Several examples illustrate
the types of fairness problems created by this format. When a question
was directed to Perot about how he would work with Congress he
responded—but the moderator did not give either Clinton or Bush an
opportunity to respond. Perot was clearly advantaged on this question.
Moments later an audience member asked Clinton "where do you stand
on gun control and what do you plan to do about it?" Clinton forcefully
responded, "I support the right to keep and bear arms," and went on to
justify his position. Bush was also asked to respond to this question.
Would Clinton or Bush have responded as they did if the question had
been asked of them the way Moderator Simpson reworded it for Ross
Perot? Simpson said, "Mr. Perot, there are young black males in America
dying at unprecedented rates—the fact [is] that homicide is the leading
cause of death among young black males 15 to 24 years old. What are you
going to do to get the guns off the streets?" Clearly Perot was not address-
ing the identical question that had been given to Clinton and Bush. In the
exchange on health care reform all three men were given an opportunity
to respond to the same question, but then Moderator Simpson recognized
Clinton for additional comments. After Clinton's rebuttal of Perot and
Bush, Simpson immediately moved to the next question. Clinton was
clearly advantaged on this exchange. He was given more time to speak
than either of his opponents; he had the opportunity for both the first and

the last word. Examples such as these clearly suggest that the talk show format is not designed, as is a debate or the "joint interview" format of most recent presidential debates, to provide for identical treatment of each candidate. Inherent in such a format is the possibility of unfair treatment.

The format of this debate was widely credited for keeping the candidates on the issues ("Real People Focus," 1992: Dowd, 1992). The basis for this judgment was that less time was spent in this debate on such matters as the personal integrity of the candidates, and the petty jockeying for position and name calling evident in the first debate, and especially evident in the immediately preceding vice-presidential debate. Questions such as the following were largely credited with keeping the candidates on the issues: "The amount of time the candidates have spent on this campaign trashing their opponents character and their programs is depressingly large. Why can't your discussions and proposals reflect the genuine complexity and the difficulty of the issues to try to build a consensus around the best aspects of all proposals?"

Such credit seems largely unwarranted. First, this debate was not appreciably more issue oriented or dignified than the first presidential debate. At several points in the debate, and in his closing statement, Bush attacked Clinton's character, much as he had in the first debate.

This debate was more issue oriented and dignified than the vice-presidential debate that preceded it by only two days. But the more issue-oriented and dignified tone of this debate, when contrasted to the immediately preceding vice-presidential debate, was no doubt largely a function of the different participants. Vice presidents are surrogates, and surrogates are typically used for harsh personal attacks (Trent and Friedenberg, 1991, 171). Presidential campaigns frequently delegate harsher, often personal, petty and partisan attacks to surrogates. Doing so allows the principal candidate to treat major issues and thus appear "presidential."

Second, even if we hypothetically concede that this debate was more dignified and issue oriented than the prior presidential debate, this change might well have been a function of President Bush's awareness that his attacks on Clinton were not working. The very morning of the debate, the front page of the *New York Times* featured an article indicating that Bush's popularity had dropped by 3 percent in the preceding ten days, while Clinton's had dropped by only 2 percent over the same period. Moreover, 79 percent of registered voters claimed they were unaffected by Bush's criticism of Clinton's anti-war activities. An overwhelming majority of those who did view Bush's attacks positively reported they were already committed to him (Toner, 1992a). If there were a change in the president's behavior between the first and second presidential debates, it is as easy to believe that that change was a reflection of campaign strategy as it is to believe that the change was a spontaneous reaction to the immediate audience.

In sum, while the immediate reaction to this debate format was positive, it does not—upon close inspection—deserve praise. It was a format that almost guaranteed that time would be wasted on weak questions by uncommitted voters. It was a format unlike any other ever used, for it provided no guarantees that the candidates would be treated equally. Moreover, the liabilities of this format do not seem to be outweighed by its virtues. The belief that the format was responsible for a more issue-oriented and dignified tone in this debate seems questionable at best.

Nevertheless, regardless of format, this debate had a winner—and that winner was Governor Clinton. Clinton handled the format better than his opponents. By this point in the campaign Clinton was debating not to lose. Often utilizing stock responses, and continually returning to his overarching theme that the nation needed economic change, Clinton effectively avoided any potential problems.

Moreover, he created an exceedingly positive image of himself on economic issues, particularly in contrast to President Bush. This was especially evident when the two men responded to a question asking each man to indicate how the nation's economic downturn personally affected them. Perot responded first, claiming that it was the impetus for his making the sacrifices of time and money to get into the presidential race.

Bush had difficulty with the question. He started hesitantly, "Well, I think the national debt affects everybody. Obviously it has a lot to do with interest rates. It has." At this point Moderator Simpson interrupted. "She's saying *you personally.* On a personal basis how has it affected you—has it affected you personally?" Bush tried again. "Well, I'm sure it has." Before he could finish his next sentence he was again interrupted. Eventually he was able to answer by returning to his original point, that the recession affects all Americans by impacting on interest rates and the national debt. Bush may have been flustered by the question and the interruptions of Moderator Simpson. Nevertheless, given an opportunity to portray himself in a caring and concerned fashion, as Perot had done, his response seemed disturbingly impersonal.

Moreover, the negative image Bush created stood in sharp contrast to the image voters received of Clinton when he followed. Clinton said that as the governor of a small state he could see that the taxes of people in his state had gone up, and the services they received had been decreased. He observed that when people were laid off in his state, he often knew them. He claimed that when factories closed in Arkansas he knew the owners. Clearly Clinton was trying to portray himself as a leader with empathy who could identify with the economic hardships facing Americans. He made the point effectively, in distinct contrast to Bush's difficulty.

Clinton appeared comfortable in this format. During the exchange just described, he moved toward the questioner and responded to her directly, as he did on several occasions throughout the evening. He repeatedly stressed his basic theme, that he would be an effective agent of change, working it into a variety of answers, including those on health care, education, and the economy. Moreover, he built his concluding remarks around this basic thesis, challenging the American public "to decide whether you want to change or not." As the evening closed it was clear that Clinton had done well and that neither of his opponents had done anything to impede his candidacy. Moreover, without competition from baseball, Clinton's good night was viewed by over 6 million more households than had witnessed the first presidential debate ("More Saw Second Debate," 1992).

THE THIRD PRESIDENTIAL DEBATE

By the final presidential debate, Governor Bill Clinton was clearly ahead of President George Bush in virtually every poll, and comfortably ahead in projected electoral college votes as well. Indeed, by the final debate many observers were suggesting that it was virtually impossible for Bush to win (Toner, 1992b). Nevertheless, this debate drew the largest audience of any of the 1992 debates ("Final Debate," 1992). For Clinton, the clear priority was to debate not to lose.

Returning to a more traditional format, the first half of this debate consisted of Moderator Jim Lehrer of PBS asking questions in sequence to the candidates who were each given two minutes to respond. After each question had been answered by the candidate to whom it was directed, the remaining two candidates were given one minute to respond. During the second half of the debate the same procedure was followed, but the questions were provided by a panel of journalists consisting of Susan Rook of Cable News Network, Gene Gibbons of Reuters, and Helen Thomas of United Press International.

Perhaps the biggest distinction between this debate and the two presidential debates that preceded it is found in the remarks of Ross Perot. In prior debates, Perot had frequently lumped Clinton and Bush together and attacked both. In this final debate, he got the loudest laugh at Governor Clinton's expense, but his attacks on Bush's policies were much more substantial and damaging. Early in the debate, Bush criticized Clinton's Arkansas record and after Clinton defended it by reiterating statistics about Arkansas's economic growth under his administration, Perot was asked who he would believe. He responded by suggesting that it was a mistake to "cast the nation's future on a unit that small." Asked for clarification, Perot created laughter at Clinton's expense by claiming that what Clinton did as governor of Arkansas was "irrelevant." When the laughter subsided, Perot clarified by observing that "I could say I ran a small grocery store on the corner, therefore . . . I could run Walmart; that's not true."

However, for the rest of the evening Perot's comments hurt Bush far more than Clinton. He indicted the influence of foreign lobbyists, citing 1988 examples involving Reagan/Bush administration figures and policies. Similarly, he claimed that the domestic airline industry was being "dismantled." Adding, "and I doubt, in all candor if the president knows it." Perot went on to indict the impending purchase of part of Northwest Airlines and other domestic lines by foreign interests: "Now guess who's on the president's campaign big time? A guy from Northwest. This deal is terribly destructive to the U.S. airline industry." He attacked Bush for being a party to "creating Saddam Hussein over a ten-year period using billions of dollars of U.S. taxpayer money." He followed up his attack on Bush's role in creating Saddam Hussein by claiming minutes later that the Bush administration had indirectly contributed to Hussein's invasion of Kuwait by telling him "we wouldn't get involved with his border dispute." Perot challenged the Bush administration to make public diplomatic documents that he asserted would clearly prove the truth of this claim. Similarly, he credited Bush with being a party to creating Manuel Noriega, "using taxpayer money."

Though Bush was more animated in this debate than in his preceding efforts, he offered little in the way of new attacks or evidence. He continued to attack Clinton as a tax-and-spend Democrat, warning, "Mr. and Mrs. America, when you hear him say we're going to tax only the rich, watch your wallet. . . . [H]is figures don't add up and he's going to sock it right to the middle-class taxpayer and lower, if he's going to pay for all the spending programs he proposes." Bush renewed his attacks on Clinton's integrity and character. After one of Clinton's answers Bush jumped in to illustrate his perception of an inconsistency in Clinton's answer. "I think he made my case. On the one hand it's a good deal, but on the other hand I'd make it better." He reiterated his belief that the issue of Clinton's Vietnam draft status was important because it illustrated Clinton's inability to speak truthfully. Though Bush was more forceful in his delivery and by comparison this was his best debate, he did little to develop new issues or extend old ones.

Like Bush, Clinton did little to develop new issues or extend old ones in this debate. But unlike Bush, Clinton entered the debate well ahead.

The lack of new issues, or new materials vivifying old issues, worked to his advantage. Debating not to lose, Clinton used much of the same material that he had used throughout the campaign, including prior debates.

In this debate, Clinton did an exceptionally good job of defending himself against the attacks on his character targeting his actions during the Vietnam War. First, he noted that he was "very strongly" in opposition to the war in Vietnam, and that though he might have been clearer in first answering questions about events that were twenty-three years old, the fact that he did not serve did not make him ineligible to be commander in chief. He cited Abraham Lincoln, Woodrow Wilson, and Franklin Roosevelt as presidents with no prior military experience who had made outstanding wartime presidents. Bush responded that it was Clinton's evasiveness in responding to questions about his activities, not the activities themselves, that was troubling. In the next round of answers, dealing with a question on taxes, Clinton returned to questions of evasiveness by pointedly observing that Bush's 1988 "read my lips" campaign promise not to raise taxes was made "just to get elected." Clinton's defense of his own character and subsequent attack on the president's character in this debate was his strongest treatment of these issues in the entire series of debates.

As he had in prior debates, Clinton again closed with a strong appeal for change. He claimed to offer "a new approach," saying he represented "the kind of change that can open up a whole new world of opportunities to America as we enter the last decade of this century." Though Clinton broke no new ground in this debate, he effectively reiterated the arguments that had thus far contributed to his large lead.

In sum, although Bush was more aggressive and animated in this debate he faced two opponents who attacked him at every opportunity. Perot's sharper indictments of Bush, coupled with the criticisms he had been receiving constantly from Clinton, made it extremely difficult for Bush. Though it was Bush's best debate it was a case of too little, too late.

CONCLUSIONS

Ideally, presidential debates should provide the public with information about the candidates that will assist voters in making informed decisions. Though one may quibble about the desirability of specific formats, the 1992 presidential debates did provide voters with information upon which to base a decision, and to that extent they were a success.

The 270 minutes of presidential debates illustrated clear differences between the candidates on such issues as gun control, pollution control standards, and free trade with Mexico. But, while the candidates were relatively clear in responding to such questions, more complex questions elicited unclear answers. The candidates concurred that the economy needed improvement, and that deficit reduction should be a priority in the next four years, yet, although frequently alluded to, specific plans were never explicitly spelled out for the viewers to compare and choose between. Similarly, the candidates claimed that military spending could be reduced, yet the specific plans for cutting that spending, though again frequently alluded to, were never explicitly spelled out for the viewers.

In addition to the positions of the candidates on issues, the debates presented voters with an opportunity to know the candidates better. All of the candidates strove to present themselves as vigorous active leaders. The *Cincinnati Enquirer* succinctly characterized the images the three candidates presented of themselves in a headline summarizing the three debates: "Mr. Experience, Mr. Change or Mr. Fix-It?" (Hess, 1992). Bush strove to present himself as a vigorous leader who met national aspirations for an experienced chief executive. Similarly, Clinton strove to present himself as a vigorous leader who met the national aspirations for change, particularly economic change. Moreover, Perot positioned himself as a vigorous leader who would fix our government, taking it away from career politicians and special interests to restore many of its old virtues.

The debates presented voters with information on issues and the opportunity to acquire an impression of the candidates themselves. Some voters clearly utilized the debates this way in making their decisions. In election day exit polling, *ABC News* found that of those who claimed that the debates were an important factor in influencing their vote, 45 percent favored Clinton, 30 percent favored Perot, and 25 percent favored Bush (ABC, 1992).

Clinton's achievement was in large part a function of his ability to master many of the seven criteria that characterize successful political debaters. All three candidates seemed to have targeted audiences, but the very fact that all three candidates called for change seemed to make that theme and its principle spokespersons, Clinton and Perot, dominate the debates and prove more attractive to audience members concerned about the economy—at the expense of the more cautious change agent, Bush. Clinton's tight focus on a single overall theme, the need for economic change, served him well. Bush's call for change had to be tempered by his need to defend many of his administration's policies, while Perot called for a host of government reforms as well as economic change.

The widespread avoidance of specifics and the frequent use of safe previously tried responses prevented each candidate from making a serious error. This worked to the clear advantage of Clinton who entered the debates leading. It worked to the clear disadvantage of Bush and Perot, who hoped Clinton would stumble, causing his supporters to waver and switch their support.

Both Clinton and Perot presented themselves as more vigorous and active leaders than Bush. Clinton's more animated delivery and his direct confrontations with Bush made the contrast between these two men especially evident during the first two debates. Though Bush worked to identify himself as the most experienced candidate and the candidate of character who could best be trusted with the presidency, his claims were to some extent undermined by the attacks of both Perot and Clinton who reminded voters that Bush had broken his 1988 pledge of "no new taxes," and may have contributed to foreign policy problems in the Middle East. The fact that Bush called his repudiation of his 1988 tax pledge a mistake also served to undermine his claim that he had the necessary experience and character to serve well. In contrast to Bush's questionable efforts to identify himself with the national aspirations for a responsible president of unquestioned character, both Clinton and Perot were able to identify themselves as clear agents of change.

Presuming that the Commission on Presidential Debates is the sponsoring organization of the future debates, it may learn several lessons from the 1992 experience. First, by the third debate much of what was being said was repeated from earlier debates. This may be, in part, a function of timing. Three presidential debates and a vice-presidential debate were all held in approximately two weeks. New issues that might have been the subjects of questions did not have time to develop between debates. This may also have been because each debate did not have a clearly defined subject or subject matter area. These problems were caused by the candidates and not the Commission, but they suggest the desirability of spacing the debates farther apart and identifying specific topic areas for each debate. Second, the 1992 debates involved a variety of formats. The least successful of them seems to have been the talk show format utilizing undecided voters. This approach inherently creates the likelihood of weak questions and unequal treatment of the candidates. If this format is used in the future it needs to be modified. Third, the Commission was faced with the awkward situation of having a third candidate join debates that were originally arranged for two candidates. It might be appropriate to consider whether the addition of a third candidate warrants a different format. Perhaps, if nothing else, the presence of a third candidate warrants an expansion of time from the 90 minutes used in 1992 to 120 minutes. Such a change would help provide candidates with a greater opportunity to express themselves. Unfortunately, these and a variety of other potential reforms that the Commission might consider must ultimately meet the approval of the major candidates. And again as 1992 illustrated, political debates take place in the real world, not the ideal world. Laudable reforms that the Commission may well consider prior to future debates must still gain the approval of candidates whose goals are to influence voters, not educate the public. Gaining such approval may be a difficult task, but it is one that the Commission on Presidential Debates should not abandon in its admirable quest to improve what have become the capstone events of our presidential elections.

REFERENCES

All direct quotations from the debates are taken from the transcripts of the debates, which appeared in the *New York Times* the morning following each debate. These transcripts were checked against videotapes of the debates as broadcast directly into viewers' homes on the American Broadcasting Company (ABC) network.

ABC Television. 1992. "Election Eve Coverage: Report of the Michigan Exit Poll," Nov. 3.
"Among Omens for Clinton, Straw Poll of the Most Literal Kind." 1992. *New York Times*, Oct. 23, A20.
Broder, David. 1992. "Don't Count Out the Super-Salesman." *Cincinnati Post*, Oct. 14, 9A
"Bush, Clinton Take Taunting Attack Tone." 1992. *Cincinnati Enquirer*, Sept. 23, A6.
CBS Morning News. 1992. September 29.
"Clinton: Bush Should Explain Debate Refusal." 1992. *Cincinnati Enquirer*, Sept. 5, A4.
"Clinton Continues His Attack." 1992. *Cincinnati Enquirer*, Sept. 20, A3.
Commission on Presidential Debates. 1992. *A Viewers Guide to Political Debates*. Washington, DC.
"Debate Cancelled: Deadline Ignored." 1992. *Cincinnati Enquirer*, Sept. 17, A1.
"Debate Commission Offers Plan." 1992. *Cincinnati Enquirer*, Sept. 23, A6.
"Debate Scorecard." 1992. *Newsweek*, Oct. 19, 43.
"Debates' Fate Unclear." 1992. *Cincinnati Enquirer*, Sept. 17, A3.
"Details of Campaign Debates Are Settled in Hours of Talks." 1992. *New York Times*, Oct. 4, A15.
Dowd, Maureen. 1992. "A No-Nonsense Sort of Talk Show on Issues, Issues, Issues." *New York Times*, Oct. 17, A12.
"Face to Face to Face." 1992. *Newsweek*, Oct. 19, 20–24.
"Final Debate Tops Ratings." 1992. *New York Times*, Oct. 21, A19.
Friedenberg, Robert V. 1990. "Patterns and Trends in National Political Debates: 1960–1988." In *Rhetorical Studies of National Political Debates: 1960–1988*, Robert V. Friedenberg, ed., 187–207. Westport, CT: Praeger.
Goldman, Peter, and Tom Mathews. 1992. "Election Special." *Newsweek*, Nov./Dec.
Hess, David. 1992. "Mr. Experience, Mr. Change or Mr. Fix-It?" *Cincinnati Enquirer*, Oct. 20, A4.
Mitchell, Andrea. 1992. "Report on the Today Show." NBC Television, Sept. 23.
"More Saw Second Debate." 1992. *Cincinnati Enquirer*, Oct. 17, A8.
Paeth, Greg. 1992. "CBS Skips Debate, Airs Playoff." *Cincinnati Post*, Oct. 12, 8B.
"Poll Watch." 1992. *Boston Sunday Globe*, Oct. 4, 16.

Popyk, Lisa, and Rick Van Sant. 1992. "Clinton Overall Debate Champion." *Cincinnati Post*, Oct. 20, 3A.

"Real People Focus on Real Issues." 1992. *Cincinnati Enquirer*, Oct. 16, A1.

Rosenthal, Andrew. 1992. "Bush Didn't Score the Needed Knockout." *New York Times*, Oct. 12, Al.

"Round One: Who Won?" 1992. *Cincinnati Post,* Oct. 12, Al.

Shapiro, Walter. 1992. "Countdown Mentality." *Time*, Sept. 28, 43.

Toner, Robin. 1992a. "Clinton Fending Off Assaults." *New York Times*, Oct. 15, Al.

———. 1992b. "Democrats' Hopes Soar, Republicans' Grow Heavy." *New York Times*, Oct. 18, A1.

Trent, Judith S., and Robert V. Friedenberg. 1991. *Political Campaign Communication: Principles and Practices*, 2d ed. Westport, CT: Praeger.

Van Sant, Rick. 1992. "Viewers Score Perot Winner." *Cincinnati Post,* Oct. 12, 8B.

Wilkinson, Howard. 1992. "Panel Saw Bush Bark, But No Bite." *Cincinnati Enquirer*, Oct. 20, A4.

Wines, Michael. 1992. "Debating Done, Bush and Clinton Begin Final Push." *New York Times,* Oct. 21, A1.

5

Political Advertising in the 1992 Campaign

Lynda Lee Kaid

After the excessive attention focused on paid television advertising in the 1988 campaigns, expectations about the role that television spots would play in the 1992 presidential campaign were very high. Researchers and political observers alike had attributed a great deal of Bush's success in his 1988 campaign to his skillful use of television advertising to create a positive image for himself and a negative image for Michael Dukakis (Devlin, 1989; Grove, 1988; Martz et al., 1988; Kaid, Leland, and Whitney, 1992). In this chapter we consider the extent to which the 1992 ads lived up to expectations by examining the content and characteristics, styles and strategies of the 1992 advertising campaigns from the primary and general election campaigns. After a brief overview of the prior research on political advertising, this analysis of the 1992 ad campaigns draws on several original datasets, including the University of Oklahoma's Political Commercial Archive Catalog Database, an extensive content analysis of the 1992 general election commercials, and the results of experimental tests of general election commercials using continuous computerized audience-response data.

POLITICAL ADVERTISING:
EXPECTATIONS FROM RESEARCH

Although the first presidential campaign to make extensive use of television spots was the 1952 Eisenhower campaign, academic researchers did not show much interest in the subject until nearly twenty years later. However, since the early 1970s, researchers have concentrated considerable attention on political advertising. Although it is always difficult with social science research methods to establish strict causal relationships, the body of research on political advertising has established strong evidence that political television spots do have a verifiable effect on the American political system. In fact, political television ads may come closer than any other political message to paralleling a "direct effects" model of communication. In an early review of political advertising research, substantial evidence showed that televised political advertising has cognitive, affective, and behavioral effects on voters (Kaid, 1981). Such evidence includes the early findings that political spots overcome selective exposure (Atkin et al., 1973); that spots directly affect candidate images (Kaid and Sanders, 1978; Cundy, 1986); and that higher issue recall results from exposure to television ads in comparison to news (Patterson and McClure, 1976) or televised debates (Just, Crigler, and Wallace, 1990).

Researchers have also amassed a substantial body of evidence indicating that negative ads do have direct effects on candidate images and evaluations, particularly when the negative ads (1) are sponsored by independent sources (Garramone, 1985; Garramone and Smith, 1984; Kaid and Boydston, 1987; Patterson and McClure, 1976) and (2) concentrate on *issue* attacks rather than *image* attacks (Roddy and Garramone, 1988). A recent study further suggested that negative ads influence voter evaluations of candidates and perceptions about candidate image (Garramone et al., 1990). Negative ads have been shown to make up between 35 and 37 percent of the ads in the presidential campaigns from 1980 through 1988 (Kaid and Johnston, 1991b).

Research has also shown that some of the criticism of television spots for being too "image oriented" is unjustified. Content analyses have clearly shown that issues make up a greater amount of political advertising content than do images (Joslyn, 1980; Kaid and Johnston, 1991b). Researchers have also demonstrated a superiority of issue over image commercials related to a variety of campaign effects (Kaid and Sanders, 1978; Geiger and Reeves, 1991; Roddy and Garramone, 1988).

Despite the findings that issue content is more prevalent and that issue ads are more successful with voters, researchers remain concerned that emotional response plays a significant role in audience reaction to televised political spots. Research on voting behavior has suggested the existence of an association between feelings and emotions, and political candidate evaluations (Abelson et al., 1982) and has shown connections between positive and negative feelings and evaluations of candidates (votes) (Marcus, 1988). Montague Kern (1989) has argued that emotional content has become an important component of political ads; and in an experimental study of political spots, Eunice Thorson, W. G. Christ, and Clarke Caywood (1991) found that the "pleasure" dimension of emotional responses to spots had a significant effect on voting behavior. Annie Lang (1991) has found that emotional aspects of political spots may relate to audience memory, particularly in negative ads. In conjunction with research on the 1988 campaign showing strong relationships between specific emotions elicited by Bush and Dukakis ads and audience evaluations of candidate images (Kaid, 1991; Kaid, Leland, and Whitney, 1992), these findings suggest that the role of emotion in political spots should receive greater attention as a source of advertising effect.

This brief overview of previous research on political ads is by no means comprehensive, but it does offer some clues about what researchers and political observers should have been anticipating in the 1992 presidential campaign: (1) a high expectation that the ads would play a major role in the election's outcome, (2) a concern for the negativity of the ads, and (3) greater attention to the components of ad content, particularly the continuing issue/image discussion and new concerns about the effects of emotional content. The high visibility of the television spots in the 1988 campaign was unprecedented. The spots themselves became a major aspect of media reporting about the campaign. In 1988, there were more stories on network news covering political spots than in all the presidential campaigns from 1972 through 1984 combined, suggesting that the extensive coverage may have legitimized television ads as voter decision-making tools (Kaid et al., 1993). The attention to the ads and the unprecedented concern about their role in the political process led to "Ad Watches" in many prominent newspapers and on television newscasts, as journalists sought a way to help voters interpret what they were seeing in candidate-controlled messages. Not only were there high expectations that the ads would play a major role in the campaign, but there was a repeated concern that the campaign might be even more negative than the 1988 campaign had been perceived to be (Grove, 1988; Martz et al., 1988; Taylor, 1989).

CONTENT AND APPROACHES OF THE 1992 SPOTS

The Primary Advertising Campaign

The American presidential nominating process consists of a hodgepodge of selection devices, encompassing both caucuses and direct primaries. The most publicized early tests in this long process are the Iowa caucuses and the New Hampshire presidential primary. By that point in 1992 the major contenders on the Democratic side appeared to be Brown, Clinton, Harkin, Kerrey, and Tsongas, with Bush and Buchanan vying for the Republican nomination.

The expectations were high that this would be a very negative campaign period. As Kathleen Kendall (1991) has pointed out in her analysis of eighty years of presidential primaries, negative campaigning is integral to presidential primaries because "they are an intraparty fight, in which several candidates from the same party compete for the nomination, and must differentiate themselves from each other" (2–3). Prior research, however, has not validated that primaries tend to produce more negative ads than do general election campaigns. An analysis of primary ads from 1968 through 1988 has indicated that the percentage of negative ads in primary campaigns is only about 18 percent, or half that expected in modern general election campaigns (Kaid and Ballotti, 1991; Kaid and Johnston, 1991b).

Some researchers have suggested that the 1992 primary ads may have exceeded the negativity of prior campaigns. A preliminary examination of 1992 nominating ads by Darrell West, Montague Kern, and Dean Alger (1992) found that 43 percent of the 90 ads examined contained an attack on the opponent's issues or character and that a substantial percentage of the ads had a decidedly "negative tone."

An analysis of the 1992 primary ads contained in the Political Commercial Archive Catalog Database[1] at the University of Oklahoma produced a sample of 140 ads used by 15 different candidates in the course of the primary season. Of these 140 ads, 19 were for obscure candidates and the remaining 121 were for the major Republican and Democratic contenders. The archive database categorizes commercials according to whether they are issue ads, image ads, or negative ads, using definitions of these categories similar to those set forth in other scholarly studies (Kaid, Chanslor, and Hovind, 1992). As Table 5.1 shows, Clinton produced the largest number of ads over the primary and caucus period (n = 51), three times as many as most other candidates. Overall, 59 percent of these primary ads for all candidates focused on candidate images, 24 percent stressed issues, and 17 percent were negative. The percentage of negative ads is thus about the same in the primary campaign as in previous primaries (Kaid and Ballotti, 1991).

However, closer examination of these data indicates that some candidates used a much higher percentage of negative ads. Buchanan, for instance, focused 69 percent of his ads on negative attacks against George Bush. The best known of these ads was the "Read-My-Lips" ad that focused on Bush's broken promise not to raise taxes. Researchers have identified this ad as particularly memorable (West, Kern, and Alger, 1992). A *New York Times* reporter suggested that after many viewings, this ad "begins to acquire a surreal fascination, as if it is disclosing something deep inside Mr. Bush. . . . he begins to seem more and more desperate, more and more absurd" (Tierney, 1992b). Another one of Buchanan's negative ads also attracted considerable media attention. This ad from the

Table 5.1
Types of 1992 Primary Television Spots

	Image	Issues	Negative	Total No. Ads
Brown	50%	17%	33%	6
Buchanan	19	12	69	16
Bush	50	25	25	12
Clinton	70	20	10	51
Harkin	69	31		13
Kerrey	43	43	14	14
Tsongas	89	11		9
Other	63	37		19
TOTAL ALL CAND.	59	24	17	140

Georgia primary attacked Bush for alleged support of pornographic art. The print news media were extremely critical of Buchanan's tactics in this ad where he tried to associate Bush with pornographic and homosexual art support because of National Endowment for the Arts funding during recent Republican administrations (West, Kern, and Alger, 1992).

Clinton, Tsongas, and Harkin gave more attention to image building in their spots. Kerrey made the greatest effort to focus on issues, according to Table 5.1. Early in the primary period, Kerrey did engage in negative advertising, but his approach softened somewhat toward the end of the New Hampshire primary period (Tierney, 1992b).

Further examination of this sample of primary ads reveals that the primaries are a time when candidates seem to appear frequently in their ads. Bush appeared in 75 percent of his ads, and Clinton was personally present in 82 percent of his spots. Clinton was far more likely than other candidates to use his family in his ads, perhaps because rumors of his extramarital affairs called for a showing of family support and solidarity. None of the candidates found the primaries an occasion for levity; in the entire sample of 140 primary ads, none was characterized as "using humor" to convey its message.

The General Election Ads

Expectations that the 1992 television ads would be an important part of the general election campaign were not misplaced. The presidential campaigns spent an unprecedented amount of money on television spots in 1992. The total spending budgets for the general election campaign for Bush and Clinton were set at $65.5 million, the maximum allowed by the Federal Election Commission for candidates accepting federal matching funding. The Perot campaign did not accept matching funds, financing the campaign from Perot's personal fortune and spending about $60 million. According to L. Patrick Devlin (1993), whose figures are compiled from consultation with the campaign consultants from each campaign, the Bush campaign advertising expenditures totaled $48.8 million, including $10.3 million that came directly from the Republican National Committee. This constituted about 75 percent of the total Bush campaign budget. The Clinton campaign spent only slightly less, about $35 million in campaign money, supplemented by $9 million in campaign and generic advertising from the Democratic National Committee. Ross Perot, who spent all of his money between October 1 (when he reentered the race) and election day, spent about two-thirds of his total budget on advertising, expending just under $40 million. The most amazing part of the Perot ad story was that the Perot campaign spent a mere $1 million on production for their spots.

In an attempt to provide a basic understanding of the content and style of the ads, we will consider the results of a content analysis of the spot ads from all three campaigns. This analysis followed procedures and categories similar to those outlined in earlier research (Kaid and Johnston, 1991b; Wadsworth and Kaid, 1987). The ads analyzed consisted of all ads provided to the Political Commercial Archive by the three campaigns and included a total of 32 Bush ads, 39 Clinton ads, and 19 Perot ads. Only spot ads of 5 minutes or less were included in this analysis. Longer ads, such as the 30-minute programs utilized by Ross Perot, are discussed separately. This sample of 90 ads was coded by a group of trained graduate student coders.[2]

In many ways, the 1992 ad campaign was the most negative in history. As Table 5.2 shows, although the Perot campaign did not air any explicitly negative ads, 56 percent of the Bush campaign ads and 69 percent of the Clinton ads were classified as negative ads (negative ads are defined as ads that were primarily focused on criticism of the opponent). *The Clinton percentage is the highest percentage of negative ads ever documented in a presidential campaign.* Prior to the 1992 campaign the highest percentages of negative ads had been found in the 1952 Eisenhower campaign, which had 66 percent negative ads (Kaid and Johnston, 1991a) and the infamous 1964 Johnson campaign with 40 percent negative ads (Kaid and Johnston, 1991b). Both Clinton and Bush negative ad totals far exceed those of the past three presidential campaigns that ranged from 35–37 percent.

Not only was the percentage of negative ads the highest ever, but Devlin (1993) has documented that for the first time ever the two major campaigns admitted to spending at least half of their ad budgets on airtime for these negative ads. Interestingly, throughout the entire campaign,

Table 5.2
Characteristics of 1992 General Election Spots

	Bush (n = 32)	Clinton (n = 39)	Perot (n = 19)
Ad Focus*			
Positive	43.8%	30.8%	100.0%
Negative	56.3	69.2	0.0
Candidate Is			
Speaker in Ad*	28.1	12.8	47.4
Dominant Appeal*			
Logical	46.9	46.2	15.8
Emotional	21.9	46.2	52.6
Ethical	31.3	7.7	31.6
Fear Appeal*	56.3	5.1	15.8
Ad Type			
Issue	50.0	66.7	57.9
Image	50.0	33.3	42.1

*Chi Square test indicates differences are significant at p ≤ .01.

the press never labeled the Clinton campaign as a "negative" campaign, a label that was repeatedly attached to Bush's 1988 effort, which had only half the number of negative ads featured in Clinton's 1992 effort.

The candidates did not, however, differ much in their relative emphases on issues versus images in their ads. The ads for each candidate were contrasted on this category, and Table 5.2 indicates that no statistically significant differences among the three candidates exist.

Table 5.2 also shows that Perot was much more likely to act as the main speaker in his ads than were Bush and Clinton. Perot serves as the main speaker in nearly half his ads (47%). Bush was the speaker for 28.1 percent of his own efforts, while Clinton spoke for himself only 12.8 percent of the time.

There are also clear differences among the three candidates in their use of appeals. Perot used far fewer *logical appeals* in his ads, relying heavily on *emotional appeals*. Both Bush and Perot made much heavier use of *ethical appeals* than did Clinton. However, neither Clinton nor Perot used any substantial number of *fear appeals*. Bush, however, used some kind of fear appeal in 56 percent of his ads, an amount that is significantly higher than Clinton or Perot. A good example of Bush's use of fear appeals was a spot called "Arkansas Record" that aired late in the campaign. Showing stark black and white footage of bleak and stormy landscapes, the spot recounts the negative aspects of Clinton's record as Arkansas governor and concludes, "And now Bill Clinton wants to do for America what he'd done for Arkansas. America can't take that risk." In many ways, the ad is a replay of the famous "revolving door" ad from the 1988 campaign, down to and including the ending tag-line.

Of interest in any campaign are the specific issues candidates stress and the image characteristics that are foremost in their ads, regardless of positive or negative slant. Table 5.3 shows that there were many differences among the candidates on these points. In terms of issues mentioned, it comes as no surprise that Clinton commercials mentioned the *economy* more often than any other issue, stressing economic concerns in 30.8 percent of his spots. Bush concentrated more of his time on *social issues* and on *taxes*. Perot also spent more effort on the *economy* (21.1%) and on the *deficit* (15.8%) in his ads than on any other issues.

When it came to candidate image characteristics, George Bush wanted to talk most about *honesty and integrity*, his own and Bill Clinton's, and he emphasized this point in three out of every five ads he sponsored (59.4%). Clinton provided a more varied message, pointing to his own *competence* (64.1% of his ads) and *performance* (48.7%), his own good and Bush's allegedly poor performance. Clinton was also more likely than the other two candidates to discuss *compassion* as a quality he felt he could bring to the office of president. Perot was more concerned with portraying himself as *competent* (89.5% of his ads), *strong* (68.4%), *qualified* (63.2%), and *aggressive* (57.9%).

While the foregoing account provides some basic information about the content and approaches of the ad campaigns, it does not tell the whole story. A detailed account of the advertising strategies of all three campaigns is provided elsewhere (see Devlin, 1993), but a brief overview here will help to put this analysis in context. The Bush campaign advertising was the responsibility of the November Group comprised of Madison Avenue talent and formed for the purpose of this particular campaign effort. In the last month of the campaign, veteran Republican ad consultant Sig Rogich came on board to assist. Clinton's advertising was coordinated by Democratic media consultant Frank Greer's agency. Perot's campaign ads also used a specially formed group, the 270 Group (the number of electoral votes needed to win) that utilized a local Dallas production facility.

Table 5.3
Emphasis on Specific Issues and Candidate
Qualities in 1992 General Election Spots

	Bush (n = 32)	Clinton (n = 39)	Perot (n = 19)
Issue Mentions			
Economy	3.1%	30.8%	21.1%
Deficit	3.1	0	15.8
Social Issues	12.5	5.1	10.5
Taxes	18.8	2.6	0
Other	6.3	0.0	5.3
No Issue	56.2	61.5	47.4
Candidate Character *Mentions*			
Honesty	59.4%	33.3%	15.8%
Strength	34.4	20.5	68.4
Compassion	6.3	38.5	21.4
Competence	25.0	64.1	89.5
Performance	18.8	48.7	31.6
Aggressiveness	15.6	17.9	57.9
Activeness	12.5	7.7	5.3
Qualifications	25.0	31.6	63.2

The structures and approaches of these three different campaign models are instructive in understanding the outcomes of these three presidential advertising campaigns. Over the course of the entire campaign period, the Clinton campaign was easily the most effective in articulating a consistent and coordinated advertising message and strategy. The first ad of the Clinton fall campaign began airing September 1; it was a 60-second ad that touted Clinton's performance as governor of Arkansas and promised that Clinton would create 8 million new jobs in four years. The visuals showed upbeat pictures of Clinton campaigning and traveling around on his bus tours (Jackson, 1992). Throughout the remainder of the campaign the Clinton ads seemed to articulate a consistent message. As is clear from the content analysis data above and from examination of the actual ads, the Clinton ads stressed that the economy was the main issue of concern, that Bush had failed in his handling of it, and that Clinton, who had succeeded in Arkansas, could succeed in getting the national economy back on track.

Bush's ad team, on the other hand, was never able to get a consistent message into their ads, either positive or negative. It has been widely reported that the Bush ad team was left without centralized coordination or direction, frustrated and in disarray (Berke, 1992; Wines, 1992). The early ads, in particular, not only lacked a message, but they had poor production values and badly executed concepts (Berke, 1992). When Clinton released his first attack ads several days before Bush's September 10 Detroit economic speech, the Bush campaign still did not have ads ready to respond to the economic attacks. At a point in the campaign when most campaigns already have an arsenal of spots ready and "in the can," the Bush ad effort was still searching for a message and a strategy to convey it (Wines, 1992).

Many observers believe that independent candidate Perot had the most innovative advertising strategy of any recent presidential campaign. One of the ironies of the Perot ad effort was that before he pulled out of the race in the summer, one of Perot's biggest disputes with his campaign consultants had been over advertising strategy. Perot had initially been very reluctant to invest much money in advertising, having achieved so much success on the "talk show" circuit for free (Barrett, 1992). By the time he jumped back into the race on October 1 for the final push, he had apparently changed his mind. During his short candidacy, he concentrated most of his efforts on the debates and on paid advertising, spending millions of his own money to buy time for both long and short commercial blocks (Kolbert, 1992). Having decided that he could control his image better through paid advertising, and having learned from his earlier effort that he did not much enjoy press scrutiny, Perot stopped making public appearances. In addition to the scheduled debates, he concentrated his efforts on building his image through a series of 30-minute "infomercials" in which Perot undertook to educate the American public about the problems facing the nation, about Perot's common-sense interpretations of them, and eventually about his family and personal values (Bark and Jackson, 1992; Goodman, 1992; Sack, 1992). Perot seemed to hit his stride when he discovered that controlled media fit his style after all.

Perot's first 30-minute program aired on October 6 on CBS and received a 12.2 Nielsen rating (each rating point equals almost a million households). Perot claimed that it received such a positive response that he was forced to repeat it on October 9, instead of airing a new program (Bark and Jackson, 1992). Dubbed "infomercials" by the media, this series of 30-minute time blocks proved to be an unusual and innovative strategy that garnered Perot considerable media attention. In fact, *Time* magazine tapped the ads as among their "best advertising of 1992," noting that the strategy had also garnered Perot *Advertising Age*'s designation as "Adman of the Year" (*Time*, 1993).

As the campaign progressed, Perot also aired shorter spots, beginning with a series of three 60-second spots on several cable television networks (Bark and Jackson, 1992). Unlike the longer "infomercials," many of these shorter spots were very dramatic and emotional, but they utilized very simple production techniques, usually combining emotional background visuals with crawling print messages.

AUDIENCE REACTIONS TO THE 1992 ADS

The style and content of the 1992 ads do not suggest how the ads were interpreted by voters. Aspects of the ads that may seem salient to researchers may not be particularly important to viewers. One interesting way of assessing audience responses is offered by computerized technologies that allow audiences to register their second-by-second responses to ads as they are viewed. As audience members view a spot, they turn hand-held dials from negative to positive to indicate how they feel about the spots. Then the computerized scores are gathered by a computer and simultaneously overlayed on a video copy of the spot, allowing researchers to assess audience reaction to a spot as it progresses. The highest rating was a 7; the lowest was a 1, with 4 being a neutral point. Such a technique also allows comparisons of various demographic groups with the audience (Republicans versus Democrats versus Independents, for instance).

This technology was used to measure reactions to a sample of 15 presidential ads from the 1992 presidential contest at the University of Oklahoma. Students from basic communications classes were randomly selected to participate in a series of studies about political commercials in late October. The results described below are based on a sample of 26 students who viewed the group of 15 ads on October 26, 1992. The group consisted of 11 Republicans, 8 Democrats, and 7 Independents.[3] The group was shown the 15 ads arranged to alternate between the candidates. The tape consisted of 3 Perot spots, 7 Bush spots, and 5 Clinton spots. All ads were short 30- or 60-second spots; none of the longer ads used by Perot were utilized in this study because of the difficulty in comparing these longer "infomercials" with traditional spot ads.

A few of the highlights of the results and statistical interpretations of viewing and responding to these ads will help indicate the nature of voter responses to the 1992 ads. First, it is clear from an analysis of the video overlays that the most consistently successful spots were those of Ross Perot. In all three of the Perot spots, the audience reactions were consistently positive. At no point in any of his three ads did the ratings for Perot dip below the median point. Perot's most positive assessment came in his "red ink" ad where the overall audience mean reached a high of 5.73 toward the end of the ad as the announcer recounts Ross Perot's qualifications for governing:

In this election, you can vote for a candidate who has proven his leadership by making the free enterprise system work. Creating jobs. Building businesses. A candidate who is not a business-as-usual politician, but a business leader with the know-how to expand the tax base, reduce the national debt, and restore the meaning of "Made in the U.S.A."

The other two Perot spots were almost as effective. The "Purple Heart" ad also created an increasingly positive rating as the ad progressed, achieving an ending mean score of 5.69 as the voice-over recounting a Vietnam veteran's confidence in Perot expounds: "Like you, I firmly believe that if we stand united, we will win." The third Perot ad, showing storm clouds swirling behind discussions of the national debt, was the least effective of the three Perot ads, but it still achieved an overall positive rating, rising to a mean high of 5.31.

The 7 Bush ads received very inconsistent ratings from the audience, an indication perhaps of the lack of consistency in the Bush message and strategy throughout the campaign. One Bush spot achieved the highest ratings of any spot in the 15-ad sample. The positive Bush spot that ran early in the campaign, mixing a forceful-sounding George Bush with printed messages on the screen, achieved a high mean rating of 5.85 from the audience. In the spot, Bush stresses the need for the United States to be "an economic and a military superpower." In fact, the dial ratings move up consistently for this spot, as the audience became more and more positive with a final high as Bush concluded that he was fighting for: "open markets for American products, lower government spending, tax relief, opportunities for small business, legal and health reform, job training, and new schools built on competition ready for the 21st century."

Bush also scored well in other positive ads, and some of his attacks on Bill Clinton were well received. Audiences responded well to the ad that showed Clinton signing numerous tax increases in Arkansas (mean high of 4.23), an ad that was particularly effective with Independents and Undecideds. Bush also got a good response from a testimonial ad that attacked Clinton's trustworthiness. This ad climbs to a mean high of 4.58 as one of the testifiers says at the end "One thing that's got me definitely for Bush is that I remember what happened the last time we did things the way Bill Clinton wants to do them." Undecideds, like Bush supporters, responded particularly well to this point.

While Bush's ratings rarely fell even slightly below the neutral point on the audience dials, most of his other negative commercials did not seem to hit responsive chords with the audience. The highly publicized spots showing two-faces of Clinton and the anti-Clinton statements on the draft featuring the *Time* magazine cover did not elicit much response, negative or positive, from viewers.

Clinton spots were also somewhat lackluster in audience appeal, based on the ratings of this audience. His highest rating in all the spots was a mere 5.01 mean high in his spot on welfare reform, a spot that was particularly appealing to Perot supporters as well as to Democrats. Clinton received more negative ratings for his spots than either of the other two candidates. several times falling below the neutral point. His lowest point, and indeed the lowest received by any candidate throughout the 15-ad sample, was an anti-Bush ad that claimed that Bush had signed the "second biggest tax increase" in history, whereas under Clinton Arkansas had "the second lowest tax burden" in the nation. This ad dipped to a rating of 3.35.

Some clear conclusions can be drawn from these data. In terms of audience reactions, all candidates clearly performed best when they talked "positive." Spots that emphasized the candidate's own concerns and agendas (such as Bush's economic/military superpower spot), and Perot's "red ink" and "Purple Heart" spots were positively received. However, it is also true that the spots that received the most consistently high ratings from the audience (the Perot spots) were also spots that made great use of emotional appeals. While Perot's spots were all basically positive spots, they were also highly emotional and highly "image oriented." Unlike his longer "infomercials," these Perot spots included few pieces of concrete information, relying instead on emotional descriptions of a Vietnam veteran offering his Purple Heart and a recounting of Perot's business experience. Even more than the verbal messages, the visual messages of the Perot commercials were emotional, a flowing red-ink background that looked almost like rolling blood, storm clouds hovering and rolling, the Purple Heart imagery. Given the research we have presented, it is not possible to assess separately the impact of this visual imagery, but certainly the results suggest that such effects may be substantial and indicate the importance of more research on this topic. It may well be that the real message of the most successful 1992 spots was not in the much-discussed technique of printing words on the screen for viewers to read, but in the overlaying of those messages against emotionally stirring visuals.

During the 1992 election year, "Ad Watches" were initiated by many newspapers and some television newscasts. Such analyses were designed to dissect ads and point out weaknesses and misleading aspects. Did they work? Although the jury (academic researcher projects) is still out, there are many reasons to suspect that such analyses do not offset voter impressions of spots. Not only do the analyses often postdate the viewers' original exposure to the spot, but the analyses often do little to consider the emotional/visual aspects of the spot. If, as the computer-automated response data suggests, voters respond more to the emotional and visual characteristics of the ads, the media's concentration on breaking down and criticizing the verbal arguments may not have much impact.

CONCLUSIONS

There were other important new directions in the 1992 advertising. The 1992 campaign saw spot buys in selected markets reach new heights. The Clinton campaign particularly used this strategy on a national basis. It was also a year in which more attention was paid to cable television. Because of its low cost and its ability to target voters more precisely, cable has long been touted as an effective marketing tool for political candidates. In the New Hampshire primary, for instance, Clinton, Kerrey, and Tsongas all used cable spot buys (Boehlert, 1992). As mentioned, Perot made heavy use of cable television to run some of his early 60-second spots. Perot's use of the "infomercial" and of longer advertising buys was also viewed as innovative by many observers.

Several major conclusions can be drawn about the 1992 presidential advertising campaigns. The ad campaigns were the most expensive and the most negative in history, yet voters responded best to positive messages and to stirring emotional messages. The 1992 campaign probably also confirmed some early research findings that "quality" may be an overriding factor in advertising effectiveness (Atkin et al., 1973).

ACKNOWLEDGMENTS

The author wishes to express her appreciation to John Ballotti, Mike Chanslor, Cindy Roper, and John Tedesco (Ph.D. students in the Department of Communication at the University of Oklahoma) for their assistance in the compilation of material and the content analytical aspects of this chapter.

NOTES

1. The Political Commercial Archive is the world's largest collection of political spots (Kaid and Haynes, 1991). Most of the advertisements in the collection are provided to the archive directly from the candidate's campaigns or producers/agencies or from television and radio stations that air the ads. The database from which this sample was provided is part of a project to catalog the archive supported by the Strengthening Research Libraries Program of the U.S. Department of Education.

2. Intercoder reliability was assessed on a sample of 10 percent of the spots and averaged +.86 across all categories. The formula used to calculate intercoder reliability is that given in North, Holsti, Zaninovich, and Zinnes (1963). It is given for two coders and can be modified for any number of coders.

$$R = \frac{2\,(C_{1,2})}{C_1 + C_2}$$

$C_{1,2}$ = # of category assignments both coders agree on and $C_1 + C_2$ = total category assignments made by both coders.

3. The group also contained 16 males and 10 females, although no major differences in response to the commercials according to gender were noted in this preliminary analysis. The candidate predispositions of the group were as follows: 8 for Bush, 5 for Clinton, 4 for Perot, and 9 undecided.

REFERENCES

Abelson, Robert P., Donald R. Kinder, Mark D. Peters, and Susan T. Fiske. 1982. "Affective and Semantic Components in Political Person Perception." *Journal of Personality and Social Psychology* 42: 619–30.

Atkin, Charles K., Lawrence Bowen, Oguz B. Nayman, and Kenneth G. Sheinkopf. 1973. "Quality versus Quantity in Televised Politics Ads." *Public Opinion Quarterly* 37: 209–24.

Bark, Ed, and David Jackson. 1992. "Perot Buys Hour on ABC Next Week." *Dallas Morning News,* Oct. 9, 12A.

Barrett, Laurence I. 1992. "Perot Takes a Walk." *Time,* July 27, 32–33.

Berke, Richard L. 1992. "Bush Ads Disappoint Many in GOP." *New York Times,* Aug. 16, 19.

Boehlert, Eric. 1992. "Spot Cable Politics." *Inside Media,* Jan. 22, 1: 52.

Cundy, Donald T. 1986. "Political Commercials and Candidate Image." In *New Perspectives on Political Advertising,* Lynda Lee Kaid, Dan Nimmo, and Keith R. Sanders, eds., 210–34. Carbondale: Southern Illinois University Press.

Devlin, L. Patrick. 1989. "Contrasts in Presidential Campaign Commercials of 1988." *American Behavioral Scientist* 32: 389–414.

———. 1993. "Contrasts in Presidential Campaign Commercials of 1992." *American Behavioral Scientist* 37 (2): 272–90.

Garramone, Gina M. 1985. "Effects of Negative Political Advertising: The Role of Sponsor and Rebuttal." *Journal of Broadcasting and Electronic Media* 29: 147–59.

Garramone, Gina M., and Stephen J. Smith. 1984. "Reactions to Political Advertising: Clarifying Sponsor Effects." *Journalism Quarterly* 61: 771–75.

Garramone, Gina M., Charles K. Atkin, Bruce E. Pinkleton, and Richard T. Cole. 1990. "Effects of Negative Political Advertising on the Political Process." *Journal of Broadcasting and Electronic Media* 34: 299–311.

Geiger, Seth F., and Byron Reeves. 1991. "The Effects of Visual Structure and Content Emphasis on the Evaluation and Memory for Political Candidates." In *Television and Political Advertising, Volume 1: Psychological Processes,* Frank Biocca, ed., 125–43. Hillsdale, NJ: Lawrence Erlbaum Publishers.

Goodman, Walter. 1992. "After Commercials Full of Grim Statistics, Perot Now Offers Softer Image." *New York Times,* Oct. 25, 15.

Grove, L. 1988. "Attack Ads Trickled Up from State Races." *Washington Post,* Nov.13, A1, 18–19.

Jackson, David. 1992. "TV Ad Touting Clinton's Record to Make Debut." *Dallas Morning News,* Aug. 31, 7A.

Joslyn, Richard A. 1980. "The Content of Political Spot Ads." *Journalism Quarterly* 57: 92–98.

Just, Marion, Ann Crigler, and Lori Wallach. 1990. "Thirty Seconds or Thirty Minutes: What Viewers Learn from Spot Advertisements and Candidate Debates." *Journal of Communication* 40: 120–33.

Kaid, Lynda Lee. 1981. "Political Advertising." In *Handbook of Political Communication,* Dan Nimmo and Keith R. Sanders, eds., 249–71. Beverly Hills, CA: Sage Publications.

———. 1991. "The Effects of Television Broadcasts on Perceptions of Political Candidates in the United States and France." In *Mediated Politics in Two Cultures: Presidential Campaigning in the United States and France,* Lynda Lee Kaid, Jacques Gerstlé, and Keith R. Sanders, eds., 247–60. Westport, CT: Praeger.

Kaid, Lynda Lee, and John Ballotti. 1991. "Television Advertising in Presidential Primaries and Caucuses." Paper presented at the Speech Communication Association Convention.

Kaid, Lynda Lee, and John Boydston. 1987. "An Experimental Study of the Effectiveness of Negative Political Advertisements." *Communication Quarterly* 35: 193–201.

Kaid, Lynda Lee, Mike Chanslor, and Mark Hovind. 1992. "The Influence of Program and Commercial Type on Political Advertising Effectiveness." *Journal of Broadcasting and Electronic Media* 36: 303–20.

Kaid, Lynda Lee, Robert H. Gobetz, Jane Garner, Chris M. Leland, and David K. Scott. 1993. "Television News and Presidential Campaigns: The Legitimization of Televised Political Advertising." *Social Science Quarterly* 74.

Kaid, Lynda Lee, and Kathleen H. M. Haynes. 1991. *The Political Commercial Archive: A Catalog and Guide to the Collection.* Norman, OK: Political Communication Center.

Kaid, Lynda Lee, and Anne Johnston. 1991a. "Negative versus Positive Television Advertising in Presidential Campaigns." Paper presented at the International Communication Association Convention.

———. 1991b. "Negative versus Positive Television Advertising in U.S. Presidential Campaigns, 1960–1988." *Journal of Communication* 41: 53–64.

Kaid, Lynda Lee, Chris Leland, and Susan Whitney. 1992. "The Impact of Televised Political Ads: Evoking Viewer Responses in the 1988 Presidential Campaign." *Southern Communication Journal* 57: 285–95.

Kaid, Lynda Lee, and Keith R. Sanders. 1978. "Political Television Commercials: An Experimental Study of Type and Length." *Communication Research* 5: 57–70.

Kendall, Kathleen E. 1991. "Negative Campaigning in the Presidential Primaries 1912–1992." Paper presented at the Speech Communication Association Convention.

Kern, Montague. 1989. *30 Second Politics: Political Advertising in the Eighties.* New York: Praeger.

Kolbert, Elizabeth. 1992. "Uh-Oh, Perot: His Message and Money Drive the Race Again." *New York Times,* Oct. 25, 1E.

Lang, Annie. 1991. "Emotion, Formal Features, and Memory for Televised Political Advertisements." In *Television and Political Advertising, Vol. 1: Psychological Processes,* Frank Biocca, ed., 221–43. Hillsdale, NJ: Lawrence Erlbaum Publishers.

Marcus, George E. 1988. "The Structure of Emotional Response: 1984 Presidential Candidates." *American Political Science Review* 82: 737–61.

Martz, Larry, Margaret Garrard Warner, Howard Fineman, Eleanor Clift, and Mark Starr. 1988. "The Smear Campaign." *Newsweek,* Oct. 31, 16–19.

North, Robert C., Ole Holsti, M. George Zaninovich, and Dina A. Zinnes. 1963. *Content Analysis: A Handbook with Applications for the Study of International Crisis.* Evanston, IL: Northwestern University Press.

Patterson, Thomas E., and Robert D. McClure. 1976. *The Unseeing Eye.* New York: G. P. Putnam.

Roddy, Brian. L., and Gina M. Garramone. 1988. "Appeals and Strategies of Negative Political Advertising." *Journal of Broadcasting and Electronic Media* 32: 415–27.

Sack, Kevin. 1992. "For TV, Perot Spends Heavily on Wart Removal." *New York Times,* Oct. 25, 15Y.

Taylor, Paul. 1989. "Consultants Rise via the Low Road." *Washington Post,* Jan. 17, A1, A14.

Thorson, Eunice, W. G. Christ, and Clarke L. Caywood. 1991. "Selling Candidates Like Tubes of Toothpaste: Is the Comparison Apt?" In *Television and Political Advertising, Volume 1: Psychological Processes,* Frank Biocca, ed., 145–72. Hillsdale, NJ: Lawrence Erlbaum Publishers.

Tierney, John. 1992a. "Grace under Pressure? It's Working for Clinton." *New York Times,* Mar. 22, 14Y.

———. 1992b. "TV Viewers Get to See the Candidates, and See the Candidates." *New York Times,* Feb. 16, 12Y.

Time. 1993. Jan. 4, 70.

Wadsworth, Anne Johnston, and Lynda Lee Kaid. 1987. "Incumbent and Challenger Styles in Presidential Advertising." Paper presented at the International Communication Association Convention.

West, Darrell M., Montague Kern, and Dean Alger. 1992. "Political Advertising and Ad Watches in the 1992 Presidential Nominating Campaign." Paper presented at the American Political Science Association Convention.

Wines, Michael. 1992. "How Bush Lost: For Want of a Strategy, Chaos Ruled." *New York Times,* Nov. 29, 1, 11.

6

A Time for Change in American Politics: The Issue of the 1992 Presidential Election

Rachel L. Holloway

How did a little-known governor from a small southern state, with allegations of infidelity, draft dodging, and insincerity dogging him until election day, defeat an experienced and popular incumbent? Why did Clinton's call for change succeed in the 1992 presidential election? A simple answer might be "the economy." An analysis of the issues in the 1992 presidential election—the economy, health care, education, crime, trade, and so on—could look to the immediate problems facing the voting public, the candidates' proposals to address those concerns, and the public's response to the candidates' strategies. Yet such an analysis would fail to resolve larger questions: Why didn't Bush's character charges against Clinton stick? Why did "change" resonate so strongly with voters' attitudes? Why did the American public become so energized in 1992? Answers to these questions and a deeper understanding of what was at issue in the 1992 presidential election can be reached through a broader political and social analysis. Beyond the immediate concerns with the economy, health care, and other issues, the 1992 election marked a shift in the cycles of political commitment identified by Arthur M. Schlesinger, Jr. (1985). That shift in political commitment created a rhetorical context that constrained presidential campaign discourse in unique ways.

Although conventional wisdom advises incumbents against calling for change (Trent and Friedenberg, 1991, 63–88; Denton and Woodward, 1990, 92–96), Schlesinger's 1985 analysis predicted a shift in American thought that would embrace "change" and look for a broad-based, public-centered campaign rhetoric. Bush's refusal to become the "agent of change" during his administration cost him the election. Conversely, Clinton won the 1992 election because he defined his candidacy according to "change," using terminology appropriate to the shift in political commitments in a way that overcame its inherent and traditional disadvantages.

The purpose of this chapter is to describe how Bush gave away the *winning* terminology of the presidential election, how his chosen strategies undermined his own candidacy, and how Bill Clinton took advantage of the rhetorical opportunity created by the shift in political commitment. A preliminary step in the analysis of the 1992 campaign strategies is to present Schlesinger's cycles of American history as a rhetorical context for the election. Then, an analysis of Bush's rhetoric prior to the election will help us to identify the rhetorical potential in his own presidency that was abandoned. Given that preliminary context, we will look at the campaign itself and analyze the strengths and weaknesses of the key definitional strategies employed by Clinton and by Bush in the presidential campaign. Ross Perot's influence is noted within the analysis of Bush's and Clinton's discourse. Finally, we will consider what we can learn about political issues and campaigns from this election.

A TIME FOR CHANGE

In *The Cycles of American History,* Arthur M. Schlesinger, Jr., offers an alternative interpretation of American political change (1985, 23–48). He explains America's political history as a cycle perpetuated by the internal tension between the nation's commitment both to private interest and to public purpose. Although both sets of values are central to American thought and share commitments to individual liberty, constitutional government, and the rule of law, the dissimilarities between private interest and public purpose concerns produce competing perspectives of government. Because neither view fully satisfies the needs of the public, eventually the political tide turns from one to the other and back again. Problems left unsolved in one era generate momentum for the other. Approximately every thirty years, people become dissatisfied with their political situation and attempt to remedy their dissatisfaction by adopting the alternative set of political values for a while. As Schlesinger notes, "As political eras, whether dominated by public purpose or private interest, run their course, they infallibly generate the desire for something different. It always becomes after a while 'time for a change'" (1985, 28).

In periods of public purpose, public life dominates private concerns. People are brought together to reform their government and their society so that all citizens can prosper. Calls for reform, based on democratic values of equality, freedom, social responsibility, and the common good, overcome the values of capitalism (free enterprise, profit, and wealth) that lead to disparity among citizens. Action, idealism, and passion shape government into an affirmative agency, characterized by innovation and policy that aims to improve the conditions under which the citizenry lives. Reform is the political byword. People turn to government to create positive change. Public life, public reform, and public action outweigh public commitment to individual prosperity. What's good for the nation is good for its citizens.

Schlesinger notes that periods of public purpose, for all the good they may do, are also disillusioning and exhausting. Continuous reform and excessive innovation begin to overwhelm the public's capacity to change and cope. A time for change comes again: "Worn out by the constant summons to battle, weary of ceaseless national activity, disillusioned by the results, they seek a new dispensation, an interlude of rest and recuperation" (1985, 28). Citizens turn to their private interests.

In such periods, the values of capitalism direct national policy and action. Political action is justified by appeals to "the sanctity of private property, the maximization of profit, the cult of the free market, the survival of the fittest" (Schlesinger, 1985, 26). People draw away from social action to their own private concerns. Family and friends become the focus of life. Community is set aside. The underlying assumption is that what is good for the individual is good for society, and so laissez-faire government becomes the preferred style. Government must "stay out of the way" of individual ambition. Public problems are left to individual action. This "privatization" rejuvenates the disillusioned populous: "It replenishes the self, the family and the private economy and renews defenses against mass society and an aggressive state" (Schlesinger, 1985, 40). It is a period of political and economic rejuvenation.

The 1980s were a classic period of private interest, echoing themes from the 1850s, 1920s, and 1950s. Schlesinger called Reagan's policies the "boilerplate of every epoch of private interest" (1985, 39). Bush's continuation of Reagan's supply-side economics, New Federalism, deregulation initiatives, and his own "no new taxes" pledge were nothing new.

Periods of private interest also produce an interesting social and cultural twist. Politically, a private interest perspective attempts to remove governmental influence from economic affairs. Socially, however, government becomes increasingly involved in monitoring private behavior. Schlesinger notes that during periods of private interest, "class and interest politics subside; cultural politics—ethnicity, religion, social status, morality—come to the fore" and produce Billy Sunday and Aimee Semple McPherson in the 1920s; Norman Vincent Peale and Billy Graham in the 1950s; and Jerry Falwell and the Moral Majority in the 1980s (Schlesinger, 1985, 39). Despite the seeming contradiction, an emphasis on private interest tends to produce an invasive public concern characterized by private behavior. Public purpose creates the opposite. The emphasis on public and community turns attention away from the private lives of officials and citizens and to their public involvements and commitments.

Eventually, the emphasis on private interest generates its own dissatisfactions. Private interest policies produce divisions throughout society—economic, intellectual, social. People feel cut off from one another and begin to seek a renewed sense of community. As they do, interests and commitments shift to democratic values of equality, freedom, social responsibility, and general welfare. It becomes time for a change again.

The internal tensions and dissatisfactions of private interest and public purpose generate their corrective counterpart, but the timing of the shift is generational as well. Childhood's political socialization produces commitments and philosophies that guide political involvement in maturity. The children who came of age politically under Eisenhower conservatism parented the eighteen- to twenty-four-year-olds who elected Ronald Reagan. Those who grew up (politically) under Theodore Roosevelt elected Franklin Roosevelt. Those young people who witnessed the New Deal reforms of Roosevelt elected John F. Kennedy. Looking to future elections, Schlesinger divided the Baby Boomers into two generations, separated at 1957: "the older generation attuned to democratic purpose, the younger to private interest" (1985, 40). According to Schlesinger's model, those Americans who were socialized under Kennedy and the reform of the 1960s and their children who were just reaching voting age would form a powerful voting block in the 1992 presidential election. A "public purpose generation" would come forward to "accept the torch" of leadership again.

But change is not easy and requires significant motivation. Mere disillusionment and generational shift offer little focus or direction. The shift from private interest to public purpose requires a final element, a "detonating issue." Economic disparities and social problems left unaddressed offer a range of potential flash points. Eventually, problems become so acute that they capture public—and therefore official—attention.

In describing and explaining the cycles of political commitment, Schlesinger advised caution against deterministic application of his ideas to politics; the political cycle is neither "automatic" nor "self-enforcing" (1985, 45). A presidential candidate's party and generation do not predict election in Schlesinger's analysis. Nor does any single issue fall within the exclusive purview of a political philosophy. Joe Klein, a *Newsweek* columnist, identified an emerging middle ground in both parties that incorporated the compelling terms of both private interest and public purpose:

a tiny—but intellectually powerful—radical middle in both parties, post socialist activists who seek to achieve liberal goals (better education, housing, health care, environment) through conservative, market-oriented means like choice, competition, tax incentives for public-spirited behavior and privatization. (Klein, 1992a)

Both parties *could* embrace a "public purpose" rhetoric. Ross Perot's popularity as an independent candidate confirmed the possibilities. A Texas billionaire businessman, by most accounts a hard-line conservative, chastised *all* government officials, regardless of party affiliation, as pawns of special interests and called for government's active responsibility to the people. He discounted personal issues as irrelevant to election and action as central to political change. "The People" responded. Rhetorical position, not party, was central to election.

Nor was the 1992 election necessarily or inevitably the moment in which the electorate would choose public interest over private interest. In fact, given the historic wounds left by the 1960s, Schlesinger felt that private interest might hold the American political momentum longer in response (1985, 45). So although Schlesinger anticipated a change in national mood, opportunity for extending the private interest era, or at least the Bush presidency, was substantial.

In fact, George Bush had several rhetorical options. He could extend the Reagan-era themes hoping that the still significant fear of reform would influence political thought; he could modify the conservative private interest rhetoric to incorporate more commitment to "public" concerns; or he could dramatically redefine his presidency to meet the public's shift in attention and interest. Major shifts in international relationships and concerns offered Bush significant justification for redefinition. He could adopt a new position in accord with the "new world order"; he could become an "agent of change."

On the other hand, Clinton's challenge was to capture the symbolic momentum of impending "change" and present a Democratic position that met concerns for the public good. At the same time, Clinton's discourse would need to reassure those voters still shaken by the intensity of the 1960s that his election would bring positive change without further division and violence. Schlesinger advised that a public purpose candidate "must rise above those worthy special interests—labor, women, blacks, old folks and the rest—that have become their electoral refuge and regain a commanding national vision of the problems and prospects of the republic" (1985, 46). Unity, community, and vision would be critical to a candidate's success.

Schlesinger's analysis describes the broad rhetorical context that constrained the 1992 presidential election. To win the 1992 election, a candidate would need to articulate a unified vision of the nation's future that incorporated government commitment to public purpose. Neither political party had a "lock" on that perspective. George Bush showed early signs of moving toward the "change" terminology that was later used so successfully, first by Perot and then by Clinton. Analysis of Bush's rhetoric in 1990 and 1991 reveals the potential for Bush's rhetorical domination of the 1992 election.

BUSH'S MISSED OPPORTUNITY

Few people imagined the world events that created the "Revolution of 1989." The Berlin Wall fell. Czechoslovakia elected a poet president. The Baltic nations moved to free themselves from the Soviet Union. As George Bush prepared his 1990 State of the Union address, Cold War themes that guided American political thought and discourse after World War II lost their guiding influence. Bush needed new themes for a new time. He marked 1989 as one of the "singular moments in history" that "divide all that goes before from all that comes after." (Bush, 1990, 130). Only once before, he said, had his generation experienced such a turning point:

Many of us in this chamber have lived much of our lives in a world whose fundamental features were defined in 1945. And the events of that year decreed the shape of nations, the pace of progress, freedom or oppression for millions of people around the world. 1945 provided the common frame of reference, the compass points of the post-war era we've relied upon to understand ourselves. (130)

And then Bush explicitly identified a shift in that "frame of reference": "And that was our world—until now. The events of the year just ended— the revolution of '89—have been a chain reaction, changes so striking that it marks the beginning of a new era in the world's affairs" (130). His identification of the "new era" was explicit: "a time of change is taking place"; "we are in a period of great transition, great hope, and yet, great uncertainty" (133). Only one year into his administration, Bush defined a "time of change."

Bush also looked to domestic concerns: "Our challenge today is to take this democratic system of ours—a system second to none—and make it better" (1990, 130). He defined "better" as more jobs, quality child care, a clean environment reconciled with a strong economy. Bush extended America's freedoms to a broader citizenry through explicit identifications and inclusive pronouns:

And where every one of us enjoys the same opportunities to live, to work, and to contribute to society. And where, for the first time, the American mainstream includes all of our disabled citizens. Where everyone has a roof over his head—and where the homeless get the help they need to live in dignity. Where our schools challenge and support our kids and our teachers—and where all of them make the grade. (1990, 130)

While Bush seemed to reach out to those lost during a private-interest era, his solution was still private: "The State of the Union depends on whether we help our neighbor—claim the problems of our community as our own" (1990, 132). Bush identified the shifting context, but still offered private, individual solutions. A *Seattle Times* editorial highlighted Bush's move toward "public values": "A sincere president articulated values that a nation weary of a decade of greed and materialism is ready to embrace—family, volunteerism, cooperation" ("State of the Union–Rhetoric Gives Hope," 1990, A8). Yet public concerns were still met with private solutions. The role of government had not changed.

The impending generational shift also was present in Bush's discourse. Late in the speech, he called for personal involvement in generational terms:

So let me start with my generation—with the grandparents out there. You are our living link with the past. Tell your grandchildren the story of struggles waged, at home and abroad. Of sacrifices freely made for freedom's sake. (1990, 132)

In the opening of the speech Bush described his generation of leadership as defined by their Cold War experience. At the end, he called his generation "a living link with the past." Even as Bush defined a moment of change and looked toward the future, he offered no vision of America's future that justified his continued leadership.

Throughout the next year, Bush faced a range of issues, not the least of which was a stagnating economy. His economic advisors reassured him that the economy was not in a recession and that the downturn would shift well before the presidential election season was in full swing. As a result, Bush first refused to recognize the recession. Later, he reassured the American people that the economy was in a "temporary downturn" and that recovery was imminent. As Schlesinger predicted, disillusionment continued to grow due to increasing economic division.

On the international scene, Iraq invaded Kuwait and President Bush ordered U.S. troops into Saudi Arabia. Bush endorsed a U.N. commitment to multinational action, and Desert Shield began. Then in January Desert Shield became Desert Storm.

Bush again had an opportunity to create a perspective on national affairs in his 1991 State of the Union address. Again he emphasized the critical time. He told Americans that they stood at "a defining hour" (1991, 74) and were at the center of "a rapidly changing world." America, he said, was part of a "new world order—where diverse nations are drawn together in common cause, to achieve the universal aspirations of mankind: peace and security, freedom and the rule of law" (1991, 74).

At home, Bush called Americans to use the same spirit and character shown in Desert Storm to tackle domestic problems. Bush acknowledged that some Americans were in "genuine economic distress," but he pointed out that many economic factors were positive. The nation was not experiencing double-digit inflation, had seen no big cuts in production, and exports remained strong. He said Americans should "put these times in perspective. Yes, the largest peacetime economic expansion in history has been temporarily interrupted. But our economy is still over twice as large as our closest competitor" (1991, 76).

Bush's response to the "temporary interruption" in prosperity was to offer tax-free savings accounts, penalty-free withdrawals from IRAs for first-time home buyers, a reduced tax for long-term capital gains to increase jobs and growth. What Bush failed to explain was how these initiatives would help those Americans unable even to make ends meet. Although citizens supported Bush's action abroad, his definition of the economic situation seemed to discount the experiences of many Americans.

Reaction to Bush's speech in 1991 was not generous. Although his popularity was still unprecedented, his vulnerabilities were *beginning* to show. Columnist Richard Goodwin (1991) commented that the public "received little more than a litany of the same obsolete exhortations and abstract intentions that have become the staple of public rhetoric." Goodwin called for a shift to "democratic values" and a change to more activist government:

A democracy is not a geographical collection of leaderless people. It is, or should be, a community that selects a government to formulate policies and programs that make it possible for people to secure the basic necessities of life and build a growing economy. During the last decade, government has abysmally failed in that responsibility. (1991)

Even conservative columnist George Will criticized the president for his lack of attention to the nation's domestic problems (Will, 1991, 103).

Columnists and pundits, however, do not always reflect public sentiment. Consider the reaction of a Cape Cod woman who had written a letter to Bush, hoping to gain understanding from the president. Bush quoted her letter in his speech to demonstrate his empathy. Ironically, despite his reference, the woman felt her efforts had failed: "I mean no disrespect, but I don't think he does understand" (McLaughlin, 1991, 12). While President Bush called the recession a "temporary interruption" in long-term prosperity, prospects for the short-term had voters scared.

For two years, in the speech that each year allowed the president the opportunity to put his own "spin" on the nation's successes and problems, Bush defined a "time of change," of shifting commitments and ways of thinking. Yet he offered no vision for the future. He attempted to identify with the public's growing concern over the economy but did not make innovative proposals to respond to that change. He continued to emphasize individual action—on the economy, education, and other pressing issues.

But Bush still had time to become the agent of change well before the election. President Bush's foreign affairs success presented an opportunity available to few presidents midway in a first term. Only a few weeks after his 1991 State of the Union address, Bush personally received credit for building a United Nations coalition and for taking decisive action against Iraq. Bush's favorability ratings soared. The success of Desert Storm, one advisor noted, put Bush "in a good position to drive a new domestic agenda through Congress" (Bedard, 1991). Bush could justify a strategic change in course appropriate to the emerging public purpose era.

Bush rejected the opportunity. A *New York Times* reporter said that the president's reluctance to change his economic proposals reflected his unwillingness to listen to junior White House staff members "who wanted the President to reach out in a more dramatic way to offer the nation's poor ways to help themselves" (Dowd, 1991). Yet that "younger generation" in the White House pushed a Republican model of a public purpose agenda. Bush had ample opportunity to capitalize on the coming generational shift by surrounding himself symbolically with a "new generation" of Republicans that combined conservative fiscal policy with concerns for social problems. Yet advice to "change with the times" was rejected. Bush "stayed the course."

Bush's overall favorability hid growing discontent with his leadership. Bush's job approval rating climbed from late 1990 through Desert Storm and then began to drop rapidly:

October 1990	52 percent
January 1991	88 percent
September 1991	70 percent
October 1991	64 percent

Even greater negatives emerged when Bush's foreign policy ratings and domestic policy ratings were tracked separately. In October 1991, Bush received a 63 percent approval rating on foreign policy. In the same poll, he rated only 30 percent approval on the economy, down eight percentage points in just two months. Republicans were split in overall ratings: 46 percent favorable to 47 percent unfavorable. Seventy-eight percent of the people polled believed Bush should spend more time on the economy (*Hotline,* October 11, 1991, 18).

And yet Bush refused to put forward a plan to address growing economic problems. He also refused to enter the presidential race, believing that no Democrat had emerged that could challenge his popularity with the people. He believed, given advice from economic advisors, that the economy would turn around. He simply told the public to "wait."

Meanwhile, national events suggested that the time was ripe for Schlesinger's cyclical shift. Rising racial tensions in universities and inner cities, increasing urban decay and housing problems, mounting industrial decay and unprecedented layoffs throughout the country, escalation of violent crime, and increasing dissatisfaction with the quality of life all bubbled just below the surface, and often boiled over into riots and violence.

Behind all this discontent, the economy emerged as the detonating issue. During the Reagan-Bush years, the national debt had quadrupled. One in eight Americans lived in poverty. Unemployment affected one family in four. Household incomes had not grown since the 1970s (Goldman and Mathews, 1992, 23). Economic pain in America was a daily reality.

The public also reported disillusionment with government. A Kettering Foundation study conducted during 1990 and 1991 found that citizens believed that politicians, PACs, lobbyists, and the media responded only to their own interests (Goldman and Mathews, 1992, 22). Just at a time when Americans needed their government to address pressing economic problems, their trust in government was almost nonexistent. As Schlesinger predicted, the time for change had arrived. Americans wanted to believe in their nation again.

Finally, as his numbers continued to drop, Bush promised the "defining moment" of his presidency in his 1992 State of the Union address. He had one more opportunity to share a vision and direction to meet the "new world order" and the "time of change," but Bush's rhetoric changed little.

BUSH'S DEFINING MOMENT

He began the speech, again, with a look to recent world events: "For the past 12 months, the world has known changes of almost Biblical proportions" (Bush, 1992a, 170). He recounted the struggles of the Cold War. He talked briefly of Desert Storm and the return of hostages from the Middle East, summing it up this way: "Our policies were vindicated. . . . A world once divided into two armed camps now recognizes one sole and pre-eminent power, the United States of America" (1992a, 171). And then, Bush introduced key terms for the election campaign: "And they regard this with no dread. For the world trusts us with power, and the world is right. They trust us to be fair, and restrained. They trust us to be on the side of decency. They trust us to do what's right" (1992a, 171). Bush suggested that America's national "character" earned "trust" from the world. He would argue that the American people should do likewise with their president.

Having argued for a continued world presence and the importance of national character, Bush acknowledged the "troubles at home." He said, "Let me tell you right from the start and right from the heart: I know we're in hard times, but I know something else: This will not stand" (1992a, 172).

Bush translated his successful ultimatum to Saddam Hussein into domestic terms. This time Congress was the enemy. Bush proposed a range of actions to bring short-term and long-term economic improvement, none of them substantially new. He called for Congress to enact "bold reform proposals" on banking, civil justice, tort reform, and national energy and then drew the line in the sand for March 20. His policies, based in private interest commitments, did not change. Congress was the problem and Bush planned to stand firm. He would "do the right thing."

Beyond economic problems, Bush recognized the disillusionment of the times and a sense of division in the country indicative of the private/public shift: "If you read the papers or watch TV you know there's been a rise these days in a certain kind of ugliness: racist comments, anti-Semitism, an increased sense of division. Really, this is not us. This is not who we are and this is not acceptable" (1992a, 176). On social issues, Bush again emphasized "character" as the source of social unrest, not policies or conditions within the country. Thus, the answer to social problems would be individual, not "public," action.

An even stronger division between the people and the government emerged as Bush attempted to build a positive perspective for the people. He characterized the nation's concerns in emotional terms:

There's a mood among us. People are worried. There has been talk of decline. . . . Moods come and go, but greatness endures. Ours does. And maybe for a moment it's good to remember what, in the dailiness of our lives, we forget. We are still and ever the freest nation on earth, the kindest nation on earth, the strongest nation on earth. And we have always risen to the occasion. And we are going to lift this nation out of hard times inch by inch, and day by day, and those who would stop us had better step aside. Because I look at hard times and make this vow: This will not stand. And so we move on, together, a rising nation, the once and future miracle, that is still, this night, the hope of the world. (176)

First, Bush tells those Americans who are concerned about the state of the economy that they are in a "mood." By implication, their evaluation of the economic situation is a passing emotion, not a reasonable or thoughtful analysis. He suggests that the mood could be lifted if people would take a broader perspective, and in essence, stop thinking merely about themselves. He says, literally, that we had "forgotten ourselves." Again, the emphasis is placed on national "character"—who we are. Bush suggests that current action and evaluation of the national situation is "out of character." What must change is the perspective of the Congress and the people. From Bush's point of view, despite his own references to racial divisions and hard times, America was still, compared to the rest of the world, the freest, kindest, and strongest nation. What the people needed, literally and figuratively, was to "get some perspective." The answer to public problems was a private readjustment of attitude.

In this "defining moment" of his presidency and his campaign, Bush launched the central campaign terms. As in his two previous State of the Union messages, Bush acknowledged a time of rapid international change and continued his "global perspective" in an attempt to place national problems in an international frame. He defined the world and the nation as interconnected and interdependent. Yet, he continued to propose *individual* action as the appropriate response to change. His policies continued the private interest emphasis of the 1980s. Consonant with an emphasis on the individual, Bush introduced "character" and "trust" as central terms by which we could evaluate his presidency. Bush defined himself as a person who "did the right thing" and who should be trusted to "protect" the country from threatening external forces—whether that means Saddam Hussein or a "gridlocked Congress." In the end, Bush chose to continue his previous rhetoric relatively unchanged.

Reaction, as always, was mixed but clearly signaled the "time for change." Despite evaluations by economists and pundits, Bush's policies did not address the growing public discontent: "To a middle-class audience squeezed by recession and uncertain about the nation's long-term prospects, Bush's proposals at nearly every step may seem too modest" (*Hotline*, January 29, 1992, 3). The *St. Petersburg Times* said, "He played to Congress, he played to New Hampshire, he smiled and talked tough. He may have thought he was showing heart and spunk, but, to people out of work, their president may have sounded smug and out of touch" (*Hotline*, January 31, 1992, 17). An unemployed New Hampshire voter said only, "Propaganda." His wife added: "Nice ideas for people that have money" (12). Bush had not satisfied the public's desire for proposals that addressed their problems. It was just "more of the same."

White House insiders sensed trouble. One called the president's proposal a "'business-as-usual' package that could put Mr. Bush at high risk in a reelection year when voters are demanding something more" (*Hotline*, January 31, 1992, 11). Pete du Pont remarked that Bush still lacked "the vision thing" and "missed an opportunity to set a course consistent with the needs of most families in America" (11). The world had changed; people's lives had changed; they wanted help from their government. George Bush did not deliver.

Bush's favorability ratings continued to drop. In January 1991, Bush had a job approval rating of 79 percent. By December 1991, it had dropped over 30 points to 47 percent. After the 1992 State of the Union address, he gained only one point overall. His 24 percent approval rating on the economy a week earlier increased only to a dismal 28 percent approval. His "defining moment" gave only a little nudge to a struggling campaign. Sixty-one percent of the people polled said the president's address had no effect on their willingness to vote for him. In an analysis of all Bush's proposed plans, 79 percent of people polled reported that Bush's economic proposals would help their personal financial situations "little or not at all."

Forty-six percent reported that they had "not much of an idea" where Bush planned to lead the country (*Hotline*, January 31, 1991, 19–20). In short, just ten months before the election, the public could identify neither specific policies nor a vision that could help move the nation forward. *U.S. News* reported that the Bush campaign's own focus groups reported that the public was in more than a "mood": "voters don't believe domestic problems—the economy, crime and drugs—are under control. More troubling for Bush, voters said they did not think he had much interest in those problems and that he merely wants to be president for the sake of the office" (Baer, 1992, 38). Without significant improvement in the economy, George Bush would become the issue. Ironically, he had launched a campaign of "character."

Bush's inaction and his failure to articulate a bold, new direction for his administration opened the door for the challenger's call for change to capture the voter's imagination. With Bush vulnerable, the opposition needed to find a way to offer a positive, inclusive image that offered believable change. The American people wanted hope. How fortunate for Bill Clinton—"he still believed in a place called Hope."

CLINTON'S CALL FOR CHANGE

Recall that Schlesinger recommended a three-step process to move the cyclical shift forward: interpret events; press issues; devise remedies. The challenge for Clinton was first to capture the "time for change" in a way that called for his solutions to the "detonating issue," the economy. He needed to present plans that would tap into the public's desire for government to correct problems. Clinton needed to offer a "vision of problems and prospects" of the nation. He would have to inspire voters and, at the same time, reassure them that his "vision" was more than mere rhetoric. Given the rise of the public purpose era, Clinton needed to create ways for citizens to participate again in their national life.

To reach these goals, Clinton launched a campaign focused on change in government—including, of course, a change in president. He identified the economy as the campaign's defining issue and offered a "new covenant" of "opportunity," "responsibility," and "community" to meet the nation's needs. He added "work" to his definitional equation to focus the campaign on action and pragmatism. This strategy combined public purpose values, action, and reassurance. It drew attention away from Clinton personally and toward the role of government and the president in changing the everyday lives of the people. It met the rhetorical challenges of the "time for change."

Clinton seized the opportunity to define President Bush and his administration in ways that favored his own election. He echoed Bush's early identification of the "moment of change" but then drew attention to present economic issues. As Clinton accepted the nomination of the Democratic party, he called for "change" to overcome the problems of the present:

We meet at a special moment in history, you and I. The Cold War is over. Soviet communism has collapsed. And our values—freedom, democracy, individual rights, free enterprise—they have triumphed all around the world. And yet, just as we have won the Cold War abroad, we are losing the battles for economic opportunity and social justice here at home. Now that we have changed the world, it's time to change America. I have news for the forces of greed and the defenders of the status quo—your time has come and gone. It's time for a change in America. (Clinton, 1992, A14)

Clinton accomplished three rhetorical moves in this definition of the "moment." First, he reinforced the shift in the world political scene; he identified an exigence that called for a new direction and action. Whereas Bush attempted to extend the transition from the Cold War, Clinton argued that the era was over. Second, he contrasted American success abroad with American security at home. He placed the focus on domestic issues and current problems. With this differentiation, past successes in foreign policy offered little help with current problems. Most importantly, he explicitly identified the shift between the private interest era and the public purpose era. According to Clinton, the "forces of greed" were on their way out of political power. The "time for change" had arrived.

Part of Clinton's rhetorical challenge in defining the "time for a change" was to symbolize the generational shift his election would signal. The generational shift, in and of itself, created movement toward the future and away from what he defined as a painful and troublesome past.

Clearly, Clinton's own public image represented the shift. His relative youth, boundless energy on the campaign trail, and "blow-dry" look all identified him as a "Baby Boomer." His choice of Al Gore as running mate solidified the generational ticket. Their young families, young wives, and young campaign staffers all created visual images of a new generation coming of age in presidential politics.

It is not surprising that the Clinton campaign compared this "time for change" with the last generational shift in American politics, between Dwight Eisenhower and John F. Kennedy. The now famous meeting of a young Bill Clinton and President John F. Kennedy became almost mythic in the campaign. Always shown in slow motion video, the moment seemed to foretell Clinton's election. He also credited Kennedy explicitly as his inspiration to pursue a career in public service: "As a teenager I heard John Kennedy's summons to citizenship" (1992, A15). Clinton also echoed Kennedy's words in the introduction of his "New Covenant": "A New Covenant—a solemn agreement between the people and their government, based not simply on what each of us can take, but what all of us must give to our nation" (Clinton, 1992, A14).

Clinton reinforced the striking visual images and implicit ties to previous generational shifts with explicit references to present political currents that linked the public's desire for "change" to a change in "generation" and political party:

The Republicans have campaigned against big government for a generation. But have you noticed, they've run this big government for a generation, and they haven't changed a thing. They don't want to fix government. They still want to campaign against it and that's all. (Clinton, 1992, A14)

Time was, literally, on Clinton's side. His age clearly distinguished him from President Bush. Clinton was just "coming of age" on the national scene; Bush had been there for decades. Clinton symbolized the future. Bush symbolized the past.

Clinton's generational message alone could not produce the shift from private interest to public purpose, however. Bush could easily "pass the torch" to a new Republican generation. Voters might willingly extend the private interest era and wait four more years for Bush's Republican heir. Clinton had to convince voters that the problem was not George Bush alone but the private interest conception of government that he embraced. He did this by characterizing Bush as "an out-of-touch, failed economic manager who clings to the obsolete trickledown policies of the '80s" (Fineman and McDaniel, 1992, 25).

Throughout the campaign, Clinton challenged trickledown economics as a "failed economic theory" and President Bush, caught in its grasp, as ineffectual and unwilling to bring about significant change. In the St. Louis debate, Clinton challenged Bush head-on: "Mr. Bush, for twelve years, you've had it your way. You've had your chance and it didn't work. It's time to change" (Presidential Debate, 1992a, 60). The "private interest" conception of government was the problem, and Bush refused to change policies.

Therefore it was time for a change in leadership. Economic issues in many guises—jobs, health care, trade, and infrastructure—required immediate and innovative plans, according to Clinton, and George Bush had not only failed to address the issues during his administration, he made no proposals until late in the campaign season. Clinton argued that the Bush administration was unwilling and unable to bring about the degree and kind of change necessary to overcome America's economic problems.

But what would Clinton do? As the first step in redefining the relationship between the country's needs, the people, and the government, Clinton focused attention on the "role of the people" in bringing about change. He asserted that "this election is about putting power back in your hands and putting government back on your side. It's about putting people first" (Clinton, 1992, A14). Clinton argued that by electing him, the people would join him in a contract to bring about change, a "New Covenant."

Clinton defined the New Covenant as "a solemn agreement between the people and their government, based not simply on what each of us can take, but what all of us must give to our nation" (Clinton, 1992, A14). The covenant had three basic components: "We offer opportunity. We demand responsibility. We will build an American community again" (Clinton, 1992, A14). The New Covenant created a partnership between the president and the people. The president and government take responsibility for creating opportunities, and the people must "do their part." On health care:

Your government has the courage, finally, to take on the health care profiteers and make health care affordable for every family. But you must do your part—preventive care, prenatal care, childhood immunization, saving lives, saving money, saving families from heartbreak. (Clinton, 1992, A15)

On welfare:

We will end welfare as we know it. We will say to those on welfare: you will have, and you deserve, the opportunity through training and education, through child care and medical coverage, to liberate yourself. But then, when you can, you must work. Because welfare should be a second chance, not a way of life. That's what the New Covenant is all about. (Clinton, 1992, A15)

Government has a responsibility to the people, but the people also have a responsibility to government. Clinton's New Covenant created a relationship between government and the people that combined the activist government appropriate to a public purpose era with the commitment to individual effort and free enterprise found in private interest eras.

Given that reciprocal commitment, the president's role in the New Covenant is "co-equal" or "supportive." The president is a "partner" with the people:

I do not find anywhere . . . people wanting Washington to run their lives. I do find everywhere people wanting a partner. . . . And I am going to work as hard as I can to challenge you to assume responsibility to build a new future, and then to empower you to seize control over your own destiny. (Clinton, 1992, A14)

Clinton's covenant offered Americans control over their country and their lives at a time when they felt the nation was running out of control. The success of government and the people were conjoined. The "character of the people" was at least as important, if not more important, than the "character of the president."

To support this definition of partnership, Clinton rarely spoke in the first person singular, using instead first person plural. For example, in his acceptance address, in attacking Bush's economic record, Clinton begins to use a recurrent phrase, "Al Gore and I can do better." In the repeated cadence, the language subtly shifts to "we can do better." That "we" eventually extends from "Clinton and Gore" to include the audience and all voters (Clinton, 1992, A14).

What people make up this "we"? Primarily, in Clinton's discourse, they are "all the people who do the work, pay the taxes, raise the kids, and play by the rules . . . the hard-working Americans who make up our forgotten middle class" (Clinton, 1992). As Denton and Woodward predicted, the challenger offered himself as the voice of a "forgotten" segment of society (1990, 100–101).

As part of defining his relationship with the people, Clinton made sure that he was identified as "of the people," not *above* the people, by characterizing himself as a product of the forgotten middle class. The opposite of "out of touch" President Bush, Clinton told the people to "trust" him because he was one of them and understood their problems. His "fighting spirit" came from his widowed mother, his "passionate commitment" to racial justice from his grandfather. He developed a commitment to children and the future. He learned about "family," "hard work," "sacrifice," and "courage." Whereas Clinton shared the public's values (and not coincidentally, values that supported his domestic agenda), he was also in some ways a work in progress—adaptable, flexible, and ready for new challenges. Faced with new experiences, he would continue to learn.

To reinforce his image as "one of the people" and as a nontraditional candidate, immediately after the Democratic convention Clinton jumped on a bus with Gore and traveled to America's heartland. Clinton played his saxophone on Arsenio Hall's late-night television show and talked directly to the MTV generation on their own turf. Research showed that shortly after the Democratic convention Clinton's character as "an average guy" who might be good for the people and for the economy scored three times higher than characterizations of him as a "tax-and-spend liberal" ("The War Room Drill," 1992, 78).

The sense of shared identity with the middle class was further reinforced by the final piece in the New Covenant, a transcendent identification of Americans as a single community:

Tonight, every one of you knows, deep in your heart, that we are too divided. And yet, for too long, politicians have told the most of us that are doing alright, that what's really wrong with America is the rest of us. Them. Them the minorities. Them the liberals. Them the poor. Them the homeless. Them the people with disabilities. Them the gays. We've gotten to where we've nearly "them'd" ourselves to death. Them and them and them. But this is America. There is no them; there is only us. (Clinton, 1992, A15)

This final component of the covenant acknowledges the divisions generated by a private interest era and attempts to overcome the traditional "special interests" by subsuming them under a shared identity. Clinton simultaneously acknowledged the groups while joining them with others. Clinton summarized the central identifications in this way:

In the end, my fellow Americans, this New Covenant simply asks us all to be Americans again. Old-fashioned Americans for a new time. Opportunity, responsibility, community. When we pull together, America will pull ahead. (Clinton, 1992, A14)

Clinton's New Covenant terminology was strategic in several ways. Clinton's basic definitions asked voters to see the political situation as "a time for change," presented the presidency as a partnership with the people, and characterized Clinton as a product of the middle class, shaped by modern American experiences, and ready to adopt innovative plans to lead a new generation of Americans. He offered unity and vision to a country struggling with division. His call for change justified his own candidacy.

The idea of an interdependence between government and the people implied public involvement and participation and mutual accountability at a time when the public's frustration and distrust of government was at an all-time high. Ross Perot frequently reminded voters that no one in Washington seemed to want to take responsibility for anything that happened inside the Beltway. Clinton's New Covenant answered the accountability question with "responsibility." Moreover, Clinton could lead the country to a reciprocal relationship of opportunity and responsibility because, as a product of the middle class, he understood their problems. Moreover, the interdependence created a sense of *public* responsibility. Instead of each person looking out for his or her own interests, everyone would rise or fall together. The nation's interests would supersede personal gain. America would be a unified nation again and one where people earned government help.

It also offered a view of an inclusive American citizenship that could overcome the growing divisions in the country. "Community" answered the growing dissatisfaction with the private interest philosophy. Inclusive terminology allowed conservative and moderate Democrats, moderate Republicans, and traditional liberals all to join with the Democratic party. Everyone was included. The New Covenant cast a wide rhetorical net. In

June, Stan Greenberg, pollster and Clinton campaign analyst, advised the campaign "to concentrate on the lower half of the electorate, economically speaking—particularly working women." He said, "We can win this election by reaching Democrats broadly understood. The campaign does not need to go right to reach its targets. It needs to go broad to reach a center-left alignment" ("Manhattan Project," 1992, 55). Responsibility, opportunity, and community created the inclusive definition needed.

As a defensive strategy, the New Covenant discourse formed a preemptive strike against those opponents of the Democratic party who attempted to label Democrats as the party of "liberal special interests" and "tax-and-spend." Ross Perot helped the Democrats in this regard by labeling *all* of government as controlled by wealthy special interests. Perot's "gucci gulch" struck a chord with voters. Neither Bush nor the Republican party could cast any "special interest" label far without drawing attention to their own negative image as "Washington insiders."

Clinton's New Covenant combined opportunity, responsibility, and community into a clear "vision" essential to inspiring a skeptical and cynical public. Clinton's terminology focused the public's attention toward the future and encouraged the people to take control of their lives. Americans became the "masters of their destinies" again. The president's role in this discourse was as a leader of the people—neither above them nor below them. According to Clinton, the president should represent and share the public's values and their dreams. The president should be a "visionary."

But vision alone would not satisfy a skeptical and disillusioned public. Especially with Perot beating his "just do it" drum, Clinton had to convince the public that his campaign was more than just talk. The character issue that truly haunted Bill Clinton was that he was a "slick politician." Citizens wanted to be inspired and uplifted, to have hope and a vision, but they knew only too well that campaign promises of a glorious future do not often become realities. Clinton needed an element of pragmatism in his discourse to answer the "trust" question and he found it in the term "work."

Prior to the Democratic Convention, focus group analysis identified "work" as a positive concept for the American people. Campaign strategist James Carville recommended that the campaign "mention work every 15 seconds." Mandy Grunwald responded with what became a central campaign theme:

By the end of the convention what do we want people to know about Clinton: that he worked his way up; that his life's work had been in education and investing in people; that he values work; that he had moved people from welfare to work; that he has a national economic strategy to put America back to work. The word "work" works for us. There are no quick fixes, no hoaxes, no easy answer. We have to work our way out of this mess. ("Manhattan Project," 1992, 41)

In this short statement, Grunwald identified a range of rhetorical resources within the term "work." It offers action on Clinton's part and casts his life as "work toward goals." The term offers a contrast with the inactivity attached to the Bush administration and builds a public persona for Clinton based in goal-directed action. In times of change, voters look for leaders who take action to solve problems. "Work" offered that emphasis.

Clinton reinforced his "problem-solver" persona by framing his answers to questions in a problem-solution format. Clinton would describe the problem, indicate his understanding and experience with the problem, and then pose a rhetorical question that prompted his proposed solution. He then would usually offer a three-point plan. An example from the Richmond debate was Clinton's discussion of export issues:

I've actually been a governor for 12 years, so I've known a lot of people who have lost their jobs because of jobs moving overseas. And I know a lot of people whose plants have been strengthened by increasing exports. The trick is to expand our export base and to expand trade on terms that are fair to us. It is true that our exports to Mexico, for example, have gone up and our trade deficit has gone down. It's also true that just today a record high trade deficit was announced with Japan. So what is the answer? Let me just mention three things quickly. (Presidential Debate, 1992b, 38)

Clinton then described measures to address the problem.

With this argument structure, Clinton used his answer to reinforce his character as "problem solver" and as "someone who understands the public's problems." He also drew attention to concrete plans designed to make his vision a reality. Although Clinton always talked about the problem, his answer promoted action and often ended with a vision of a positive future: "So, more trade, but on fair terms [that favor] investment in America" (Presidential Debate, Richmond, 1992b, 38); "Those things would revolutionize American education and take us to the top economically" (Presidential Debate, 1992b, 52); "I know it can work. I've seen it happen" (Presidential Debate, 1992b, 41). Clinton used a positive rhetoric that offered action and pragmatic solutions, tested by experience.

"Work" also continued to focus attention on the problem Clinton identified as central to the nation's need for change—the economy. "Work" personalized economic concerns for voters. Talk of budget deficits, trade deficits, and enterprise zones does not adapt to the individual's concerns. The concepts are too abstract. Voters in economic distress wanted the bottom line: "Will I be able to work to support my family?" or "If I work 40 hours a week, will I be able to support my family?" Young voters want to know if they will have an opportunity to work. Clinton demonstrated his understanding of their concerns through this discussion of "work":

I was raised to believe that the American dream was built on rewarding hard work. . . . For too long, those who play by the rules and keep the faith have gotten the shaft. And those who cut corners and cut deals have been rewarded. . . . People are working harder than ever . . . and their incomes are still going down, their taxes are still going up, and the costs of health care, housing and education are going through the roof. Meanwhile, more and more of our best people are falling into poverty, even when they work 40 hours a week. (Clinton, 1992, A14)

According to Clinton, under the Bush administration, the people *were* "doing their part." The problem was that government had failed in its responsibility to "work for them." Whereas Bush believed the *people* had acted "out of character," Clinton argued that *government* was the party without character.

"Work" also reinforced the idealism of the American Dream expressed in the New Covenant. Clinton's terminology offered voters active participation: "In Arkansas we are working together and we're making progress. No, there is no Arkansas miracle. But there are a lot of miraculous people" (Clinton, 1992, A15). Again, people can accomplish needed change, if government helps them. Work makes change possible.

"Work" also tempers expectations. "Slick Willie" had to be careful not to promise too much too fast, as if his election would make everything easy. Instead, he said, "Now, I don't have all the answers. But I do know that old ways don't work" (Clinton, 1992, A14). Hard work sounds realistic. No serious voter would believe that any plan would sail through Congress and make everything right with the nation. To suggest otherwise would have doomed Clinton's campaign.

Clinton's New Covenant terms formed a unified definition of the nation's political situation that incorporated an inspiring, hopeful vision of the future with reassurance that people could make a difference in their own lives with practical, hard work. Government and the people would work in a partnership to return the nation to prosperity. In speaking about the New Covenant, Clinton summarized his commitments this way:

It will work because it is rooted in the vision and the values of the American people. Of all the things George Bush has ever said that I disagree with, perhaps

the thing that bothers me most, is how he derides and degrades the American tradition of seeing, and seeking a better future. He mocks it as "the vision thing."
But just remember what the scripture says: "Where there is no vision, the people
perish." (Clinton, 1992, A14)

Clinton offered an optimistic vision and a reassurance that the people
could take back their government and their own destinies. Clinton gave
people hope that things could really change.

Faced with a strengthening Clinton campaign, the Bush campaign
struggled to find a winning message. A strikingly new domestic agenda
would have raised questions about Bush's commitment to the people: why
only now in the election season, rather than a year or two earlier, if not
purely as a political strategy? The Bush campaign's main strategy was to
raise doubts about Clinton with a campaign based on "character," "trust,"
and "experience." What they failed to anticipate was the boomerang carried in those terms during a public purpose era. This time, "character" had
a new twist.

BUSH'S CAMPAIGN ON CHARACTER

Bush faced a difficult position as the general campaign neared. After
having denied that there was a recession for well over a year, Bush continued to refuse to address domestic issues, despite advice from administration officials and campaign strategists to take positive action. After
months of telling the public to "wait," Bush's 1992 State of the Union
address (his "defining moment") failed to generate the momentum needed
for reelection. The public wasn't buying. He offered the public an
"Agenda for American Renewal" in September but then failed to center
attention on its components. David Gergen reported that he was "stunned"
that President Bush allowed Clinton's "failed economic theory" charges to
stand without answer (Gergen and Shields, 1992). Instead, Bush adopted a
defensive strategy that attempted to divert attention from the nation's economic ills.

Between the State of the Union address and the acceptance of his
nomination, Bush's discourse changed only slightly. He continued to
argue, although now more aggressively, that the nation's economic woes
were the result of external forces; he defined his own role as "protector"
of the people; and promoted "experience," "character," and "trust" as the
central factors in the presidential race. The emphasis was not so much on
the positive direction Bush would create in a second term, but rather on a
guaranteed negative direction with Clinton and Congress.

To define the nation's condition in a way that limited George Bush's
responsibility for "hard times," as he called them, required two strategies.

First, Bush defined the United States as one nation among many in a "new world order" and as a victim of global slowdown. Second, he blamed his lack of domestic policy to address the slowdown in a gridlocked Congress.

Bush continued his emphasis on a changed world. In his nomination acceptance speech, Bush reminded Americans of the fall of the Berlin Wall, the freeing of hostages in Lebanon, peace talks in the Middle East, the free elections in Nicaragua, the fall of communism, the breakup of the Soviet Union, and the United Nations effort to free Kuwait. In the end he noted that "this convention is the first at which an American president can say, the Cold War is over, and freedom finished first" (Bush, 1992b, 1463). But despite the nation's triumph over communism, Bush cautioned Americans that "there will be more foreign policy challenges like Kuwait in the next four years, terrorists and aggressors to stand up to, dangerous weapons to be controlled and destroyed. And freedom's fight is not finished" (Bush, 1992b, 1464). Bush predicted an uncertain, threatening future.

Bush's "global" definition played to his strengths. If the world indeed was an uncertain and unpredictable place, reasoned Bush, the United States needed a leader of "experience" and "character" to respond to unforeseen circumstances. Bush argued that his military experience at a young age in World War II, his part in the fall of communism, his later success as commander in chief during Desert Storm, and his personal character all made him the best presidential candidate for these critical times. He made this argument most succinctly and explicitly at the end of one presidential debate:

If in the next five minutes, a television announcer came on and said, there is a major international crisis. There is a major threat to the world. Or in this country, a major threat. My question is, who—if you were appointed to name one of the three of us, who would you choose? Who has the perseverance, the character, the integrity, the maturity, to get the job done? I hope I'm that person. (Presidential Debate, 1992c)

Bush argued that he was the best man for the job.

On foreign affairs, a global perspective further helped Bush's cause. He could emphasize his own successes and point to his opponent's lack of foreign policy and military experience. Moreover, he attacked Clinton as a "waffler," unable to make up his mind in crisis, and any mention of military action raised Clinton's suspect draft standing from the 1960s.

Who will lead the world in the face of these challenges? Not my opponent. In his acceptance speech he devoted just 65 seconds to telling us about the world. And then he said that America was, and I quote again, I want to be fair and factual, I quote, being "ridiculed" everywhere. Well, tell that to the people around the world for whom America is still a dream. Tell that to leaders around the world, from whom America commands respect. Tell that to the men and women of Desert Storm. (Bush, 1992b, 1464)

Whereas Bush's strategy did open a line of attack on Clinton, it also emphasized one of the public's greatest concerns: that President Bush's global perspective prevented him from recognizing and attending to pressing problems at home. Perspective, literally, is a point of view based on where you stand and what you see. Bush's global perspective reassured Americans when the impending threat was one of force, but provided little hope on the domestic scene.

As with foreign policy, Bush defined the nation's economic conditions as the result of uncontrollable forces external to the United States—the emergence of the new world order and the resulting economic upheaval and slowdown globally. Continuing the attempt to reorient the public in his State of the Union address, Bush evaluated America's problems by comparing them to other nations. In effect, Bush argued that conditions in the United States were not so bad when compared to conditions globally:

I mean, we've got big economic problems, but we are not coming apart at the seams. We're ready for a recovery—with interest rates down and inflation down, the cruelest tax of all, caught in a global slowdown right now, but that will change if you go with the programs I've talked about. (Presidential Debate, 1992a, 61)

I don't think we're a declining nation. The whole world has had economic problems. We're doing better than a lot of the countries in the world, and we're going to lead the way out of this economic recession across this world and economic slowdown here at home. (Presidential Debate, 1992c, 27)

While a global perspective helped to explain the expansion at the end of the 1980s in a way that lifted responsibility from the Bush administration, this justification was a first step in what became Bush's overall defensive and reactive rhetorical stance. In Bush's definitions, the United States was a victim of external forces and appeared dependent on the decisions of other nations worldwide. Although that interconnectedness is a fact of modern political and economic life, rhetorically it placed the United States in a waiting game, anticipating and reacting to uncontrollable and often unpredictable world events. For too long Bush told the American people simply to "wait" and then when people were willing to wait no longer, he offered no significantly innovative policies to address what was perceived as a worsening situation. Bush had no economic equivalent to the Berlin Wall or the dissolution of the Soviet Union to persuade voters that in time his policies would be vindicated. His attempt to transcend national boundaries made him appear either unwilling or unable to take positive action toward change. What Americans wished to hear was that *they* could shape the world, not that the world would shape them. Bush had to explain why, even in reaction to external forces, he had been unable to address the nation's growing economic problems. He had to give people a reason to believe he could do better in a second term. His answer was to say that "things would be worse" under Clinton and again to explain his lack of movement on a force outside his own administration: Congress.

First, Bush tried to defend his record to some degree. Late in the campaign he pointed to specific positive conditions experienced by individuals due to his policy.

Are you better off? Well, is a home buyer better off [when] he can refinance the home because interest rates are down? Is a senior citizen better off because inflation is not wiping out their family savings? I think they are. Is the guy out of work better off? Of course he's not. But he's not going to be better off if we grow the government. (Presidential Debate, 1992c, 8)

For those *not* helped by his policies, Bush offered no positive response, only a promise that things would get worse under a Clinton administration: "Yes, we're having tough times, but we do not need to go back to the failed policies of the past when you had a Democratic president and a spendthrift Democratic Congress" (Presidential Debate, 1992c, 26).

Bush's description of the world situation offered little reassurance to a public faced with increasing signs of economic decline. The promised recovery was slow to materialize and more difficult to feel. The American people felt confident in their evaluation of their economic plight. Bush's admonition that "things could be worse" may have been true, but Americans were looking for ways to make things better.

Bush's own proposals were neither new nor positive. He continued to call for a balanced budget amendment, line-item veto, and cut in capital gains taxes. He offered to freeze paperwork and unnecessary regulation; to end "crazy" lawsuits; to close legal loopholes; to limit Congressional terms. On health care, Bush promised to hold the line on Social Security and put a cap on the growth of mandatory spending programs. When asked about the potential legalization of drugs, Bush responded: "I oppose it and I'm going to stand up and continue to oppose it" (Presidential Debate, 1992b, 34). An analysis of Bush's verbs shows his rhetorical style: he vetoes, cuts, freezes, ends, closes, limits, holds the line, opposes. Given his position as the incumbent and given his political philosophy, Bush's continued call for reduced government could have been expected. Yet, in a public purpose era, government action is preferred. Bush's words place him in a defensive and reactive position. Rather than moving the country forward when voters called for change, Bush's discourse prevented action at best and at worst "stayed the course" when Americans believed the ship of state was headed toward a rocky demise.

But even for voters who agreed with Bush's proposals, another question loomed large. Bush himself asked, "why are these proposals not in effect today?" Consistent with his definition of the United States as victim of "global slowdown," Bush claimed he was the victim of an internal force as well: "the gridlocked Democratic Congress." He asserted that "our policies haven't failed, they haven't even been tried" (Bush, 1992b, 1467). Bush recounted struggles against Congress: "For three quarters I have been fighting to get the Congress to pass some incentives for small business—capital gains, investment tax allowance, credit for first-time home buyers. And it's blocked by Congress" (Presidential Debate, 1992c, 8).

His response to congressional action was to counter it with a veto to protect the citizens, just when citizens did not want a "protector": "I'm going to protect the working man by continuing to veto and to threaten veto until we get this new Congress, and then we're going to move forward on our plan. I've got to protect them" (Presidential Debate, 1992a, 69). Of course, voters only had Bush's reassurance that things would be different with a new Congress: "With this new Congress coming in, gridlock will be gone, and I'll sit down with them and say, 'Let's get this done,' but I do not want to go the tax-and-spend route" (Presidential Debate, 1992a, 66). Bush does offer change—a changed relationship with a changed Congress.

Bush extended the argument further to explore the alternative. What would happen with Bill Clinton in the White House? First, he attempted to align the decision voters would have to make as a choice between George Bush and the combination of Clinton and a Democratic Congress. He did so explicitly in his nomination acceptance speech: "Governor Clinton and Congress want to put through the largest tax increase in history, but I won't let that happen. And Governor Clinton and Congress don't want kids to have the option of praying in school, but I do" (Bush, 1992b, 1468).

He then described the consequence of such an alliance as a step backward rather than forward: "Look, we tried this once before, combining the Democratic governor of a small southern state with a very liberal vice president and a Democratic Congress. America doesn't need Carter II. We don't want to take America back to those days of malaise" (Bush, 1992b, 1468). Throughout the campaign, Bush argued that with Clinton in the White House we would have something worse than a gridlocked Congress—a runaway Congress led by a tax-and-spend president.

His reliance on the election of a new Congress as the "change" needed in America was a weak strategy. First, in some districts, a change in congressional representation was unlikely. Many voters could not directly influence a change in Congress. If they desired change, they would have to accomplish it through their presidential selection.

Second, even if voters could influence a change in Congress, they still might believe that Congress as a whole was unlikely to change drastically. In a year of heightened political participation, voters wanted to make their votes count. For some, a vote for Bush was a vote for continued gridlock and a vote for Clinton was a vote for potential forward movement. Ultimately, the question came down to which would be the greater risk: continuing a Bush administration or risking the unknown with Clinton.

Voters had a third concern. Perhaps voters believed they *could* change Congress. What assurance did they have that Bush, who characterized himself as a "protector" and "steward," could lead a redirected and open Congress? Bush clearly made the case that he could and would fight *against* external forces and unpopular government action but never offered a new, positive plan for the future. He only offered this reassurance:

One hundred and fifty new members, from both parties, will be coming to Washington this fall. And every one will have a fresh view of America's future. And I will pledge today to the American people, immediately after this election I will meet with every one of these new members, before they get attacked by the PACs, overwhelmed by the staffs, and cornered by a camera crew, and I will lay out my case for change. (Bush, 1992b, 1468)

Bush's answer was for voters to give him a new Congress, and then trust him to make things right again.

The "tax-and-spend" challenge against Clinton and Congress was only one strategy used to undermine Clinton's candidacy. Attempts to raise doubts about Clinton went beyond his public character into his private character. Early reports of extramarital affairs looked like the opportunity Clinton opponents had been hoping for. Yet when the public was polled, Clinton's private life was of little interest. When Gennifer Flowers told the public that she and Bill Clinton had had an affair, seventy-eight percent of people polled reported that the question of whether Clinton had an affair should not be an issue. Seventy-three percent reported that the allegations would have no effect on whether they would vote for Clinton (*Hotline,* January 31, 1992, 19). Clinton's focus groups reported the same influence, especially among men. When asked if Clinton's morals hurt his candidacy, men in the focus groups "confessed to troubles of their own and refused to cast the first stone" ("Manhattan Project," 1992, 41).

Clinton's draft record opened another round of questioning. As bits and pieces of his record emerged, Bush began to question Clinton's "ability to tell the whole story" and to admit mistakes. Bush chastised Clinton for organizing and participating in anti-war protests in Great Britain in the 1960s when he was a student at Oxford. He even went so far as to challenge Clinton's "judgment" concerning a trip to Moscow made at about that same time. Public opinion polls and opinion leader endorsements again minimized the effect of Bush's attacks. Later, Bush again attempted to push the characterization of Clinton as a "waffler," unable to take a position and hold it. The charges were most focused in the Michigan debate:

There's a pattern here of appealing to the auto workers and then trying to appeal to the spotted owl crowd or the extremes in the environmental movement. You can't do it as president. You can't have a pattern of one side of the issue one day and another the next. (Presidential Debate, 1992c, 8)

In the final days of the campaign, Bush called Clinton a bozo, compared his foreign policy experience to that of Bush's dog, Millie, and labeled vice-presidential candidate Al Gore "ozone man" (*MacNeil/Lehrer Newshour,* 1992b).

What Bush failed to anticipate was the public's definition of "character." Having moved out of a private interest era, the people really were not concerned with a candidate's private behavior but with public performance. The "character" that the voters deemed relevant was "political character." And on "political character," Bush was potentially more vulnerable than Clinton. One commentator reported that every time Bush emphasized "trust," Clinton's unfavorable numbers went up. The problem was that Bush's unfavorable ratings climbed, too ("A Silver Bullet," 1992, 84).

Clinton attempted to heighten the negative effect of "character" and "trust" issues on Bush by pointing to shifts in Bush's own statements from the "no new taxes" pledge to campaign talk of "voodoo economics" in 1980. Late in the campaign, the media reported new findings about Bush's involvement in the Iran-Contra scandal. In the presidential debates, Ross

Perot highlighted Bush's rhetorical problem, talking about the many interpretations of "character":

I think it's very important to measure when and where things occurred. Did they occur when you were a young person, in your formative years? Or did they occur while you were a senior official in the federal government? When you're a senior official in the federal government spending billions of dollars of taxpayers' money and you're a mature individual and you make a mistake, then that was on our ticket. If you make it as a young man, time passes. So I would say just, you know, look at all three of us. (Presidential Debate, 1992a, 61)

The bottom line was that the American people simply did not want to trust *anyone*. As they stated clearly to the media and in the Richmond debate, they wanted to know what each candidate would *do*. Clinton offered clear plans; Bush did not. The people said they wanted to be involved in their government. Clinton's discourse offered that possibility; Bush's did not. The public called for a vision for the future. Clinton inspired them; Bush did not.

The "character" issue offered one more twist to the presidential campaign. Clinton wanted to define Bush as "out of touch" with the people. Unfortunately for Bush, his rhetoric subtly and pervasively demonstrated Clinton's characterization. Bush's "global" definitions and his "protector" role distanced him from the people. In defining the nation's problems from the perspective of other nations and other leaders that only he could report, he delegitimized the concerns of American citizens. He suggested that they should be thankful that they were not somewhere else where the situation was far worse. Such a perspective might make people feel *relatively* lucky, yet still not safe or happy. Telling Americans that they were not suffering as badly as others around the world would not eliminate their pain.

Worse yet, not only did Bush argue that things weren't quite as bad as they could be, he suggested that the American people were being duped into believing that economic conditions were worse than they actually were by the Clinton campaign:

[Clinton] thinks, I think he said, that the country is coming apart at the seams. Now, I know that the only way he can win is to make everybody believe the economy's worse than it is. . . . We can do much, much better, but we ought not try to convince the American people that America is a country that's coming apart at the seams. I would hate to be running for president and think that the only way I could win would be to convince everybody how horrible things are. (Presidential Debate, 1992a, 61)

Bush first denied the public's concerns, next he acknowledged but minimized them, and then he attempted to discount them. Finally, opinion polls forced Bush to address the severity of the nation's problems. Even then, his movement from "it could be worse," to "yes it's bad, but . . ." failed to fully acknowledge public concerns. He seemed to believe that if he said, "things aren't that bad," the public would reject their own experience and adopt his perspective. In the St. Louis debate, Bush was asked what he would say to a defense worker who had lost her job due to defense cutbacks:

So her best hope for short term is job retraining if she was thrown out of work at a defense plant, but tell her it's not all that gloomy. We're the United States. We've got—we've faced tough problems before. . . . I am much more optimistic about this country than some. (Presidential Debate, 1992a, 67)

To a woman recently out of work and with no prospect for employment, Bush's comment, "tell her it's not all that gloomy," does sound out of touch. In many ways, Bush's discourse seemed to say "snap out of it" to a nation convinced that their problems were not imagined but real.

Throughout his discourse, Bush attempted to explain how his point of view allowed him to adopt a different and more accurate perspective on world and national affairs than those of his opponents. The problem with the strategy was that Clinton's and Perot's descriptions of the nation's economic conditions resonated with the public's experience and observation. So, in contrasting his view with his opponents, he also distanced himself from the electorate: "And now, I know that Americans are uneasy today. There is anxious talk around our kitchen tables. But from where I stand, I see not America's sunset, but a sunrise" (Bush, 1992b, 1468). In contrast to Clinton's inclusive "we," Bush uses "I" and speaks about "where he stands." For a candidate perceived as "out of touch," such a subtle rhetorical move only reinforces negative perceptions. In describing problems faced by citizens, Bush said:

Nothing hurts me more than to meet with soldiers home from the Persian Gulf who can't find a job, or workers who have a job, but worry that the next day will bring a pink slip. And what about parents who scrape and struggle to send their kids to college, only to find them back living at home, because they can't get work. (1992b, 1465)

The voters were not interested in knowing that President Bush felt his own pain. They wanted him to feel *their* pain.

Bush's lack of strategic pronouns could easily have been outweighed by clear, personal statements of his experience with public pain. However, in contrast with the other candidates, Bush rarely spoke in terms that reassured voters that he personally understood and had touched their problems. When asked during the debates about family values, Clinton spoke of growing up with a widowed mother, and about the people of Arkansas. Perot spoke of his grandchildren. Bush, although his family is extensive and his children and grandchildren were pictured prominently at the Republican National Convention, only offered surrogates on such issues:

When Barbara holds an AIDS baby, she's showing a certain compassion for family. When she reads to children, the same thing. I believe that discipline and respect for the law, all of these things should be taught to children. Not in our schools, but families have to do that. (Presidential Debate, 1992a, 74)

Bush did not talk about his role in educating his children, or about holding an AIDS baby. He again was at a distance. Even in his policy-maker role, Bush offered a surrogate for domestic planning, James Baker: "What I'm going to do is say to Jim Baker when this campaign is over, 'All right, let's sit down now. You do in domestic affairs what you've done in foreign affairs'" (Presidential Debate, 1992a, 69). Clinton countered this statement in the third debate to highlight Bush's distance from even his own administration:

Well, I'll tell you I'll make some news in the third debate. The person responsible for domestic economic policy in my administration will be Bill Clinton. I'm going to make those decisions, and I won't raise taxes on the middle class to pay for my programs. (Presidential Debate, 1992c, 26)

Bush lashed back under his breath with "that's what we're all afraid of." But Clinton's point was made. In each case, Bush failed to create a sense of personal involvement, responsibility, or accountability. It was an ironic strategy for someone who emphasized "character" as the central issue of the campaign.

Of course, the most noted example of Bush's rhetorical distance, and the most revealing in terms of strategy, was the exchange in the Richmond debate when an audience member asked the candidates how the national debt had affected each of them personally. After Perot had answered the question with a statement of his personal motivation, President Bush said, "I'm not sure I get it." Although on the face of it, Bush was referring to the woman's specific question, he uttered before millions of Americans the exact negative words that his opponents had used to define his administration. Bush eventually answered again with an explanation from his perspective as president:

Well, listen. You ought to be in the White House for a day and hear what I hear and see what I see and read the mail I read and touch the people that I touch from time to time. . . . I mean, you've got to care. Everybody cares if people aren't doing well, but I don't think it—I don't think it's fair to say you haven't had cancer, therefore, you don't know what it's like. I don't think it's fair to say, you know, whatever it is, if you haven't been hit by it personally, but everybody is affected by the debt because of the tremendous interest that goes into paying on that debt. Everything is more expensive. Everything comes out of your pocket and my pocket. . . . But I think in terms of the recession, of course, you feel it when you're president of the United States, and that's why I'm trying to do something about it by stimulating the export, investing more, better education systems. (Presidential Debate, 1992b, 46–47)

Bush's answer highlighted the differences between the questioner's perspective and his own. He explicitly said, "you ought to be me for a day," when the woman had asked him to do the same for her. He used "I" four times in the first sentence alone. He says "it is not fair" to expect *him* to feel the pain of a struggling wage earner and yet he expects a common citizen to imagine being president. He even refers to himself in his role as "president of the United States." He argues that her question was "unfair" when, rhetorically, fairness was not at issue. The issue was compassion, empathy, and identification. Unfortunately for Bush, instead of focusing on the woman and her concerns, he turned attention to himself. Bush got defensive when it was the worst possible response.

Of course, Bush's response would not have been so bad had it not been followed by a masterful piece of rhetoric from Clinton. He specifically acknowledged the questioner's position and his understanding of it:

Clinton: Tell me how it's affected you again. You know people who lost their jobs and have lost their homes?

Questioner: Well, yeah, uh-huh.

Clinton: Well, I've been governor of a small state for 12 years. I'll tell you how it's affected me. Every year, Congress and the president sign laws that make us do more things and gives us less money to do it with. I see people in my state. Middle-class people, their taxes have gone up in Washington, and their services have gone down, while the wealthy have gotten tax cuts. I have seen what's happened in this last four years when, in my state, people lose their jobs, there's a good chance I'll know them by their names. When a factory closes, I know the people who ran it. When the businesses go bankrupt, I know them. (Presidential Debate, 1992b, 47)

Clinton first speaks in the woman's terms. He acknowledges her position, then he identifies his position and joins them rhetorically by saying "you know people who have been hurt. I do, too." He emphasizes the similarities in what, on the face, are very different experiences. He does not mention *personal* hurt or suffering or even his own feelings. In fact, his answer says little about Bill Clinton, and more about the economic plight of voters. Then, with similarity established, Clinton shifts to *his* agenda:

What I want you to understand is the national debt is not the only cause of that. It is because America has not invested in its people. . . . It is because we are in the grip of a failed economic theory and this decision you're about to make better be about what kind of economic theory you want. Not just people saying, "I'm going to fix it," but what are we going to do. What I think we have to do is invest in American jobs, American education, control American health care costs and bring the American people together again. (Presidential Debate, 1992b, 47)

Having acknowledged her perspective and the difficult economic situation, Clinton then goes on to *add* to that perspective. He takes the woman's position and uses her ideas to reinforce his own. As a result, through her question he refocused the choice before the American people as a choice of economic theories first—and candidates second.

Through all these strategies, Bush attempted to explain his own behavior and cast enough doubt on Clinton's to preserve his presidency for a second term. His blaming of economic problems on forces external to his administration—global slowdown and Congress—might have sufficiently explained the country's seeming lack of positive movement in a way that minimized blame on the administration. Those very same strategies raised concern that Bush was unable to change the situation. His "experience" was also divided. On foreign policy, American voters clearly preferred Bush over the other two candidates. But, on the domestic side, Bush's own term "experience" undermined his position. As Ross Perot noted, "I don't have any experience in running up a $4 trillion debt. I don't have any experience in gridlock government where nobody takes responsibility for anything and everybody blames everybody else" (Presidential Debate, 1992a, 61). Neither "experience" nor "character" nor "trust" offered Bush sufficient leverage against Clinton. In the end, all of Bush's key definitional strategies were double-edged swords.

Bush also participated in Clinton's strategy to cast him as "out of touch." At a theoretical level, when presidents contrast their perspective with that of the voters they create *division* from the public, not identification. Bush indicated that the American people who worried about the economy were somehow wrong or narrow in their perspective. Bush's analysis of the political situation discounted voters' concerns and led them to despair of economic recovery and their own participation toward such recovery under Bush. Unlike the shared vision offered by Clinton, Bush's discourse, to some degree, asked voters to turn over their evaluations and decision-making power to someone "above them."

An intellectual analysis might reveal Bush's perspective to be more accurate. And his use of the transcendent perspective of the presidency might be a successful strategy when people wish to relinquish political decision to elected officials. But a public purpose era generates the opposite interest and commitment from voters.

CONCLUSIONS

What was "at issue" in the 1992 presidential election stretched far beyond economic initiatives, health-care reform, trade agreements, crime legislation, or other policy proposals. The issue was the relationship between the American people, their government, and their president. Although many factors influenced the outcome of this election, the political visions articulated in the candidate's discourse played a significant role. The 1992 election presented a particularly unique rhetorical context because the overarching shift in political commitments invalidated the one central rule of incumbency: do not call for change. Despite George Bush's overwhelming popularity throughout his administration and the apparent weakness of Democratic contenders, Bush's status quo rhetoric failed to meet the rhetorical demands of the election. Clinton became the "agent of change" in what was perceived as a "time for change." And his definition of the situation resonated with the public's change in political commitments.

Analysis of the central terms "covenant" and "trust" indicates the differing conceptions of government, the governors, and the governed presented in the campaign rhetoric of Clinton and Bush. "Covenant" is derived from the Latin word that means to come together, be of one mind, agree. The term draws on conceptions of government that are well documented in American history. Its legal origin contributed to the Mayflower Compact, and its religious meanings defined the Puritans' New Covenant with God in North America. A covenant by definition is "a binding and solemn agreement by two or more persons, parties, etc., to do or keep from doing some specified thing." Legally, a covenant is "writing, under seal, containing the terms of agreement or contract between two parties." The term "covenant" creates a relationship between legal parties based on commitment to specific future action.

Now, consider the term "trust." One meaning of trust is "confidence, a reliance or resting of the mind on the integrity, veracity, justice, friendship, or other sound principle of another person or thing." A second meaning is "something received in confidence; that which is confided to one's faith." Yet another meaning is "confident expectation of any event; anticipation, hope." To trust means "to commit to one's care; to allow to do something without fear of consequences; to allow to be exposed." Each of these definitions creates a relationship between the person trusting and the person being trusted. The person who trusts another predicts the future based on evaluation of the other's past acts. The person who trusts gives up control of something and places it into the other's care. Thus, the legal conception of a trust is "the confidence reposed in a person by giving him nominal ownership of property, which he is to keep, use or administer to another's benefit."

Consider the relationship between the governed and the governor when the two terms are used in a political context. A covenant by definition unites parties in a mutual agreement about action. A trust actually delegates action to another, without consultation or approval. A covenant entails participation, partnership, and control by both parties. A covenant demands mutual responsibility. A trust involves a giving up of responsibility. A covenant guides behavior despite individual differences or character. Parties are judged according to their "works." Trust is dependent on character and faith. So, given Schlesinger's discussion, a covenant fits a public purpose era. Trust fits private interest. To use one or the other in its opposite context produces a rhetoric that fails to "fit the times."

In an era of unprecedented cynicism, emphasis on any individual was ill advised. Americans did not want to "trust" *anyone*. However, voters might be willing to trust some *thing*, namely, a detailed plan of action. A vote for character gives away participation and control. You simply cast your support behind a belief that someone will act "in character" with little knowledge of what action that may entail. Indeed, Bush ran on his promise to "do the right thing," as if the "right thing" would not be contested. If a vote is for a plan or criteria for action, however, the "character" of the individual assigned to carry out that plan becomes *less* significant, although not *in*significant. Factors of competence, energy, persuasiveness—pragmatic skills—become central. With a plan in place, voters need not consider the candidate's morality per se. The candidate's charge is to implement the mandated policy direction. Private character is of little relevance, but public political character is critical.

The campaign terminologies define the appropriate role of the president accordingly—one that fits the public purpose era and one that does not. Bush's "protector" definition was appropriate when people felt embattled by government. Yet, when people turn to government again to solve neglected social and economic problems, the "protector" role is the antithesis of what voters desire. Clinton's "partner" designation met the public's political demands: participation and leadership. Moreover, a partner can be called to give an accounting at any time. When you trust someone, you not only give up some ability to make decisions but to challenge those decisions as well. The idea of being "partners" in government met the public's desire to assert some control and accountability. For better or worse, voters could achieve a feeling of participation without experiencing the frustration of governing.

These elements may be obvious, but Gronbeck highlights another essential definitional challenge for candidates. While the candidates' discourse obviously must create a believable connection between the nation's problems and the candidate's ability to solve those problems, it also defines the role of the people in the political process. He says campaigns "ultimately tell us who we as a people are, where we have been and where we are going" (Gronbeck, 1984, 496). Campaign discourse invites the public to adopt a particular political identity. Inasmuch as a candidate's discourse meets the voters' perceptions of who they are, the discourse resonates with their experience and desires. When the rhetoric develops a preferred and ideal conception of voters, it may also inspire. Through analyzing a candidate's discourse, a critic can discern "a model of what the rhetor would have his real auditor become," or what Ed Black discusses as the "second persona" (1970, 113). Campaign messages communicate not only the candidate's conception of the role of president and the government but an equally strategic conception of the people. As one journalist noted, "Voters know the candidates up close and personal. The voting process is so intimate because what they are looking for is a reflection of themselves: their trials and turmoils, virtues and values. The political campaign is a search for connection—from both sides, candidates and voters alike" (Roberts, 1992, 15).

The 1992 presidential election revealed the paradoxical nature of American national identity; individualism promotes conceptions of private interest and private behavior. A sense of American destiny leads us to consider ourselves in relation to a higher good demonstrated in public purpose politics. Candidates must balance these themes. At times, individual interests will outweigh public concerns. At other times, the public good must override individual interests. What works in one era will fall on deaf ears in another.

Clearly, 1992 was a "time for change." The shift will come again. When it does, discourse similar to Clinton's will be as unsatisfying and inappropriate for many citizens as Bush's was in 1992. Words that define political perspectives must fit not only the immediate instrumental situation but the symbolic forces of the times. Strains of American discourse emerge from the raucous din of political talk to guide public evaluation and action. That is why a candidate's ability to give voice to the public's rising concerns and desires and to offer meaningful responses contributes to political success.

ACKNOWLEDGMENT

The author would like to thank Dr. Matthew P. McAllister for his helpful comments.

REFERENCES

Alter, Jonathan. 1992. "The Real Character Issues." *Newsweek,* Mar. 30, 33.

Baer, Donald. 1992. "The Race." *U.S. News and World Report,* Aug. 31–Sept. 7, 34–40.

Bedard, Paul. 1991. "For President, All's Quiet on the Home Front." *Washington Times,* Jan. 31, A3.

Black, Edwin. 1970. "The Second Persona." *Quarterly Journal of Speech* 56: 109–19.

Bush, George. 1990. "Address before a Joint Session of the Congress on the State of the Union." *Public Papers of the Presidents, George Bush, 1990,* vol. 1, 129–34. Washington, DC: U.S. Government Printing Office.

———. 1991. "Address before a Joint Session of the Congress on the State of the Union." *Public Papers of the Presidents, George Bush, 1991,* 74–79. Washington, DC: USGPO.

———. 1992a. "Address before a Joint Session of the Congress on the State of the Union." *Weekly Compilation of Presidential Documents,* vol. 28, 165–90. Washington, DC: USGPO.

———. 1992b. "Remarks Accepting the Presidential Nomination at the Republican National Convention in Houston." *Weekly Compilation of Presidential Documents,* vol. 28, 1445–1470. Washington, DC: USGPO.

———. 1992c. "Remarks and a Question-and-Answer Session at the Economic Club of Detroit in Michigan." *Weekly Compilation of Presidential Documents,* vol. 28, 1571–1634. Washington, DC: USGPO.

Clinton, Bill. 1992. "Transcript of Speech by Clinton Accepting Democratic Nomination." *New York Times,* July 17, A14–15.

"Democrats Generally Applaud Speeches' Tone." 1990. *Washington Post,* Feb. 1.

Denton, Robert E., and Gary C. Woodward. 1990. *Political Communication in America,* 2d ed. Westport, CT: Praeger.

Dowd, Maureen. 1991. "President, in State of Union Talk, Dwells on War and the Economy." *New York Times,* Jan. 30, A1.

Duffy, Michael. 1992. "No Miracles Yet." *Time,* Sept. 21, 22–24.

Fineman, Howard, and Ann McDaniel. 1992. "Can He Beat Bush?" *Newsweek,* Mar. 30, 24–27.

Fineman, Howard, with Eleanor Clift, Ginny Carroll, and Vern E. Smith. 1992. "Wondering Who's 'Electable.'" *Newsweek,* Mar. 2, 24–26.

Gergen, D., and M. Shields. 1992. *MacNeil/Lehrer Newshour,* Oct. 16.

Goldman, Peter, and Tom Mathews. 1992. "America Changes the Guard." *Newsweek,* Nov./Dec., 20–23.

Goodwin, Richard N. 1991. "Bootstrapping Won't Work without Shoes." *Los Angeles Times,* Jan. 31, B7.

Greenhouse, Steven. 1992. "Looking to Short Term." *New York Times,* Jan. 29, A1.

Gronbeck, Bruce. 1984. "Functional and Dramaturgical Theories of Presidential Campaigns." *Presidential Studies Quarterly* 14: 487–98.

Hotline. 1991–1992. Vol. 4, no. 224–vol. 6, no. 68.

Klein, Joe. 1992a. "Little Lies and Big Whoppers." *Newsweek,* Aug. 31, 36.

———. 1992b. "Prisoner of the People." *Newsweek,* Nov. 2, 58.

McLaughlin, Jeff. 1991. "Cape Woman Not Sure Bush Got Message of Hard Times." *Boston Globe,* Jan. 31, 12.

MacNeil/Lehrer Newshour. 1992a. October 16.

———. 1992b. October 30.

"'Manhattan Project,' 1992." 1992. *Newsweek,* Nov./Dec., 40–56.

Morganthau, Tom, with Ginny Carroll, Bill Turque, and Michael Meyer. 1992. "The Wild Card." *Newsweek,* Apr. 27, 21–25.

Presidential Debate. 1992a. President George Bush, Republican Candidate; Governor Bill Clinton, Democratic Candidate; Ross Perot, Independent Candidate (Campus of Washington University, St. Louis, Missouri). *Federal News Service,* Oct. 11, 59–84.

———. 1992b. President George Bush, Republican Candidate; Governor Bill Clinton, Democratic Candidate; Ross Perot, Independent Candidate (Richmond, Virginia). *Federal News Service,* Oct. 15, 31–58.

———. 1992c. President George Bush, Republican Candidate; Governor Bill Clinton, Democratic Candidate; Ross Perot, Independent Candidate (East Lansing, Michigan). *Federal News Service,* Oct. 19, 2–30.

Raskin, James. 1992a. "Inside Bush Headquarters." *Campaigns and Elections,* July, 29–30.

———. 1992b. "Inside Clinton Headquarters." *Campaigns and Elections,* September, 28–29.

Roberts, Steven V. 1992. "Looking for the Light in Their Souls." *U.S. News and World Report,* Sept. 7, 15.

Schlesinger, Arthur M., Jr. 1985. *The Cycles of American History.* Boston: Houghton-Mifflin.

"A Silver Bullet." 1992. *Newsweek,* Nov./Dec., 82–85.

"State of the Union–Rhetoric Gives Hope: Program Still Lacking." 1990. *Seattle Times,* Feb. 1, A8.

Trent, Judith S., and Robert V. Friedenberg. 1991. *Political Campaign Communication: Principles and Practices,* 2d ed. New York: Praeger.

"The War Room Drill." 1992. *Newsweek,* Nov./Dec., 78–81.

Will, George. 1991. "The Nation's Hard Work of Freedom." *Newsday,* Jan. 31, 103.

Zuckerman, Mortimer B. 1992. "George Bush: Evening in America." *U.S. News and World Report,* Sept. 14, 88.

7

Voter Rationality and Media Excess: Image in the 1992 Presidential Campaign

Alan Louden

> There is no evidence that people learn less from campaigns today than they did in past years.
>
> Samuel L. Popkin, *The Reasoning Voter*

THE SCENE

The sober predictability of the 1992 presidential contest gave way to a memorable election when a little-known governor from the rural backwater of Southern politics challenged and defeated the reigning political establishment. Explanations for the outcome are abundant, ranging from the hangover of economic woes to the charm of a blow-dried "image," each of which likely contributed to the outcome. At a more basic level, however, American voters were introduced to their "neighbor," Bill Clinton, and in a comparative sense, they liked what they saw.

The political season did not disappoint the most avid observer with its entertaining cacophony of charges and countercharges, stupefying in their soap-opera dimension. Voters learned that Quayle intellectual prowess collapsed to the spelling of "potato(e)"; that Clinton was so concerned with his semblance that he "didn't inhale"; and that Bush was sheltered to the degree that a supermarket scanner elicited adoration. Campaign sideshows, several that directly assassinated candidates' character, beguiled voters. This was no less the case with "substantive" theatrical firestorms that included everything from "family values" and "patriotism," as expressed by military service, to paranoid "snooping" on family and friends. Although any of these "diversions" may have contained the seeds of serious campaign issues, arguably media coverage largely ignored the solemn angle. The family values debate, in particular, entered a surrealistic zone when "prime-time entertainment" met "evening news entertainment" in a pseudo debate featuring the vice president and an FYI anchorperson. Columnist John Hall shared the exasperation, noting: "The real Vice President Dan Quayle has written in his own hand to the fictional newborn son of a television character, the husbandless Murphy Brown, and then watched television with a group of real-life single mothers as the fictional Brown . . . read a statement on her fictional newscast attacking Quayle for criticizing Murphy Brown and thereby fostering values inimical to the American Family" (1992, A17).

Indeed, it would be easy to conclude that the media's reporting rendered a "reasoned" decision nearly impossible. One might ask, how could voters, distracted by a media carnival of excess, reach or appreciate the import of their decision? Some observers maintain that media's emphasis on manifestations of character threatens the very cornerstones of Democracy (Graber, 1992). What follows is a reconsideration of this unitary hypothesis, questioning the dominant critical posture of communication scholars and advancing a more favorable assessment of voters' ability to reach "informed" judgments. The approach examines the practice and utility of media coverage in the 1992 election, employing image as the organizing construct.

IMAGE "CHARACTERIZED"

Image is an elastic term that assumes disparate meanings depending on the perspective taken. From the voter's viewpoint, image is generally conceived as a "subjective reality" encompassing many types of impressions. Usually the term includes voters' beliefs about candidates' traits, policies, values, and campaign activity, based on both what is learned about the candidates and evaluative responses to that information. From the standpoint of candidates, political image usually means what candidates project to voters. Image is typically conceptualized as source- or message-dependent, and is assessed by examining the content and form of campaign messages. Image, however, is more precisely an evaluation negotiated and constructed by candidates and voters in a cooperative venture. The interdependence of source and receiver lies at the heart of inquiry from a communication orientation. Dan Nimmo alludes to the richness and complexity of viewing image in this manner: "Candidates formulate and project not only images of themselves and each other but also imagine what voters think of them as office-seekers. Voters construct and project self-images and images of the candidates—the qualities they perceive in each candidate and how they think the candidates, in turn, respond to them as voters" (1976, 36). It is the *practice* of political persuasion, however, that frustrates many observers and leads to the third delineation of image. Unfortunately, most of the literature examining political communication (as well as media pundits and commentators) regards image irreverently, placing image in opposition to issue (Hellweg,

Dionisiopoulos, and Kugler, 1989). Issues are the "right-stuff" of decision making whereas *image* becomes synonymous with extraneous character judgments. In this chapter I argue that the resultant issue/image dichotomy is artificial and misleading in that both the messages projected by candidates and perceived by voters are, in fact, a complex blend of issue and image information. Issue and image representations should be considered not as oppositional but rather as harmonized constructs; they are reciprocal, reflexive, and transformable. Issue and image are conceptions whose meaning blends in voters' minds; however, this more integrative approach is often under siege from critics and pundits alike.

THE CRITIC'S STANCE

Communication scholars are more reasoned than their on-screen counterparts when deriding the mediated political scene. Seldom does one read a critique of media presentations without a nod of agreement. Commentary is typified by Kathleen Jamieson's (1992) precise and lively pleas for more "argument, engagement, and accountability," or Bruce Gronbeck's (1992) contention that political reporting is little more than "rhetorical condensation," replacing deliberative discourse with slogan, and David Zarefsky's (1992) warning that the media's contribution is a transitory trivialization "truncating the public sphere."

Contemporary scholarship generally centers on exposing the dysfunctional political milieu. The "politically correct" theme resonant in political communication research offers sharp warnings about the pallid condition of political discourse, concluding that television is more proficient in conveying images than promoting political discussions and debate (Bertelsen, 1992). Most agree with Neil Postman's judgment that viewers are simply entertained, embracing unexamined image as experience (1986).

Democratic theory, conceptualizations of rationality, and a rhetorical tradition grounded in Aristotle have long influenced evaluations of the electoral process (Blumler, 1987). These perspectives share an ideal of an "informed" citizenry, making rational decisions. It is not surprising that many conclude with Richard Joslyn that campaign information, as served up by the media, becomes more a choice endorsing "cultural icons and values than . . . an appreciation of policy alternatives" and is "much more likely to restrict elections to choices between competing images of candidate personalities . . . than to a choice between competing programs of governmental action or political beliefs." Somehow grounding candidate selection in individuals' value systems is viewed as "irrational." This censorious perspective holds that image undermines informed decisions while issue constitutes "good reasons" (1986, 183).

The tendency of critical form is to place issue and image into an opposition of *preferred and seditious* message forms. Although most critics do not subscribe to the position that issues are the only "legitimate" form of message, they nevertheless tacitly separate issue and image in their commentary. Part of the reason that "image" is less valued than issue-talk is that the partition is seductive. Not only is the dichotomy continually reinforced in commentary, but our personal experience authenticates a distinction between the verifiable/consequential and the intuitive/ephemeral. The separation is so ingrained that it is difficult to talk about campaign coverage outside the issue/image framework, relegating campaign accounts hostage to the dichotomy.

Critics' dismay with mediated political discourse is not entirely fair, however, as Americans have throughout their history elected candidates based on subjective image (Lemann, 1980; Jamieson, 1988, 1992). Television per se has done little to change the role of imagery in elections (Melder, 1986), and as Lee Sigelman points out "it makes no sense to blame the media for a decline and fall from what never was" (1992, 409; Sigelman and Bullock, 1991). *Image has always been the issue.*

The viewpoint advocated here is decidedly more optimistic regarding media's contribution to voters' knowledge. This is based on three suppositions: information providers have decidedly improved the political fare; voters are more sophisticated in assessing media output than customarily assumed; and campaign "hype" is itself valuable information in reaching sensible voting decisions.

MEDIA AND CANDIDATE REFLEXIVITY

Although it remains fashionable to consider media practice as chronically flawed, election coverage is not static, and in the 1992 campaign cycle, programming often enlightened voters. Media semantics place ample restrictions on what constitutes news. The frame of storytelling remains a serious limitation to voter enlightenment (Altheide and Snow, 1991; Brummett, 1991; Postman and Powers, 1992), but in all fairness, mainstream media has cleaned up its act in many instances. Media handling of elections seems to be evolving since the 1970s and 1980s when it appeared that candidates had gained domination of media: controlling timing, staging of events, and capitalizing on television's appetite for the visual (Simons and Stewart, 1991; Schram, 1987). There is some indication that media providers, perhaps feeling pressure from constant criticism or seeking a way to reassert (justify) their influence, have "improved" coverage during the 1992 election.

Claims that the media and campaigns have elevated their offerings are, of course, made cautiously. The sheer volume of frivolous coverage and the expected hyperbole from candidates provide grounds for concluding that media sources did not do much better in 1992 than before. Yet there is room for optimism.

Omitting the "contribution" of tabloid journalism, it is useful to think of media input as a spectrum anchored on one end by CNN's modish *Inside Politics,* and C-SPAN's uninterrupted coverage on the other. Most instances of television coverage fell somewhere between extremes such as "horserace" and "non-mediated" media coverage. In 1992 the network news departments increasingly abandoned photo-opt journalism, scrutinizing candidates' claims night after night (Goodman, 1992). Much that was aired was substantive and often interactive, as with Koppel's town halls or ABC's *Nightline.* The ratings and audience shares for the presidential debates were the highest ever, with the Richmond debate outdrawing a baseball playoff game (Fouhy, 1992). Around 16 million people witnessed Ross Perot's initial, lengthy "infomercial" ("The Second Coming," 1992), and there was even the occasional audience for C-SPAN's *Road to the White House,* all of which suggest that voters' media intake went beyond half-hour news programming. It is important to remember that many, if not all, political consumers receive information *across* this spectrum.

One important change in 1992 was that candidates became more accomplished at bypassing network's 30-second sound bites. This was accomplished, in part, by candidates redefining their relationship with media coverage. Traditionally candidates have staged events, dependent on media for amplification. Although competition to get on the news continued unabated in 1992, candidates nonetheless found "new" ways to appear unfettered on television. Many opportunities seized were traditional, as in past elections (conventions, debates, and ritualistic interviews), but there were innovations in the 1992 election cycle.

On the more conventional side, several appearances were not only relatively lengthy events but drew large portions of expectant voters. The three presidential debates, for example, rose above the "prepared" sound bite, providing a glimpse of policy directions and intimating the candidate's character and mode of operation. After the conventional debate in St. Louis, spiced only by the uncertainty of a third candidate, audience comments in Richmond and strong follow-up questions in East Lansing allowed contrast unavailable elsewhere. Comparably large segments of the electorate reported basing their voting decisions on the debates (Fouhy, 1992). It appeared that voters were hungry for information on the candidates, and they were prepared to sit through extended statements.

The 1992 candidates adopted a less orthodox approach toward "serious" television, transforming entertainment-talk with political talk. Clinton's forays into late night with Arsenio Hall and his generational crossover on MTV were groundbreaking events. The *Larry King Show* as conduit for Perot's entry, exit, and reentry dramatically utilized uninterrupted exposure to reach voters. The election season also introduced a myriad of talk shows that, across time, became "legitimate" forums for the candidates. Jamieson recently observed that talk shows enfranchise voters since "participation rather than spectatorship is invited by its interactive form." Additionally, she notes "it attracts an audience otherwise largely inaccessible to candidates" (1992, 266). Perot's sidestepping of traditional media may not have elevated the campaign, but he nonetheless illustrated the power to reapportion media's authority (Zoglin, 1992).

Of course, talk shows as purveyors of substantive campaign discourse have been uneven. It was more than a little embarrassing for the earnest observer when, on *Donahue,* the host relentlessly pursued Bill Clinton's alleged philandering. Even so, such programs allow candidates to counter the brevity of nightly news with details, and even to short circuit potential scandals. As candidates get better at exploiting entertainment formats, issue elaboration, and scandal abatement, talk-show programming becomes a more important vehicle to drive out specious and immaterial campaign sideshows.

Toward the end of the campaign, candidates had perfected the art of canvassing free time on the media. Across morning, afternoon, and evening television, as well as alternative outlets via linkups to local networks, radio, and surrogates, any interested viewer could watch or hear each of the willing candidates for hours each day. Often Bush and Clinton were scheduled in rotations of back-to-back appearances, mimicking mini-debates on the campaign's more salient issues. The candidates answered difficult and often pointed questions, reflecting the maturation gained during the campaign (e.g., Bush and Clinton fielding Sam Donaldson's questions on *Prime Time Live*). It is difficult to imagine how the voters could expect or profit from any greater exposure to the candidates and the views they choose to share. One could argue that the questioning should be tougher or that only joint appearances suffice, yet the public was as informed as in any election year.

Adaptations to the dominate media form create an altered framework for dialogue with voters—one in which issue complexity is transformed into accessible personalizations. Responding to television's domination of popular culture, image making is increasingly wrestling political dialogue away from past examples of popular culture. An appearance on *Arsenio*

Hall, mixing celebrity status with concern for health care, is not a cheapening of politics as much as it is candidates' repossession of the audience. Although one may criticize the sophistication of the message content, this adaptation to the dominant media is not noticeably different from the Lincoln-Douglas debates that graced the domain of the public square and family picnics, or Roosevelt's fireside chats that achieved a comfortable adaptation of radio's gathered intimacy. Michael Gurevitch and Anandam Kavoori confirm as much when they note that the rush to television's talk shows, call-in programs, electronic town meetings, and late-night entertainment programs "could foretell a movement where the instrumentality of popular culture may eventually come to replace (at least in part) the formalized institutional/cultural apparatus of power" (1992, 419). In this sense, candidates found culturally relevant means to preempt the imperious control of news clips and sound bites.

Candidates' tendency to stage numerous debates, talk formats, and lengthy proclamations may represent little more than the demands of a competitive race. Kathleen Jamieson (1992) provides evidence that perceptually close elections, as in 1960 and 1980, produce "engagement on policy and useful predictions about governance." As she argues, "the longer the statement the more likely it is to compare and contrast [differentiate] candidates' positions, providing either oppositional evidence discrediting the opponent's stand or supportive evidence for one's side or both. So, for example, speeches are more likely to engage than spots, the longer soundbites of 'MacNeil/Lehrer' more likely to engage than those on other network news" (259). However, Jamieson cites evidence that segments of fifteen minutes or longer have continued to decline. It seems that 1992 reversed that trend. This is, in part, because candidates have redefined the "dignified campaign," affirming alternatives to traditional media coverage. Obviously, exposure is not without risk and lopsided elections might entice the leading contender to lie low, but challengers who warrant interest may be increasingly capable of forcing engagement by taking to the airwaves.

Skeptics would point out that despite availability, extended length, and greater interaction with voters, candidates' messages are just more of the same barren discourse. A partial answer and the position advanced in the next section is foreshadowed by columnist Philip Gailey's question: "Which does a better job of helping voters size up a candidate, a 20-minute conversation with Arsenio Hall or a 15-second sound bite on the evening news with Dan, Peter and Tom?" (1992, 11). The answer depends, in part, on how voters make sense of campaign communication.

VOTERS "RATIONALLY" ASSESS IMAGE

Voters are not nearly as whimsical as we give them credit for, nor are they as misinformed (Page and Shapiro, 1992). Notwithstanding polls reflecting displeasure with campaign hyperbole, voters do not view political communication in a vacuum, nor do they succumb to every political charlatan. Voters are adept in reaching sound decisions, especially in high-profile elections. The electorate's rationality often escapes critics because voters are not always articulate in accounting for their decisions *and* because they often base their voting decisions on a candidate's character. Arthur Miller's examination of national samples of presidential voters (1952 to 1984) found that "perceptions of candidates are generally focused on 'personality' characteristics rather than on issue concerns" (1986, 521). Findings of this sort feed critics' contention that media's fixation on character hinders voters. The standard becomes "unless voters' political judgments are reducible to propositional statements, we mistrust those judgments." An impressional foundation is "not enough." Voters must be able to articulate restricted axioms within the confines of pollsters' and researchers' questionnaires. Voters are not asked to reach a rounded decision but to "oversimplify" their calculus.

Although individuals willingly judge coworkers and friends largely based on character, it remains dubious for the same individuals to decide the leadership potential of a candidate based on personal attributes. It is acceptable to support Clinton because one understands and agrees with a distinct policy, yet it is questionable to conclude, for example, he'll exercise reasoned responses based on his management of controversy during the campaign. Recent work by cognitive researchers serves as a reminder that:

Candidate evaluations are not necessarily cognitively superficial, irrational, or short-term. Voters may focus on the personal qualities of a candidate to gain information about characteristics relevant to assessing how a person will perform in office. Voting for a candidate based on personal characteristics therefore does not in and of itself imply "irrationality"; it may suggest reasonable and intelligible performance evaluations. (Miller, Wattenberg, and Malanchuk, 1985, 184)

The argument condemning content of mediated messages includes the notion that the public cannot truly *know* the character of candidates. The unstated fear is that candidates are indeed "packaged," or at least inadequately refracted in the media's spotlight. For example, Jamieson argued that "when we see a potential leader through the filter provided by pseudo-events, news bites, or nuggetized ads and then can know for certain only that most politicians do not speak their own words, *ethos is* a less reliable anchor for belief" (1988, 240). Although there is always the feeling in a campaign that voters could know candidates more thoroughly, they nevertheless have ample opportunity to observe their actions and tendencies. Most have watched the candidate "handle crowds, speeches, press conferences, reporters, and squabbles," all of which Samuel Popkin argued provide "information with which they imagine how he or she would be likely to behave in office" (1991, 62). I doubt most voters questioned *their* personal judgments of George Bush or Michael Dukakis after the 1988 election.

In his persuasive book *The Reasoning Voter,* Popkin reviewed a sizeable body of research assessing the manner in which voters make sense of often fractured and sometimes shallow campaign information. He concluded that voters use cognitive "shortcuts" in assessing candidates that are reliable and clear sighted.

Voters remember past campaigns and presidents, and past failures of performance to match promises. They have a sense of who is with them and who is against them; they make judgments about unfavorable news and editorials and advertisements from hostile sources, ignoring some of what is favorable to those they oppose and some of what is unfavorable to those they support. In managing their personal affairs and making decisions about their work, they collect information that they can use in a reality test for campaign claims and media stories. They notice the difference between behavior that has real consequences, on the one hand, and mere talk, on the other. (1991, 235)

Voters' stress on character is more than a simple reflection of media's emphasis on personal qualities. The intrinsic nature of campaigns and the manner in which individuals assess social situations ensure a character's continued authority. Even when campaigns revolve around discernible issue agendas, the peculiarity of the campaign process keeps the issue of character at the apex. Built into the process is a forced choice among identifiable actors who willingly assume the symbolic mantle for issues. Campaigns inherently associate praise or blame with *particular* candidates. Negative campaigning produces messages designed to debunk, subvert, and unmask; this process of depreciating the image of the opponent is, at its heart, about character.

In addition, candidates' actions—issuing positions, statements, decisions—are intentionally displayed, left open to criticism by the opposition and media. Lance Bennett (1992, 403) observed that mediated political dramas "are personalized, both because they dwell on the political fates of individual actors, and because they are thematized around the psychological concerns of individual viewers." It follows that character is always salient in high-profile races, and 1992 was no exception. As Roger Ailes, who has masterminded a number of successful campaigns, advised, "You can present all the issues you want on the air, and if at the end the audience doesn't like the guy, they're not going to vote for him" (Diamond and Bates, 1988, 387).

Ultimately, it is the manner in which voters reason that places character at the decisional core. Individuals reference their own experience, much of which is gained interpersonally, to understand political candidates, employing standards that have fidelity in their own lives. Donald Kinder (1986) believes that individuals look at a candidate and wonder what sort of person he or she is. Voters answer this question "in a way analogous to the way in which they answer similar questions about their friends and neighbors, that is, partly by consulting their implicit theories regarding the organization and antecedents of character itself" (253). As in daily life, where individuals regularly assign attributes based on the consistency of actions and character, voters note the behaviors of candidates, apply appropriate personal standards, and derive an evaluation of a candidate's character (Gamson, 1992; Graber, 1984; Husson et al., 1988; Kendall and Yum, 1984).

An example from the 1992 campaign illustrates how voters make use of character and, in part, compensate for media's abbreviated analysis. A standard campaign tactic is to advertise the challenger's failure of experience, calling into question the competence of a candidate. We saw this in several recent elections, notably Carter's Georgia, Reagan's California, and Dukakis's "Massachusetts Miracle." In the 1992 campaign the focus was shifted to Arkansas, attacking Clinton's record as governor. Voters were likely to know specifics beyond the fact that Arkansas was a poor, but improving, state, lead by a governor who "created" jobs for chicken pluckers. Popkin (77) indicated how voters, confronted with an information deficit, go about reaching arguably sound inferences. He maintained that voters in 1976, armed only with the knowledge that Carter was governor of Georgia, "decide[d] what kind of governor Carter was and what kind of president he [would] be *not* on the basis of knowledge about his performance as governor but on their assessment of how likely it [was] that Carter, as a person, was a good governor." Past performance as a measure of future performance was an issue dependent on a character evaluation. Similarly in the 1992 election, it was not so much the specifics of what voters knew about Clinton as governor, but how they thought a candidate with Clinton's character would *act* as governor.

Naturally the electorate makes use of a variety of criteria when casting their ballots, including knowledge about numerous issues (Popkin, 1991), yet certain criteria appear to carry more weight than others. Character attributes, especially integrity and competence, seem more important than friendliness, appearance, family, and so forth (Kinder et al., 1980; Miller, Wattenberg, and Malanchuk, 1985, 1986). Minimal competency is usually demanded and often overpowers specific issue positions. Similarly, integrity is more probative than other character assessments. As Doris Graber (1984) noted, "While honesty is no assurance of other good qualities, lack of honesty presumably depreciates sharply the value of other good qualities" (161). Steven Sharp (1986), testifying before a Senate committee reviewing spot advertising, previewed the argument made here when he noted:

[Voters] are primarily concerned with the ability and integrity of the candidate, and they want to know how that person is going to handle themselves on an issue that they may have never even heard of. They may not understand the issues, but whether through watching television or shaking hands or looking them in the eye or whatever it is, they want to have the feeling that person is someone they can trust to do a good job. (38–39)

The question voters are asked to evaluate is how will a candidate act in future situations; information that can only be known indirectly. Are voters best served by candidates' overclaims and media's "invented" past record, or are both the past and future better understood when tempered through the lens of the candidate's character?

TRANSFORMATION FROM ISSUE TO IMAGE

The certitude that voters utilize information shortcuts and have at their disposal less than ideal information leads critics to offer numerous suggestions for improvement. What is needed, critics propose, is to reform media excess and address voter apathy. Their answer is to inform voters and "return" campaign dialogue to a discussion of issues. But efforts are frustrated, in part, because voters integrate issue and image evaluations when assessing candidates. Even when voters know "substantive" facts and figures regarding candidates' issues or situations, this information is often translated by voters into perceptions of character. Graber, who looked at responses to news stories highlighting candidates' issues, observed that viewers engage in an "alchemy" whereby issues serve as the basis for making assessments of candidates as capable or compassionate, or smart, or likable (1984).

Indeed, even if selection criteria were restricted to issue-based information, the result would not be cause for celebration. The evidence is very strong that when voters are presented with issue content they habitually infer image-based judgments. This was illustrated by Deirdre Johnston's (1989) study of political advertising that found for most subjects, messages that focused exclusively on candidate's issues—a laundry list of issue positions—elicited a majority of image evaluations. It appears that auditors easily and automatically make character assessments even when these attributes were overtly absent in the messages (Louden, 1990; Popkin, 1991).

The manner in which voters integrate information can profitably be thought of as an inferential process where issue information informs image evaluation (issue → image). The evidence is persuasive that voters' inferential patterns move from issue to image evaluation. Determinations of this sort are not surprising given the nature of campaigns. Candidates usually frame issues by either doing or not doing something, or proclaiming they will do or not do something. Candidates also frame their opponents' actions or lack thereof in a similar manner. Character judgment, therefore, necessarily draws on the exposition of issues, because to witness issue-talk is to see actors act. Judgment embedded in the reality and appropriateness of actions provides clues to the candidates' character. Additionally, voters *experience* candidates' actions and accounts of issues, a personalization of judgment that enhances observers' certainty.

The downside of voters' tendency to translate action into issue projections is that it elevates current campaign conduct at the expense of other relevant information. Popkin summarized the notion, "Because we generate narratives about kinds of people, it is easier to take personal data and fill in the political facts and policies than to start with the political facts and fill in the personal data. This has an important political implication in decision making and evaluation: campaign behavior can dominate political history" (1991, 78).

META-CAMPAIGN JUDGMENTS

Most observers reluctantly acknowledge that candidates and the media will likely continue to produce messages offensive to critics. Some solace can be found in the observation that voters are accomplished at sorting through the barrage. This last section takes a precarious turn, asking if the mediated campaign drama—campaign-as-spectator-sport—serves voters in reaching "informed" voting decisions. The goal is not to defend media and candidate excess but rather to recognize how the very act of campaigning is a major and legitimate source of information for voters—a campaign-about-the-campaign, or the *meta-campaign*.

Media critics adamantly dismiss the frivolity of mediated campaigns. Jamieson, for example, described much of media's (and consequently voters') controlling lens as "strategy schema" that direct thinking about campaign events.

So enmeshed is the vocabulary of horse race and war in our thoughts about politics that we are not conscious that the "race" is a metaphor and "spectatorship" an inappropriate role for the electorate. Press reliance on the language of strategy reduces candidate and public accountability. . . . [R]eliance on the strategy schema means that campaigns are shifting from communication to metacommunication, thereby reducing the information content available to voters. (1992, 165, 187)

Of course, there is much to this claim, yet it is premature to categorically disregard meta-campaign information. A preoccupation with campaign strategy is a reminder that campaigns *interact*; they engage in an *ongoing dialogue* where candidates employ ritualized turn-taking, send and address accusations, work the press and politicians, manage an unruly campaign apparatus, and generally go about the business of being a candidate. How then does this exchange serve the voter?

Messages are deployed in a campaign to engage one another, creating interpretive contexts that are, across time, integrative. Voters cannot isolate their understanding to a single event or message, even if a particular campaign episode appears to carry all the importance in the individual's voting rationale. Any voter who is exposed to the media (and who is not?) cannot avoid adopting a viewpoint that is temporal, cumulative, and includes information from both campaigns. During a campaign, as Popkin relates, "Voters learn about the traits and characteristics of the new candidates, and they also see their behavior in contrast to that of the other candidates in the field. They learn directly from observing the candidates, and indirectly from seeing how the candidate fits into the array of candidates" (1991, 133). It is helpful, therefore, to conceive of spots, speeches, news stories, and tracts as part of the strategic fabric of a campaign; a web of relationships building friendly and unfriendly story lines; an unfolding that provides fodder for the electorate's inferential competence.

Sometimes this interaction is direct, as in the debates, where voters were provided a direct reading of the candidates' relational postures and command of the issues and situation. More often the interaction is separated temporally, as when the three major candidates responded to viewer questions on the *Larry King Show*. In these forums voters could, relatively unhindered, assess how candidates interacted. The most common communication pattern, however, is dialogue separated spatially and temporally, employing the media as conduit. Even though messages are hostage to media grammar, voters still learn about the candidate's values, tenacity, and artistry. An interesting example from the 1992 campaign involved Clinton's posture during the Vietnam War. The Bush campaign, hoping to elevate Clinton's history to an "issue" of patriotism, raised his draft status repeatedly. Bush contended, when pressed by reporters, "It is wrong to demonstrate against your country when your country is at war. Clinton ought to answer for not serving when black kids from the ghetto were the ones forced to go fight in his stead" (Monroe, 1992). Clinton's lapse in recalling his draft-age feelings and actions was troublesome to many, but the patriotism question diffused when Clinton was able to shift the evaluative standard. He refocused the discussion into a question of Bush's motives, simultaneously providing an interpretative frame that diminished the importance of the draft issue. Clinton's response to Bush's charges included a doleful retort on the way to the St. Louis presidential debate, "I just think he's desperate. I felt real sad for Mr. Bush yesterday. Here we are on the way to debate the great issues facing this country and its future, and we've descended to that level ("Clinton Slams Bush," 1992). But even if the charges and countercharges were contrived, voters watching the interaction of the candidates did learn about skills in handling "public deliberation" and about the quality of the person making or answering the charges, however unflattering. Campaign voyeurism should not be confused with substantive programming, yet much that is thought to be germane for voters may be less insightful than the unvarnished dialogue in the day-to-day campaign. For example, candidate biographies provide factual grounding, yet watching Clinton's and Bush's sanitized convention films and Ross Perot's hour-long character testimonial by his "world class" family and close friends, give one pause for consideration as to which is more informative. The introduction of pseudo issues also has a way of generating serious media coverage and discussions, as with shattering the political myth of the archetype of the American family.

One important way in which meta-campaign judgments operate to define candidate image is in terms of competence, a central character judgment. Evaluation of competence includes past political experience, ability, and comprehension of political issues. It also carries over into how candidates conduct their campaign. Competence in unfamiliar arenas is simply inferred from the perceived capacity of the candidate in the more familiar arena, the candidate as campaigner. The dexterity with which candidates manage interactions is, itself, an important *action* by the candidate. Voters arrive at meta-campaign evaluations that aid their comparison of candidates, leave impressions regarding which candidates can control the agenda, and, potentially, reveal the lack of ability to perform in office.

For example, Dukakis's "incompetence" in challenging Bush in 1988 undermined his "campaign of competence." Management of a campaign, per se, is not conclusive evidence for acceptance or rejection, yet when cross-referenced with other information about candidates it contributes to an "informed" perspective.

RESERVATIONS ABOUT THE META-CAMPAIGN

Jamieson strongly contended that favoring a "strategy schema" funnels voters' attention to the wrong questions. Strategy criteria elicit questions such as: "How effective were the strategies? In the process an effective strategy implicitly becomes a 'good' strategy." The alternative she defended is to value "performance." Natural questions might include: "What is the candidate's record in dealing with this sort of problem? In dealing with the sorts of problems a president faces?" (1992, 171).

This is accurate to a degree. Certainly the choreographed dance with the media increases attention to missteps and discordant movement. The point to be appreciated is that dexterity in mastering campaign complexities is additive to the assessment of past accomplishments and future promises. Even if it is true that the meta-campaign is less probative than alternative information, it is impossible, within the context of a campaign, to avoid such judgments. For voters, *strategy is performance.* The demands of the campaign provide a window, however opaque, on how candidates handle pressure and function within the glass house constructed around the presidency.

Additionally there are evident limits to fitness, fidelity, and fair play that serve as *tangible* boundaries for understanding the candidate-as-candidate. Candidates' actions must be responsive and relevant to exigencies, have the quality of truthfulness, and stay within standards mirroring voters' sensibilities. Campaigns cannot invent reality, insulated from the candidate's history and actions, in part, because voters use interactive cues in appraising character. Certainly there is latitude between the "private" person and his or her "public" image, yet the candidates, as public actors, knowingly or unknowingly provide hundreds of sensible cues that voters judge for credibility.

Campaigns, of course, are aware that voters apply meta-campaign judgments and the campaign-about-the-campaign serves as an additional avenue for influence. Even with staged events, campaigns often reveal a tongue-in-cheek bravado, inviting the media to present not only a staged photo-op but to "reveal" the behind-the-scenes strategy. The enthymematic posture, as one columnist wrote, is, "we are deceiving you, but look how skillfully we do it" (Schell, 1992, 11). Omnipresent is a latent judgment of the campaign's ability to guide its own symbolic unfolding. The aim is to appear enigmatic, even as the magician reveals the secrets of his magic trick. What is interesting about the practice is that campaigns, unlike critics, implicitly acknowledge that voters *know* they are being influenced. Not only are the voters savvy to the process, they simultaneously appreciate the deftness of such tactics even while abating its weight in their calculation. Any doubts that voters are sophisticated in understanding the process of campaigning are answered when one hears the insights of "unsophisticated" focus groups.

CONCLUSION

Critics will continue to prescribe solutions and warn the "simple-minded" public that mediated political discourse hovers just above platitudes and opprobrious attacks. We should attend less to how voters are duped and more to how they "make sense" in assessing campaign rhetoric. The evidence examined shows that voters are not fanciful in reflecting character in their decisional matrix. Notwithstanding critics' honorable motives, there remains a paucity of alternatives that candidates, the media, and voters are willing to accommodate.

Models of electoral rationality endeavor to view voters as comparison shoppers selecting among untangled policy options (issues). Yet the picture that emerges here is that voters have always chosen and will continue to choose among actions that reveal candidates' characters. Issues are important in a race but they do much more than position a candidate's policy stands. Voters attend to candidate's actions (including issues) as evidence of character and form an evaluation of the candidate's projected reliability. Voters, therefore, are rational when they endorse the person whose character can be relied upon to embody their values. Those who would argue that "issue-messages" are preferred in that they avoid the problem of "style becoming substance" should note that "issue-messages" effectively work with "substance becoming style."

Changes that emerged in the 1992 campaign included greater media responsibility and candidate cunning in appropriating alternative television access. As a result, voters were presented with endless information on candidates, easily permitting character assessment. One might ask: were voters mislead in concluding that Bush was voluntarily insulated from voters' concerns? or feeling that Clinton's proclivity for getting into tight corners educed a certain verbal artistry? or believing that Perot's self-assurance was matched, in scale, only by his mistrust of others? Perhaps. However, to answer "yes" is to underestimate the electorate, media, and candidates. Typifying American elections, images that resonated in

1992 were negotiated among the players, each adopting a strategy that was simultaneously self-serving *and* reflexive to the other's demands. Critics need to occasionally reconsider how the process serves dynamic, reasoning participants. Ultimately, the 1992 election cycle was encouraging in its ability to accommodate the electorate's decisional predisposition.

REFERENCES

Altheide, David L., and Robert P. Snow. 1991. *Media Worlds in the Postjournalism Era.* New York: Aldine De Gruyter.

Bartels, Larry M. 1988. *Presidential Primaries and the Dynamic of Public Choice.* Princeton, NJ: Princeton University Press.

Bennett, W. Lance. 1992. "White Noise: The Perils of Mass Mediated Democracy." *Communication Monographs* 59: 401–6.

Bertelsen, Dale A. 1992. "Media Form and Government: Democracy as an Archetypal Image in the Electronic Age." *Communication Quarterly* 40: 325–37.

Blumler, J. G. 1987. "Election Communication and the Democratic Political System." In *Political Communication Research: Approaches, Studies, Assessments,* David L. Paletz, ed. Norwood, NJ: Ablex.

Brummett, Barry. 1991. *Rhetorical Dimensions of Popular Culture.* Tuscaloosa: University of Alabama Press.

"Clinton Slams Bush Comments about his '70 Visit to Moscow." 1992. *Winston-Salem Journal,* Oct. 9, 5.

Diamond, Edwin, and Stephen S. Bates. 1988. *The Spot: The Rise of Political Advertising on Television,* 2d ed. Cambridge, MA: MIT Press.

Fouhy, Ed. 1992. "Election Debriefing" videotape, Dec. 12. Philadelphia, PA: Annenberg School for Communication.

Gailey, Philip. 1992. "And Now the News—with Phil and Geraldo." *Winston-Salem Journal,* June 19, 11.

Gamson, William A. 1992. *Talking Politics.* New York: Cambridge University Press.

Goodman, Walter. 1992. "TV Audiences Are Victors in This Election." *New York Times,* Nov. 3, C17(L).

Graber, Doris A. 1984. *Processing the News: How People Tame the Information Tide.* New York: Longman.

———. 1992. "News and Democracy: Are Their Paths Diverging?" *Roy W. Howard Public Lecture in Journalism and Mass Communication Research,* no. 3. Indiana University.

Gronbeck, Bruce E. 1992. "Electric Rhetoric: The Changing Forms of American Political Discourse." *Iowa Gazette,* University of Iowa, Fall, 4–5.

Gurevitch, Michael, and Anandam P. Kavoori. 1992. "Television Spectacles as Politics." *Communication Monographs* 59: 415–20.

Hall, John. 1992. "'All the World's a Stage' Was Never More True Than in This Election." *Winston-Salem Journal,* Sept. 27, A17.

Hellweg, Susan A., George N. Dionisopoulos, and Drew B. Kugler. 1989. "Political Candidate Image: A State-of-the-Art Review." In *Progress in Communication Sciences* 9, Brenda Dervin and Melvin J. Voight, eds. Norwood, NJ: Ablex.

Husson, William, Timothy Stephen, Teresa M. Harrison, and B. J. Fehr. 1988. "An Inter-personal Communication Perspective on Images of Political Candidates." *Human Communication Research* 14: 397–421.

Jamieson, Kathleen Hall. 1988. *Eloquence in an Electronic Age: The Transformation of Political Speechmaking.* New York: Oxford University Press.

———. 1992. *Dirty Politics: Deception, Distraction, and Democracy.* New York: Oxford University Press.

Johnston, Deirdre D. 1989. "Image and Issue Information: Message Content or Interpre-tation." *Journalism Quarterly* 66: 379–82.

Joslyn, Richard. 1986. "Political Advertising and the Meaning of Elections." In *New Perspectives on Political Advertising,* Lynda Lee Kaid, Dan Nimmo, and Keith R. Sanders, eds. Carbondale: Southern Illinois University Press.

Kendall, Kathleen, and June Ock Yum. 1984. "Persuading the Blue-Collar Voter: Issues, Images, and Homophily." *Communication Yearbook* 8.

Kinder, Donald R. 1986. "Presidential Character Revisited." In *Political Cognition: The 19th Annual Carnegie Symposium on Cognition,* Richard R. Lau and David O. Sears, eds. Hillsdale, NJ: Lawrence Erlbaum.

Kinder, Donald R., Mark D. Peters, Robert P. Abelson, and Susan T. Fiske. 1980. "Presi-dential Prototypes." *Political Behavior* 2: 315–37.

Lemann, Nicholas. 1980. "No; Seriously; I Want You to Look at the Camera and Say 'Ride with Me, Wyoming.'" *Washington Monthly* 12: 8–15.

Louden, Allan D. 1990. *Transformation of Issue to Image and Presence: Eliciting Char-acter Evaluations in Negative Spot Advertising.* Paper presented at a meeting of the International Communication Association, Dublin, Ireland.

Melder, Keith. 1986. "Creating Candidate Imagery, Part I: The Man on Horseback." *Campaigns & Elections* 6: 6–11.

Miller, Arthur H., Martin P. Wattenberg, and Okasana Malanchuk. 1985. "Cognitive Representations of Candidate Assessments." In *Political Communication Yearbook, 1984,* Keith R. Sanders, Lynda Lee Kaid, and Dan Nimmo, eds. Carbondale: Southern Illinois University Press.

———. 1986. "Schematic Assessments of Presidential Candidates." *American Political Science Review* 80: 521–40.

Monroe, Keith. 1992. "Bush Campaign is Ill-Served by Illogical Mudslinging." *Winston-Salem Journal,* Oct. 18, 17.

Nimmo, Dan. 1976. "Political Image Makers and the Mass Media." *Annals of the Ameri-can Academy of Political and Social Science* 427: 33–44.

Page, Benjamin I., and Robert Y. Shapiro. 1992. *The Rational Public: Fifty Years of Trends in Americans' Policy Preferences.* Chicago: University of Chicago Press.

Popkin, Samuel L. 1991. *The Reasoning Voter: Communication and Persuasion in Pres-idential Campaigns.* Chicago: University of Chicago Press.

Postman, Neil. 1986. *Amusing Ourselves to Death: Public Discourse in the Age of Show Business.* New York: Penguin Books.

Postman, Neil, and Steve Powers. 1992. *How to Watch TV News.* New York: Penguin Books.

Raspberry, William. 1992. "Much Ado about Little: Debates Fail to Show Who Is Fit for Office." *Winston-Salem Journal,* Oct. 19, 10.

Schell, Jonathan. 1992. "Unmasking the Exposing of Clinton Campaign." *Winston-Salem Journal,* Sept. 7, 11.

Schram, Martin. 1987. *The Great American Video Game: Presidential Politics in the Television Age.* New York: William Morrow.

"The Second Coming: Perot Rode Back into the Race on the Airwaves, as Star of 60-Second Spots and Hit Mini-Series of Chart Talks." 1992. *Newsweek* 120, Nov./Dec., 87–88.

Sharp, Steven A. 1986. "Clean Campaign Act of 1985." *Senate Hearing 99-49.* Committee on Commerce, Science, and Transportation. Washington, DC: U.S. Government Printing Office.

Sigelman, Lee. 1992. "There You Go Again: The Media and the Debasement of American Politics." *Communication Monographs* 59: 407–10.

Sigelman, Lee, and D. Bullock. 1991. "Candidates, Issues, Horse Races, and Hoopla: Presidential Campaign Coverage, 1888–1988." *American Politics Quarterly* 19: 5–32.

Simons, Herbert W., and Don J. Stewart. 1991. "Network Coverage of Video Politics: 'A New Beginning' in the Limits of Criticism." In *Television and Political Advertising, Vol. 2: Signs, Codes, and Images,* Frank Biocca, ed. Hillsdale, NJ: Lawrence Erlbaum.

Trent, Judy S., and Robert V. Friedenberg. 1991. *Political Campaign Communication: Principles and Practices,* 2d ed. Westport, CT: Praeger.

Zarefsky, David. 1992. "Spectator Politics and the Revival of Public Argument." *Communication Monographs* 59: 411–14.

Zoglin, Richard. 1992. "It Just Wasn't That Simple." *Time* 140, Nov. 16, 70.

8

Television News and the Advertising-Driven New Mass Media Election: A More Significant Local Role in 1992?

Montague Kern and Robert H. Wicks

In the 1980s a new political communication process emerged that we term the "New Mass Media Election." Unlike the "Old Mass Media Election" of the 1960s and 1970s, its underlying values are based on commercial advertising, with rhetoric that draws on emotional and entertainment-based appeals, including character narratives, not documentaries or news.

The influence of such commercial advertising on political messages was twofold. First, it affected media consultant philosophies and the content of the ads they produced. Second, media consultants holding these commercial values had an increasing influence on the shaping of televised campaign news, which served to legitimize rather than question the messages contained in the political advertising (Kern, 1989, 1991).

An increasing number of news stories covered political advertising as effective campaign strategy in a manner that gave more credibility to its use (Kaid, 1991). Such news accounts aired large segments of the ads themselves, which were indeed visually compelling, and thus further authenticated the advertising messages therein (Jamieson, 1992). Furthermore, staged events were employed to create news "sound bites" and photo opportunities that were coordinated with paid advertising in order to dominate the airwaves on both congressional and statewide levels.

By 1988, as voters cited televised political advertising as their main source of information (Buchanan, 1991) the New Mass Media Election had moved to the presidential level. So it was that a George Bush advertising campaign was able to link Democratic candidate Michael Dukakis with escaped criminals in a fashion that devastatingly shaped public perceptions of the respective candidates' positions on law and order (Hershey, 1989).

Accordingly, 1988 post-mortems not only focused on the customary view that election news should abandon its "horse race" orientation, but also held that the media should devote critical attention to paid political advertising. Other changes occurred in local and national network news over the course of the 1992 campaign as voters, increasingly concerned about the ability of the American political system to address the faltering economy and soaring budget deficit, expressed dissatisfaction not only with the candidates and the political process, but with the news media itself. The public was disturbed by excessive sensational coverage, such as Gennifer Flowers's alleged affair with Bill Clinton, which rapidly spread from the tabloid press to mainstream news. The view was frequently expressed that the combination of commercialized political messages, sensational journalism, and abbreviated sound bites drowned out a voice for the public during democracy's defining moment, the electoral process. In June, after the Los Angeles riots, public concern escalated regarding the political process and the role of news coverage, and Ross Perot peaked in the public opinion polls. In short, 1992 brought major changes in the self-perceived role of the public, candidates, and press in the electoral process (Just et al., forthcoming).

In 1990 *Washington Post* columnist David Broder, the dean of American political writers, asked journalists to closely examine political messages as speech in order to limit or break consultant influence on the campaign process. This inaugurated the era of what has come to be called "Ad Watches" by major American newspapers. Broder also called for journalists to accept a new sense of responsibility and a willingness to focus their coverage around issues that were of concern to the public, as first measured by early public opinion polls and followed by periodic reassessments of the "public pulse" throughout the campaign. From this process, he believed, journalists might move toward the perennially expressed goal of a greater focus on coverage of issues (Broder, 1990).

From another perspective, Larry Sabato of the University of Virginia offered his own criticism that news reporters, driven by competitive pressures, had abandoned their traditional concern with balance and accuracy and were engaging in a "feeding frenzy" of dubious sensational stories, of which the Gennifer Flowers story was only the most recent example. This problem was particularly acute in the networks, as shortened airtime increased such competitive pressures (Sabato, 1992).

From a campaign perspective a reassessment was also taking place as candidates perceived what they did not consider to be a "pretty picture": frustrated journalists, newly determined not to be manipulated as they had been in the 1980s, became a persistent problem as daily exemplars of the "feeding frenzy" phenomenon. Seeking alternatives to reach voters directly, campaigns turned to the talk shows. Beginning with Bill Clinton's appearance on *Donahue* in the midst of the Gennifer Flowers controversy during the New York primary, and continuing to Ross Perot's announcement of his candidacy on *Larry King Live,* campaigns moved rapidly into yet another entertainment-oriented form of political expression.

In one sense this phenomenon was simply an extension of the New Mass Media Election of the 1980s, which had combined a less dominant role for news with advertising increasingly based on entertainment values. Yet there was a difference. To these two key elements—further decline in the role of the journalist and campaign-driven expression as entertainment—was added a new role for the public as personified by the talk-show caller. By early summer, A.M. soft news and entertainment programs such as *Good Morning America* were adding candidates and callers; by the fall, network newscasts were featuring "ordinary voters" expressing themselves in focus groups conducted by veteran network anchors Dan Rather and Peter Jennings. Jennings emerged from one of these sessions amazed at the voters' failure to understand candidate positions on even the most elementary issues (Kurtz, 1993). David Broder's call for a new form of news, more aware of and responsive to voters' real concerns, was finding important converts at the networks.

In the meantime, candidates had discovered how to take full advantage of the other major phenomenon of the 1992 election: the spread of satellite technologies and the new significance of local news, whose audience was growing as the network audience declined. Ronald Reagan had discovered the combination of satellite broadcasts and local reporters hungry for a story in the 1984 election, and beamed interviews directly from Washington to Peoria, bypassing "cynical" national network reporters. Senate and House candidates made the same discovery during the late 1980s and began to be interviewed by satellite by local news reporters from studios on Capitol Hill. In 1992, a new wrinkle emerged. On the presidential level, it began at a June conference for local journalists in Los Angeles sponsored by the Joan Shorenstein Barone Center of the John F. Kennedy School of Government at Harvard University and the *Los Angeles Times* (Kurtz, 1993). A star local reporter from WSB-TV Atlanta, Bill Nigut, asked Clinton press aide Jeff Eller if his candidate would "come into the local market to be interviewed, talk show style, by a live audience." Since some 30 percent of all local stations can now beam their programs to a group of affiliated local stations, candidates found a new way to reach a regional audience in a fashion that satisfied the public desire for a "real" (not a canned) media event. For a candidate such as Bill Clinton, who excelled in such a format, the opportunity was great. He subsequently came into the hometown studios of a number of other local stations before a live audience. The candidate as "genial host" bypassed the national press with local messages amplified by satellite feeds.

Would this bring an end to the New Mass Media Election with its limited role for in-depth televised journalism? Or did it not constitute its logical extension as candidates utilized not only national but also statewide and local outlets to reach mass audiences on a more personal basis?

We will examine the emergence of the New Mass Media Election with particular reference to the congressional and statewide races where it became pervasive in the 1980s. Its underlying theory is then compared with that of the Old Mass Media Election concept developed by political scientists Thomas Patterson and Robert McClure in 1976. We focus particularly on local news coverage of political advertising in 1992 because, along with satellite use, this augmented coverage was the principal change by the increasingly significant local stations. We will consider whether local stations' coverage of political advertising in fact provided more critical analysis of ads for accuracy and the underlying messages conveyed through such visual symbols as Willie Horton, black "death shot" pictures of opponents, or warm fuzzy pictures of a bride at her wedding. Or did coverage of political advertising focus instead on the strategic use and effectiveness of political ads while duplicating their evocative visuals, and thereby magnifying their messages?

THE EMERGENCE OF THE NEW MASS MEDIA ELECTION

Survey research and focus groups both demonstrate that political advertising can shape voters' images of candidates (West, 1993; West, Kern, and Alger, 1992). Although fundamentally different, both "Old" and "New" theories suggest that such advertising can have an impact when it resonates with salient voter affect and values (Kern and Just, 1992a; 1992b). To this end, the commercially oriented New Mass Media Election televised political messages have become increasingly personal. In the mid-1970s the political party as such disappeared from individual candidate advertisements. This coincided with the rise to prominence of television news in the electoral process. In the 1980s New Mass Media Elections, other organized political groups and institutions were also dropped from positive, but not negative, campaign advertising. The result may be a loss for the Democratic process, because it is through organized entities that voters have historically aggregated and mediated their interests and effectively engaged in politics with their power enhanced. Negative messages directed at politicians, political institutions, and even such concepts as equal employment opportunity, furthermore, have played a pivotal role in some recent American elections (Joslyn, 1984; Kern, 1989).

Competing with commercial advertising on a medium saturated with messages tailored to individual consumers, political advertising messages focus heavily on character and appeal to the solitary home viewer in highly personal ways. Truth, exaggeration, and even the occasional falsehood now commingle in a confusion of campaign messages that can, particularly on the nonpresidential level, overwhelm televised election news. More thorough daily newspaper examination of complex issues, the substance of local governance, reaches only a declining number of voters.

By the end of the 1980s, politicians were caught in a budget-related gridlock of paralyzed governance and growing public perceptions of economic decline. Virtually all were forced to raise significant campaign war chests to pay for advertising time and other campaign expenses. Yet voters at all levels were the targets of messages that focused neither on the realities of our current political dilemmas nor on any positive role for the politician in it. It was not surprising that there were frequent expressions not only of voter anger toward incumbents but also of cynicism regarding the entire electoral process.

Welcome, therefore, to the New Mass Media Election. A slightly modified *cri de coeur* from the commercial world of the 1980s—"Reach Out, Reach Out and Touch (or Knife) Someone"—is its metaphor. It largely repudiates the Old Mass Media Election of the 1960s and 1970s that dominated the airwaves and consequently the research literature for over two decades. Commercial advertising principles, rather than news values, so dictate its tone and content that most ads from the past seem both remote and ineffectual.

THE OLD MASS MEDIA ELECTION YIELDS TO THE NEW

In Thomas Patterson and Robert McClure's study of 1972 presidential level advertising and news, the dominant force on the airwaves was network news. This baleful "unseeing eye" was horse race oriented, and geared to covering "who is winning," rather than significant campaign issues. In the continuing tug of war between news media and campaigns, the news media clearly had the upper hand. Consultants and candidates shaped their strategies accordingly, and avoided rhetorically emotional and negative political ads in the belief that intensive news media scrutiny would cause them to backfire on candidates who used them (Sabato, 1981; Diamond and Bates, 1988).

The 1970s was the decade of Watergate and post–Vietnam War suspicion of government, which strengthened the investigative television reporter tradition established in the 1950s by Edward R. Murrow of CBS. Few then foresaw that the documentary investigative news effort, the *bête noire* of errant politicians, would largely fade away in the more commercially oriented buoyant 1980s of the Reagan presidency.

In its own time, broadcast news and documentaries had significantly influenced advertising genres. One-half of the data included in the Patterson and McClure study was the work of Charles Guggenheim, whose five-minute and longer documentary ads featured such scenes as 1972 Democratic presidential candidate George McGovern, seated in a working class restaurant, discussing the Vietnam War at length with blue-collar voters. Unfortunately for the future cause of reasoned political dialogue, McGovern lost overwhelmingly to the advertising style described by Patterson and McClure as "mindless emotional," as skillfully employed by presidential candidate Richard Nixon and his media consultant Roger Ailes. Guggenheim, but not Ailes, had retired from the field of political advertising by the 1980s and the more discursive longer ads were forced off the airwaves as airtime became more costly. This first occurred in commercial advertising in 1976 and soon thereafter was the rule in all political advertising except for extremely high budget campaigns (Napolitan, 1976; Kern, 1989).

In various scholarly studies made in the 1970s, which noted both the lackluster performance of network television news and its predominance, issue-oriented ads were believed to offer an antidote to network news by providing the American voter with useful information concerning policy-related campaign issues. In the Patterson and McClure presidential election study, such ads occupied four times the airtime and provided four times as much information about campaign issues as news programming. The more credible news programming, however, was still the major force on the airwaves. In this atmosphere of news media influence, a phenomenon such as negative advertising was believed to be the sole province of underfunded challengers, desperate ideological political organizations, and would-be crusaders.

Traditional election strategy in the 1960s and 1970s involved the slow tripartite evolution of a campaign. It began with positive introductory spots featuring the candidate, perhaps with his coat casually slung over his shoulder. Then began a middle period of comparative spots contrasting the candidate's background and issue positions with those of his opponent. These utilized ads that in competitive races might strike a more strident but rarely wholly negative tone. Finally, a return to positive advertising at the close of the campaign was recommended by the experts in order to give the viewer a reason to get out and vote for the aspiring candidate (Sabato, 1981).

A new pattern emerged on the state and local level in the 1980s, however, so radically different as to be properly termed the "New Mass Media

Election." It surfaced clearly on all levels in 1984, although it was little recognized amidst all the talk of Ronald Reagan's "feel-good advertising." That year was one of "feel-bad" advertising as well, beginning with the primary election campaign period on both the presidential and Congressional levels in competitive districts. Little noticed in the academic literature at that time, candidates and consultants discovered that "negative advertising works." In the 1986 midterm election the New Mass Media Election came into full bloom as more consultants and candidates applied the "lessons of 1984" in competitive state and local races around the country (Kern, 1989). In 1988 the new technologies dominated the airwaves as citizens began to cite political advertising as their major source of campaign information.

At the end of the 1980s elections were still mass media events, with the networks the preferred source of news. But now on the state and local level, commercial advertising messages rather than news values set the tone. This was compounded by problems in local news where "horse race" coverage tends to crowd out the examination of issues (Kaniss, 1991; Kern, 1989). Overall, state government news reporting is quite limited (Hess, 1990; Gormley, 1978). Reporters tend to rely heavily on established news sources, including police and fire scanners, press releases and press conferences, wire service stories and local newspapers (Kaniss, 1991). Television stations tend to have general assignment, rather than political reporters (Berkowitz, 1987; 1992) further facilitating sound-bite journalism. Large news holes and multiple daily deadlines prompt television news departments to seek out stories that are visually strong and easy to complete. Pressures to attract large audiences also create a demand for emotional and compelling visual news stories. Political stories, unlike fires and crime stories with their elements of action and suspense, frequently lack compelling visuals. Therefore, political news may be crowded out by other matters that offer more interest (Altheide, 1976; Fishman, 1978).

All of these conditions facilitate the candidate-driven election news coverage and New Mass Media Election of sound-bite journalism and emotional political advertising that became America's principal election news source (Buchanan, 1991; Kern, 1989).

WILL THE NEW MASS MEDIA ELECTION CONTINUE?

In the 1990 election and even more widely in 1992, in response to such concerns, the *Miami Herald, Los Angeles Times, Sacramento Bee, San Francisco Chronicle, Atlanta Journal-Constitution,* and *Boston Herald,* among others, assigned reporters to review all TV ads in state and local races. Some papers, including the *Washington Post* and the *New York Times,* examined races across the nation. The reviews (which came in some instances to be called "truth boxes" or "ad watches") offered a line-by-line analysis of assertions made in the ads, along with commentary on their production qualities and, in some cases, underlying symbolic meaning.

Interestingly the results of some of these critiques were used by candidates in ads to respond effectively to an opponent's negative attacks. For example, in Michigan in 1990 Republican challenger Bill Schuette attacked Democratic Senator Carl Levin with ads linking him with the savings and loan scandal and implying that Levin's votes against new warships and other weapons programs endangered American troops serving in the Middle East. Levin's response ad featured press critiques labeling the Schuette attacks as "innuendos and guilt by association." The press subsequently reported that Levin's response ads effectively defused the issue. Press critiques of media consultants also grew in magnitude, and consultants themselves sometimes became the issue. In 1984, Roger Ailes and his "slick ads" on behalf of the Illinois Republican Senate candidate had been effectively used as a major issue by the successful campaign of Democrat Paul Simon. In 1990, Ailes again became controversial together with Democratic consultant Robert Squier (Kurtz, 1993).

Some consultants expressed the view that the press watchdog effort had an impact on their efforts, forcing them to verify charges more carefully and make changes. Early in the 1990 campaign cycle, David Broder of the *Washington Post* had critiqued ads for their "increasingly sophisticated insinuation" and called journalists to the task of a major critical effort. The week before the election he argued cogently that press critiques had indeed affected the course of several elections. In Texas, both WFAA-TV in Dallas and KVUE-TV in Austin joined the print press in scrutinizing political advertisements in the extremely negative gubernatorial race. These were two of three major television stations that made such an effort (the other was KRON-TV in San Francisco).

Given this fact, some consultants questioned the value of the newspapers' efforts. For pollster Paul Maslin: "A newspaper piece saying whether an ad is truthful or not that's seen by 30 percent of the public isn't enough to reduce the actual impact of a TV ad seen by 80 percent of the public" (Rothenberg, 1990b). Media consultant Frank Greer commented: "The press [in critiquing political ads] gives us ammunition we can use on the air. Most people won't read or see one article, but we can run it on the air and run the hell out of it" (Rothenberg, 1990a). With ads in Congressional races not receiving the critical attention devoted to ads in state races, a significant proportion of candidate ads in 1990 were simply not examined by the press. And few of these were positive ads, although they too serve an important purpose for both incumbents and challengers.

In 1992, in response to criticism of the news media's failure to critique the 1988 Willie Horton ad, among others, the examination of political ads became a priority not only for the leading newspapers, but for the national networks as well. Cable News Network, with the help of a major Markle Foundation grant, also inaugurated a program, *Inside Politics,* including regular critiques of political advertising headed by former *Wall Street Journal* reporter Brooks Jackson. What changes would emerge on local television? Would it take a more proactive role in election coverage, reflecting its increased role as an information source? Would a larger number of stations follow the pattern of the handful of local stations that critiqued political advertising in 1992? Would the focus be on analyzing accuracy and symbolic meaning as well as the effectiveness of political advertising, thereby challenging the candidate-driven New Mass Media Election?

NEWS DIRECTORS POLL

We decided to determine news directors' views on this subject, as well as, more generally, how their 1992 national, statewide, and local campaign coverage differed from that of 1988. We decided that we would interview the news directors at local stations, because they are responsible for news policy. Literature suggests that they are more innovatively conservative, at least compared to local television news reporters. News directors have typically worked in news 14 years longer than broadcast reporters and producers. They have been less concerned with the criticism that local news may stress the wrong features of a political campaign, such as the horse race or "hoopla," and more often succumb to ratings pressure and allow "a lot of non-news stories to get on local news because they are so easy to do 'live'" (Smith, 1988). A conservative approach to change might therefore be expected. Still, in early 1992 satellite technologies were offering them an opportunity to try new approaches to political coverage, and viewers had more competitive choices, including cable, new independent stations, and lower-power stations. Hence news directors might be expected to forgo their conservative inclinations in the interest of attracting and maintaining audiences. Accordingly, we developed a questionnaire to determine whether news directors planned any major changes in their coverage in 1992 as compared with 1988. After the election we followed this with in-depth interviews with a randomly selected subsample to determine whether they followed through on their stated plans.

Methodological Overview

A mail survey of television news directors in the United States and its territories was conducted in the spring of 1992 to find out how local news directors planned to cover the 1992 election. We chose a mail survey to reach as many news directors as possible and to encourage honest responses (Babbie, 1992; Dillman, 1978). The population of all commercial television stations listed in the *Broadcasting Yearbook* (1991) (excluding religious, home shopping, and satellite stations, which simply carry the signal of another station) was included to ensure representation of stations of all sizes from all regions of the country, including Puerto Rico and Guam. Rosters of news directors were obtained from the Radio-Television News Directors Association to cross-check the accuracy of the listings in *Broadcasting Yearbook* (1991) .

One pretest was conducted in January 1992 to ensure that items were clear and correctly understood and that the questionnaire could be completed in less than eight minutes. Two mailings were then conducted during the 1992 primary season to obtain the greatest rate of response (Dillman, 1978).[1] The first mailing was planned to arrive at stations on or near the date of the New Hampshire primary. A second questionnaire was sent to nonrespondents on or near the date of the "Super Tuesday" primaries. Reminder postcards were also sent after each of the two stages of surveys. The mailings were sent to coincide with these particular events because it seemed probable that news directors would have considered or decided on their coverage strategies by that point.

Out of the 1,008 stations queried, 397 questionnaires were completed and returned, producing a 39-percent response rate. Seventy of these stations notified the researchers that they had either abandoned their news effort or had never engaged in news coverage; their responses were therefore not tabulated in subsequent analyses. Of the 327 usable cases, 83 percent were from stations affiliated with the three major broadcasting networks, 8 percent were from public television stations, and 8 percent were from independent television stations. Less than one percent were from local cable companies that produce local television news. Eighty-one (25%) were from stations in the top 30 markets, 128 (39%) were from medium-sized markets between market numbers 31 and 100, and 114 (35%) were from stations in small markets not in the top 100.

The Questionnaire and Statistical Procedures Employed

The questionnaire contained 51 questions dealing with general reporting and analysis issues, plans to critique political advertising, and plans to take advantage of the new satellite technologies. This analysis will focus specifically on the advertising questions. Fifteen questions (variables) concerned how news managers planned to address the question of covering political advertising. Ten of these items asked whether news managers planned to report on the accuracy and underlying themes of advertising aired by presidential, state, and local candidates as well as that which is largely issue oriented, on either the national (e.g., abortion) or local (a proposition campaign) level. Five variables queried whether news directors planned to report on the effectiveness of advertising in these same categories. Each of the questions offered a forced five-point Likert scale with values ranging from "definitely will" to "definitely not." Completed questions were then coded and sorted based on market size.

After appropriate steps were taken to eliminate multicollinearity in the data, principal axis factor analysis was performed. The analysis revealed the presence of five factors accounting for 60 percent of the variance. The political advertising items loaded on the first and largest factor indicated political advertising was indeed an important issue for the news directors.[2] Then, each item was cross-tabulated by market size (1 to 30 = large; 31 to 100 = medium; and 101 to 214 = small).

The items dealing with political advertising produced significant findings. News directors expressed a broad interest in analyzing and reporting on political advertising. By wide margins, they believed that political advertising was "manipulative" and overused by voters who "rely too much on messages designed to persuade rather than inform."[3] Fifty-seven percent indicated that they planned to increase their coverage of advertising produced by state and local candidates. Thirty-eight percent said they planned to analyze political ads about presidential candidates and national issues.

There were major differences based on market size. Large market stations indicated a stronger interest in analyzing the accuracy of the political advertising for all three classes of candidates: presidential, state, and local. Smaller stations expressed an interest in focusing primarily on advertising in local races. For example, 59 percent of the large market stations planned to report on the accuracy of advertising by presidential candidates, 42 percent of the medium-sized stations planned such analysis, and only 25 percent of the small market stations expressed such plans. Chi-square analysis suggested a significant difference in this area based on market size (Chi-square = 39.5; df = 8; p < .0000). A similar pattern held for plans to cover the accuracy of national issues-based advertising, producing a difference based on market size (Chi-square = 42.4; df = 8; p < .0000). These results indicate that although stations in large markets expressed an interest in moving into the area of covering presidential-candidate and national issues–based advertising, medium and small market stations were less interested in doing so, following the traditional view that examination of presidential candidates and national issues should be the terrain of the national, not the local, news media.

Such a striking difference based on market size did not emerge in the area of planning increased coverage of the accuracy of advertisements for local candidates. Similar to the findings above, 64 percent of the large market news directors reported plans to cover local candidate advertising. However, 61 percent of the news directors at medium-sized stations and 55 percent of the small-market news directors also planned to cover such advertising by local candidates. The difference based on market size is not statistically significant. Hence, it appears that larger stations, with greater resources, planned to provide across-the-board coverage of political advertising, whereas small and medium-sized stations appeared most interested in covering the accuracy of local candidates' ads.

On the issue of covering the underlying messages of presidential candidates' ads, 47 percent of the large market stations expressed "definite" or "probable" plans to do so, while another 33 percent reported that they "may" provide such coverage. By contrast, only 25 percent of the medium-sized stations and 16 percent of the small market stations expressed "definite" or "probable" plans to provide coverage of underlying messages by the presidential contenders. Chi-square analysis again suggested a difference based on market size (Chi-square = 47; df = 8; p < .0000). A similar pattern held for plans to cover underlying messages of national issues–based advertising (Chi-square = 36.4; df = 8; p < .0000).

Unlike coverage of the accuracy of local political candidates' ads, large-market news directors were more interested in examining the underlying messages of local candidates than their medium and small market counterparts. For example, 50 percent of the large market compared to 32 percent of the medium and 35 percent of the small market stations planned such coverage. Chi-square analysis again suggested a difference based on market size (Chi-square = 23.9; df = 8; p < .01).

Finally, a familiar pattern with respect to market size recurs with the questions concerning plans to examine the effectiveness of political advertising by presidential candidates. In this area, large market stations again led the way with 44 percent of them planning such analysis. By contrast, 20 percent of the medium-sized markets planned such coverage. Finally,

15 percent of the small market stations reported such plans. Chi-square analysis indicated a statistical significance based on market size (Chi-square = 36.7; df = 8; p < .0000). A similar pattern was also found for plans to cover the effectiveness of national issues–based advertising (Chi-square = 29.0; df = 8; p < .001).

Concerning plans to cover the effectiveness of local candidate advertisements, large stations again expressed the greatest interest in this type of reporting with 42 percent planning to expand coverage in this area. Twenty-three percent of the medium-sized markets also planned to increase their efforts. Interestingly, 28 percent of the small market stations, five percent more than medium-sized stations, also planned to expand their attention to the effectiveness of advertisements by local candidates. Chi-square analysis suggested a statistically significant difference (Chi-square = 17.9; df = 8; p < .05). Finally, a statistically significant difference was also found for the question of plans to evaluate the effectiveness of local issues–based advertising, with large market stations planning the most coverage (Chi-square = 21.9; df = 8; p < .01).

The news directors' plans to develop greater coverage of political advertising came in conjunction with a similarly significant plan to use more satellites. Forty-one percent of the large market stations, 25 percent of the medium-sized market stations, and 11 percent of the small market stations planned to rely more on new technologies such as satellites. There was also a less pronounced but nonetheless significant trend to offer more coverage of candidates whenever they appeared within the station's own market and to focus more on coverage of important state and local issues (Wicks and Kern, 1993).

POSTELECTION INTERVIEWS

Did the stations follow through on their plans to cover political advertising? Was their focus, in fact, on analyzing accuracy and symbolic meaning as well as the effectiveness of political advertising, thereby challenging the candidate-centered pattern of the New Mass Media Election? Did they find that the effect of their efforts would be fodder for the mill of the political campaigns that would air segments of their ad critiques in their own political ads? How did they feel about their overall experience covering political advertising in 1992?

These questions were asked after the election. We decided to conduct postelection telephone interviews with news directors selected at random from the pool of interviewees from the spring. We also decided to sacrifice the possibility of generalizing based on the large survey research sample for the richness of depth interview data. A sample of 48 valid cases emerged. Thirty-six of these (75%) were interviewed for 10 to 15 minutes during the weeks of January 11–15 and February 22–26, 1993. The market-size breakdown of this sample resembled that of the original population of respondents: 7 (19%) were from major markets, 13 (36%) from medium markets, and 16 (44%) from small market stations. Following the pattern of the spring survey, the data was analyzed by market size.

Many of the same closed-ended political advertising questions that we asked in the spring were again asked in the fall; this time, however, we used open-ended questions designed to stimulate open-ended discourse (Neumann, Just, and Crigler, 1992). Concerning political advertising we asked: "How would you evaluate the experience that you had with the coverage of political advertising? Could you describe some of the major issues that emerged? How did you deal with them?" We also asked whether they had run regular "Ad Watch" features, and whether political consultant Frank Greer's dictum had held true that candidates would win any "ad wars" battle with the news media, because candidates can reach a greater audience with their ad critiques than the media.

In this chapter we report on the results of the medium-sized and small market interviews, focusing particularly on statewide and local elections. We focus particularly on the results of the closed-ended questions, and offer illustrations from the open-ended discourse concerning issues of concern to the news directors.

Although the postelection interview sample was small, the results indicate that for many the major changes described in our analysis of the spring survey were implemented.

First, the medium- and small-market news directors had indicated that they did not intend to compete with the networks and the national media in the area of covering presidential advertising. Close to two-thirds of them reported that they did not develop their own coverage of presidential ads, stating that these were covered by newspapers and the national electronic media, including their parent networks.

In a second major area, coverage of the accuracy of political advertising, change also occurred as planned in the spring survey. The spring 1992 sample firmly indicated that the news directors in markets of all sizes had plans in this area. Sixty-nine percent of the postelection in-depth interviewees in the medium-sized markets said that they carried out their plans. Fifty-four percent of the small-market stations said they had also done so.

Also, as expected, underlying messages and advertising effectiveness of statewide and local political advertising were less often examined than was accuracy. Thirty-eight percent of the medium-sized market and 15 percent of the small market stations interviewed in the postelection period reported covering underlying symbolic messages, while 38 percent of the medium-sized and 25 percent of the small market stations said they ran stories examining the effectiveness of advertising.

From this analysis, it is clear that many local television news directors reported that they carried out their 1992 plans to cover political advertising. Most of them, however, did not air a regular "Ad Watch" feature. And, although it is clear that a significant number of stations attempted coverage of political advertising, it must also be pointed out that in comparison with the actual number of stories that news directors said that they aired in the various categories, political advertising still dominated the airwaves in total airtime, surpassing the ad critiques. Most of the stations that produced stories said that they produced between five and ten over the course of the whole election. These stories might offer their own reporter's analysis of the ads, or feature a local professor or, in one case, local citizens' groups offering an ad critique. Such stories represented a clear voice for change in local news coverage.

Although few news directors reported that their stories were used as the subject of political ads (8% of the medium-sized and 12% of the small market stations), for a news director such as Al Zobel of KHGI-TV, Kearney, Nebraska, who experienced this phenomenon, his first reaction to the open-ended question concerning his experiences with political advertising this year was "gut-wrenching." KHGI examined both the accuracy and underlying messages of local political ads, and, like many of the news directors this year, Mr. Zobel was faced with such difficult decisions as how to cover anti-abortion ads depicting dead fetuses.

Other reactions to the open-ended questions are worth pointing out. Two represent points on the extreme ends of political advertising coverage by local stations in 1992. WSTM-TV in Syracuse, New York, a medium-sized market station (ADI 68), was one of the most active stations reached.[4] The airwaves were flooded throughout the electoral season with negative advertising from a competitive and particularly nasty New York Senate race involving, in the primary, Democrats Liz Holzman, Geraldine Ferraro, and Bob Abrams. WSTM aired a regular Ad Watch feature, with at least four or five stories in the primary and 20 in the general election dealing with accuracy, underlying messages, and strategy. The news director's overall experience? "We had no impact on the tenor of the campaign. The media was critical of the statewide Senate campaign, but to no avail. . . . There were no real issues, just lots of mudslinging." Yet because of this major difference in his 1992 coverage as compared with 1988: "Our news coverage was much better. We took more time to examine what's being said by candidates and to hold these people accountable."

KNDO-TV in Yakima, Washington, was a small market station (ADI 126) that produced one story critiquing negative campaigning. An ultimately successful female Senate candidate, Patty Murray, was on the ballot. So, according to news director Shelley Swanke, "we had the Year of the Woman from a statewide perspective." With redistricting and "a lot of incumbents not running for reelection, there was a lot of interest in the elections this year, and candidates came into our area making appearances," which her station covered. She also produced a story that highlighted negative advertising because, she said, "there was a candidate who said that he was going to campaign in a clean fashion and he didn't. Our story about his campaigning analyzed statements which he made in an ad. We ran a point-counterpoint: here's what he said, here are the facts." The major issues that emerged in this regard? "He went ballistic on us. He didn't pull his advertising, though."

It is important to note that the experiences of the news directors were predictably diverse, representing the wide range of political and economic environments within which they worked.

CONCLUSION

We have described the growth of a New Mass Media Election format that resulted in increasingly negative, emotional, and commercially driven political advertising—becoming the voters' main source of election information.

The election year of 1992 was a major year of change for both the national and the local press. In the area of local television journalism, two major changes occurred: satellite-based reporting and the attempt to cover political advertising in an analytical fashion. In this latter area, a significant number of local news directors planned and implemented coverage that focused not just on strategy or effectiveness, but on accuracy, and in some cases underlying symbolic meaning as well. In undertaking this type of coverage, local news took an important step in the direction of establishing a more significant role for local televised journalism in the electoral process.

NOTES

1. Reminder postcards were also sent to nonrespondents after the questionnaires were sent out.

2. The political advertising factor had an eigenvalue of 7.6 percent and accounted for 32 percent of the variance.

3. The question was worded as follows: "Some news managers think that politicians are trying to manipulate voters by hiding messages in the campaign advertising. For example, some journalists thought several messages were conveyed in the 'Willie Horton' ad. Do you have plans for any of the following?"

4. ADI is a marketing and advertising term standing for "area of dominant influence." The nation is divided into media markets that are ranked from 1 (New York) to approximately 144.

REFERENCES

Altheide, David. 1976. *Creating Reality: How Television News Distorts Events.* Beverly Hills, CA: Sage.

Babbie, Earl. 1992. *The Practice of Social Research,* 6th ed. Belmont, CA: Wadsworth.

Berkowitz, David. 1987. "TV News Sources and News Channels: A Study in Agenda Building." *Journalism Quarterly* 64, no. 1: 61–95.

———. 1992. "Non-Routine News and Newswork: Exploring What-a-Story." *Journal of Communication* 42, no. 1: 84–95.

Broder, David. 1990. "Putting Sanity Back into Elections." *Washington Post,* Jan. 21.

Buchanan, Bruce. 1991. *Electing a President: The Markle Commission Research on Campaign 88.* Austin: University of Texas Press.

Diamond, Edwin, and Stephen S. Bates. 1988. *The Spot: The Rise of Political Advertising on Television,* 2d ed. Cambridge, MA: MIT Press.

Dillman, D. 1978. *Mail and Telephone Surveys: The Total Design Method.* New York: Wiley & Sons.

Fishman, Mark. 1978. "Crime Waves as Ideology." *Social Problems* 25: 531–43.

Gormley, W. T., Jr. 1978. "Television Coverage of State Government." *Public Opinion Quarterly* 42, no. 3:354–59.

Hershey, Marjorie. 1989. "The Campaign and the Media." In *The Election of 1988,* Gerald M. Pomper, ed. Chatham, NJ: Chatham House.

Hess, Stephen. 1990. "Washington as Seen in Local Television News." Paper presented at the Annual Meeting of the American Political Science Association, San Francisco, August 31.

Jamieson, Kathleen. 1992. Lecture at the Joan Shorenstein Barone Center on Press, Politics, and Public Policy, Harvard University.

Joslyn, Richard. 1984. *Mass Media and Elections.* Reading, MA: Addison-Wesley.

Just, Marion, Ann Crigler, Dean Alger, Timothy Cook, Montague Kern, and Darrell West. *Constructing Campaigns: The 1992 Presidential Election in Prime Time* (forthcoming).

Kaid, Lynda Lee. 1991. "The Legitimization of Political Advertising." Paper presented at the Annual Meeting of the International Communication Association, Dublin.

Kaniss, Phyllis. 1991. *Making Local News.* Chicago: University of Chicago Press.

Kern, Montague. 1989. *30-Second Politics: Political Advertising in the Eighties.* New York: Praeger.

————. 1991. "The 'New' Mass Media Election on the Congressional and Statewide Levels: Will 80s Patterns Persist into the 90s?" Paper presented at the Annual Meeting of the International Communication Association, Chicago, Illinois.

Kern, Montague, and Marion Just. 1992a. "The Focus Group Methods, Ads, News and the Construction of Candidate Images." Paper presented at the Annual Meeting of the American Political Science Association.

————. 1992b. "News, Advertising and the Construction of Candidate Images: A Campaign Simulation." Paper presented at the Annual Meeting of the New England Political Science Association, Providence, Rhode Island.

Kurtz, Howard. 1993. *The Media Circus.* New York: Random House.

Lacy, Stephen, and James Bernstein. 1992. "The Impact of Competition and Market Size on the Assembly Cost of Local Television News." *Mass Communication Review* 19, nos. 1 and 2: 41–48.

Napolitan, Joseph. 1976. "Media Costs and Effects in Political Campaigns." *Annals* (American Academy of Political and Social Science) 427, Sept., 119.

Neumann, Russell, Marion Just, and Ann Crigler. 1992. *Common Knowledge: News and the Construction of Political Meaning.* Chicago: University of Chicago Press.

Patterson, Thomas E. 1980. *The Mass Media Election: How Americans Change Their President.* New York: Praeger.

Patterson, Thomas E., and Robert D. McClure. 1976. *The Unseeing Eye.* New York: G. P. Putnam.

Pfau, Michael, and Michael Burgoon. 1988. "Inoculation in Political Campaign Communication." *Human Communication Research* 15: 91–111.

Pfau, Michael, Roxanne Parrott, and Bridget Lindquist. 1992. "An Expectancy Theory Explanation of the Effectiveness of Political Attack Television Spots: A Case Study." *Journal of Applied Communication Research* 20, no 3: 235–54.

Rothenberg, Randall. 1990a. "Newspapers Watch What People Watch in the TV Campaign." *National Journal,* Oct. 27, 2595.

————. 1990b. "The Press Plays Referee on Campaign Ads." *New York Times,* Nov. 4, A1.

Sabato, Larry J. 1981. *The Rise of the Political Consultants: New Ways of Winning Elections.* New York: Basic Books.

————. 1992. *Feeding Frenzy.* New York: Free Press.

Smith, Carl. 1988. "News Critics, Newsworkers and Local Television News." *Journalism Quarterly* 65, no. 2: 99–102.

West, Darrell M. 1993. *Air Wars: Television Advertising in Election Campaigns, 1952–92.* Washington, DC: Congressional Quarterly Press.

West, Darrell M., Montague Kern, and Dean Alger. 1992. "Political Advertising and Ad Watches in the 1992 Presidential Nominating Campaign." Paper presented at the Annual Meeting of the American Political Science Association, Chicago, Illinois.

Wicks, Robert H., and Montague Kern. 1993. "A Shift Toward More Reporting on Political Advertising and Use of Satellite-Based Technologies by Local Television News in Election Coverage." Paper prepared for the Annual Meeting of the International Communication Association, Washington, DC.

9

The Electronic Town Hall in Campaign '92: Interactive Forum or Carnival of Buncombe?

Dan Nimmo

"When people look back at this year and ask, 'What really happened?' I think two-way communication on TV between the candidate and the people will be the story," Bill Clinton told interviewers a few days after his election (Golson and Range, 1992a, 15). Small wonder. It was just such two-way communication that had, in his mind, salvaged his campaign at a bleak moment months earlier.

"Nobody wanted to talk about the issues anymore," he said of his travails in the early primary contests. Dogged by charges of marital infidelity and draft evasion, Clinton sought to refocus his campaign.

We'd done a couple of local town-hall meetings in New Hampshire, and there was a huge disconnect between questions the press was always asking me and those the voters were asking. [So] I just took that [town hall] idea to television in the final weeks of the primary. (Golson and Range, 1992b, 17–19)

Thus was born the electronic town hall in Campaign '92. Clinton went on to exploit the town meeting in almost every primary state. And, on February 20, potential presidential candidate Ross Perot, on *Larry King Live,* tried the format. Asked by King if he was going to run, Perot said "No." "Flat no?" asked King. Perot avoided a direct answer by mixing metaphors: "You, in effect, have sort of an electronic town hall, so I think we can serve the country by really getting down in the trenches." Perot entered King's "electronic town hall" six times in Campaign '92. Finally, President George Bush, after earlier calling such forums "wacky," relaxed on the White House lawn before cameras of *CBS This Morning* on July 1, answering questions of tourists in what the show's co-hosts labeled a live "town hall meeting."

This chapter examines the electronic town hall in the 1992 presidential campaign. It looks first at the uses, functions, and variations of this direct-access, interactive tool of TV campaigning, as well as the pros and cons regarding such "New News" (Daley, 1992, 4-3). Second, we examine the origins of the tradition of town meetings in American politics with an eye toward sorting fact and fiction. Third, drawing upon an analysis of video-tapes and transcripts of a sample of 28 town hall meetings conducted in the presidential campaign, we explore whether the format resulted in forums of deliberation between citizens and candidates. Finally, we raise questions regarding future electronic town halls in U.S. elections.

MEET THE PEOPLE, BEAT THE PRESS

"The audience is part of the show. And that's the whole point. It's a television show. Our television show. And the press has no business on the set. And god-dammit, Harry, the problem is that this is an electronic election." These words were uttered about the electronic town hall not in 1992 but in 1968 (McGinnis, 1969, 66). They came not from Bill Clinton's TV advisers (Hollywood producers Harry Thomason and Linda Bloodworth-Thomason of *Designing Women, Evening Shade,* and *Hearts Afire*) but from a Richard Nixon handler (28-year-old Roger Ailes, then executive producer of the *Mike Douglas Show*). Ailes's remarks were as pertinent in 1992 as they had been six presidential election campaigns earlier.

In 1968, campaign strategists for Richard Nixon designed the "Hills-boro Format," named after Hillsboro, New Hampshire, where Nixon announced his candidacy employing the device. Nixon faced a panel of citizens and fielded seemingly unrehearsed questions in an engaging, informal style. Videotaped and then edited, the programs aired as half-hour town hall style meetings. Criticisms of editing the shows led to live videocasts. The technique proved so successful in portraying the "New Nixon" that Ailes exploited it throughout the campaign. He placed Nixon before a studio audience of 300 people, seeming to respond spontaneously to questions from a panel of seemingly ordinary citizens. He added also a seeming icon, noted football coach Bud Wilkinson who presided as host. We know today that the "seemings" were carefully contrived: the audience stacked, the panel carefully "balanced," Nixon's responses crafted. Wilkinson was less an impartial moderator than a cheerleader.

One other "seeming" came into play: this live town meeting seemed to be a live news event, not a paid commercial. It presented the "New Nixon" as warm, caring, capable of establishing intimate personal relations with voters, informed, enthusiastic, and worthy of applause and deference. Moreover, the Hillsboro Format bypassed journalists. Indeed, journalists were locked out of the TV studio, forced to watch on monitors the same "seemings" as Joe Six-Pack in Peoria. Certainly there would be a Joe Six-Pack watching, for Ailes insisted that the program be entertaining, not boring.

The contemporary electronic town hall of Campaign '92 had the same fascination and practicality for political candidates as it did in 1968. One thing differed. After he popularized it in New Hampshire, Bill Clinton and other candidates found they no longer paid for broadcast time. The town meeting format popped up in candidate appearances on *Donahue, Larry King Live, Today, CBS This Morning, Good Morning America, Peter Jennings Reporting, Nashville Now,* even MTV's *Choose or Lose.* TV producers eagerly cooperated with the candidates' media consultants to put the polish of the celebrity on the ambitions of the politician.

The TV town halls of 1992 had links to more than Nixon's Hillsboro Format; they were also closely related to a staple of radio programming, the listener call-in show (the "talk-radio" format). Indeed, when not appearing in video town forums, the presidential candidates could be found on the radio dial—Bill Clinton, Jerry Brown, and others as callers, George Bush as a guest on Rush Limbaugh's popular network program and on numerous regional call-ins while phoning in from Air Force One. Moreover, the electronic town hall format also borrowed from talk radio's most notable televised imitator, C-SPAN's viewer call-ins with its 15 calls per hour, more than 17,000 calls in 1991. (See Chapter 10 for Janette Muir's discussion of C-SPAN in 1992.)

So enamored with the electronic town hall were presidential candidates that two of them, Clinton and Perot, promised to institutionalize them as a means of keeping in touch with the people when elected president. Perot's plans were the most ambitious. They called for the president, congressional leaders, and selected experts to set forth the essentials of major issues on national TV. Viewers, organized by congressional district, would express their policy choices by dialing a toll-free (800) number, pressing a button on an interactive TV hookup, or mailing in a postcard. Walter Goodman, television critic of the *New York Times,* wrote of Perot's proposal, "Mr. Perot seems to be dreaming of a politics of consensus, with the American orchestra playing in tune under the direction of Maestro Perot like a 'Great Performances' special" (1992, H25).

The town meetings of 1992 were not always national. Candidates also took part in televised town halls with local, regional, or special-interest audiences. For example, to preempt potential damage he might suffer in the key state of Texas by the GOP's ad campaign, "September Storm," a blitz of anti-Clinton spots, the Democratic candidate appeared on August 25 on the CBS Dallas affiliate for a "Face to Face with Bill Clinton." An ad hoc network carried the town meeting into 8 states via 25 TV stations. Questions originated from studio audiences in Dallas, St. Louis, Austin, and Birmingham. Clinton's aides also actively sought to place him before specific voter groups through appearances on The Nashville Network (calling hogs), Lifetime, and Black Entertainment Television. The frequency of Clinton's performances in town halls moved Dana Summers, editorial cartoonist of the Orlando *Sentinel*, to depict a couple, their son, and dog watching a TV set blaring out a Clinton question, "O.K. Big Bird, Bert and Ernie, gather round now. Who knows what the word 'vote' means?" The irritated father responds, "Sheesh! Is there a TV show Clinton hasn't done?" (Summers, 1992, 30-A).

Interactive TV was also exploited by candidates who did not make it through to the general election. In his underfinanced challenge for the Democratic nomination, for example, Jerry Brown utilized quasi–town meeting formats on local public access channels. *We the People,* half-hour programs, had several variations; one was a mini-telethon publicizing Brown's 800 number to solicit funds (Carter and Beiler, 1992, 24). And, using satellite feeds as a basis for interactive TV, candidates appeared simultaneously before issue groups gathered in various locales throughout the nation both to hear the political pitch and to ask questions.

As a feature of the 1992 presidential election season the engineered town hall meeting provoked questions and judgments regarding what the format was doing for and to the body politic. *TV Guide,* ever raising and lowering the mercury in its unflagging efforts to measure the barometric trends of popular television, "hesitantly" gave "cheers" to talk shows for becoming the "whistle stops" of the 1992 campaign. The "unbroken stretches" of video time were a welcome relief to sound bites and 30-second commercials, said the TV weekly. But, "we'll reserve judgment on how much of a circus this becomes" (1992, 7). A week later the magazine's editorial judgment might still be reserved, but the verdict of a feature article was not. In an interview with former uncle (now gray eminence) Walter Cronkite, *TV Guide* asked, "What about politics by talk show? *Donahue, Larry King Live,* the rest. Should candidates be able to avoid journalists in favor of callers and show hosts?" Cronkite responded that "everybody" in the media was asking that question. Moreover, he warned, "we're going to demand answers." Cronkite's judgment was that, "It is a phenomenon of the moment." And, he stressed (his emphasis), "*It will not stand!* There will be a backlash." In the meantime, he urged that talk-show appearances "be taken apart, analyzed, put under the microscope: what did he *really* say on this?" (Range, 1992, 16).

Some of those who accepted the challenge and asked what candidates were saying on interactive town hall TV came away unimpressed. For example, in an October 12, 1992, editorial the *Dallas Morning News* voiced a complaint that many in print journalism had about the town hall format. Noting that the three presidential candidates had done a "lot of talking" on *Larry King Live, Donahue,* and *Oprah,* the editorial added, "it's impossible to overlook that much of their verbiage has emanated in response to singularly polite questions." Was this development, the editorial continued, good or bad? The short answer was, "not necessarily bad, but it could certainly be better." And "better" would mean having interviewers "asking relevant and intelligent questions" rather than conducting "softball interviews." "Better" does happen "when the phones start ringing and audience members begin raising their hands." Then, "the unmistakable authority of the *vox populi* is suddenly present."

Along with political correspondents and editorial writers, media consultants and TV critics added their pros and cons on the innovation wrought by the 1992 electronic town halls. Democratic consultant Robert Squier, in contradiction to Cronkite's view, opined that viewer interactions with presidential candidates should become a staple of modern campaigning: "What could be better than the candidates answering real questions from real people?" (Bark, 1992a, 9-A). ABC's TV critic Jeff Greenfield also extolled the merits of the new formats: "nontraditional campaign forums . . . have become major political arenas, giving candidates greater access and voters more direct information than they have ever had before" (1992, 11).

Setting aside for the moment the question of how much citizens benefited from electronic town halls in Campaign '92, there is little doubt that at least two personae in the theatrical halls did so a great deal. As far as the candidates were concerned they managed to garner free airtime on TV programs with access to target audiences not easily reached by conventional modes of campaigning such as rallies, speeches, interviews on nightly news shows and weekly forums such as *This Week with David Brinkley,* or via paid TV advertising. So great was the cash value of the electronic forum in 1992 that Bill Clinton canceled a half-hour paid political program on NBC scheduled for Sunday, June 21, on grounds that it was pointless to pay money for what was being given away free. Said a representative of a firm handling Clinton's time-buys: "Due to the campaign's successful free media strategy, it feels the half-hour program is unnecessary at this time" (Bark, 1992b, 18-A).

Moreover, candidates could exploit interactive TV without facing embarrassing or potentially hostile questions from reporters probing sensitive areas. This proved particularly useful to Ross Perot who, having shadow-boxed his way through the primary season using *Larry King Live* as a forum, was able to keep his phantom candidacy alive after "dropping" out of the campaign in midsummer by returning to the same venue.

In short, Perot and all candidates reaped the benefits of the Hillsboro Format.

In addition, for the first time interactive TV formats in presidential campaigning helped candidates exploit the burgeoning audiences supplied by cable TV. As political scientist Samuel Popkin, an adviser to Bill Clinton, pointed out in an interview, "If the network news had held the same central dominant position in American culture as it did in 1972, you would not be seeing people spending as much time on talk shows" (Kolbert, 1992, 2-E). But in 1992 the combined ratings for the network evening news shows—*ABC's World News Tonight, CBS Evening News,* and *NBC Nightly News*—declined to their lowest point since 1961. On an average, 56 percent of all TV viewers watched nightly network news in 1992 compared with 76 percent who did so in 1980. On the other hand, 60 percent of American households now have cable television.

Thus, whereas the battlefields of presidential campaigns in the 1960s through the 1980s were the TV networks, in the 1990s major conflicts aired on syndicated and cable TV grounds. This has made a second set of personae beneficiaries of the electronic town hall. That was the generation of TV phenomena who act as hosts of talk shows, shaping the pace and content of the palaver while building audience ratings and bringing in advertisers' dollars. Phil Donahue made the point, perhaps via self-promotion, when he told a reporter:

Since Kennedy, the only outlets electronically for the presidential process were Huntley, Brinkley, and Cronkite. I mean no disrespect, but now with the television industry having changed, with a picture for every letter in the alphabet on your TV screen now, the process has to change, and I think that's a good thing. (Kolbert, 1992, 2-E)

Yes, a "good thing" for Phil Donahue, Larry King, Oprah Winfrey, and the moderators of *Today, Good Morning America,* and *CBS This Morning*—but what is the verdict for *vox populi*? In de Tocqueville's essay, "From Town Halls to Television Studios," he wrote: "Only the selectmen have the right to call a town meeting . . . [and] there explain the need felt; they state the means available for the purpose, how much it will cost" (1969, 65).

If Walt Whitman deserves accolades for being the chief poetic voice of Democracy in *Leaves of Grass* and *Democratic Vistas,* Norman Rockwell deserves equal billing for his numerous sketches and paintings forever preserved in reprints of covers of the *Saturday Evening Post*. It was Rockwell who reminded us often of the simple virtues of direct, popular

Democracy, often depicted in pictorial representations of the New England town meeting.

It has been three-and-one-half centuries since the adoption of the "Body of Liberties" by the Great and General Court of Massachusetts in 1641 that established the town meeting as a governing form—depicted by Alexis de Tocqueville in realistic ways, later to be rendered by Rockwell with romantic nostalgia. The "Body of Liberties" asserted the liberty of "every man" to attend town meetings and "either by speech or writing to move any lawful, reasonable, and material question." "Every man" was restricted to the adult male population; moreover there were distinctions between freemen and men who were not free. As the practice evolved participation extended to all "qualified voters," thus broadening the base of local politics (Sly, 1930, 48–49). Tocqueville wrote of the unique quality of the exercise in direct Democracy: "The body of electors . . . gives directions in everything beyond the simple, ordinary execution of the laws of the state . . . a state of affairs . . . contrary to our ideas and our habits" (1969, 64).

With the growth of population and extended complexities of governing, electors giving "directions in everything beyond the simple execution of the laws" became, if not impossible, impractical. Hence, "representative town meetings" supplanted the original form in many areas (Sly, 1930, 165–66). Yet, even in many of those areas where they possessed no legislative authority, annual town meetings continued to be held as forums for the exchange of views between representatives and constituents. As generations have come and gone, with the help of Rockwell paintings and civics textbooks, with some inaccuracy, we fondly look back on the legendary town meeting as providing a forum of self-governance where *vox populi* issued the mandate. Here was an institution of direct Democracy that encouraged individual expression and public accountability.

We forget, however, that the town meeting was more than a mere forum. The town meeting was a device to solve a problem and, thereby, was a paradox. The problem was how to govern peacefully without force or fraud. It was brought about by the fact that "the town was the locus of effective authority, yet the town hardly had such authority" (Zuckerman, 1970, 92). Towns possessed relatively small measures of coercive judicial power. Local constables could *command* but they could not *demand*. There were courts of law, but the townspeople were loath to use them for airing grievances. How then could authority be made to stick? The town meeting was the answer. Forum of deliberation? Perhaps. Forum of contrivance? Most certainly.

Zuckerman wrote that the town meeting was "the essential element in the delicate equipoise of peace and propriety which governed the New

England town" (1970, 93). Since there was no satisfactory means of traditional or institutional *coercion*, the recalcitrant could not be compelled to adhere to what to the town's populace, especially its selectmen, was the "common course of action." Therefore the common course had to be coordinated to leave *none* recalcitrant. That was the vital function of the New England town meeting, not the open give-and-take over what would be the course of action. As a forum, said Zuckerman, "the town meeting solved the problem of enforcement by evading it." Convocations of the community "gave institutional expression to the imperatives of peace; in them consensus was reached, and *individual consent and group opinion were placed in the service of social conformity*" (emphasis added). Zuckerman concluded, "In the town meeting men talked of politics, but ultimately they sought to establish moral community" (1970, 93).

Viewed from this perspective the town meeting as a deliberative body rendered recalcitrance unthinkable. The orchestration of the town meeting was in strict adherence to a constituted taken-for-granted code of power, namely, moral injunctions. Those injunctions directed deliberations "bent toward securing unanimity. That was the prime purpose of the town meeting and was the essential thrust of its politics of consensus" (Zuckerman, 1970, 93–94). Through generations of town meetings the "doctrinal rigidity of the men who had once sought a city on the hill" (i.e., who *knew* what policies should be with "intolerable pride") "bore sons who expected to submit their judgment to the judgment of their peers" (Zuckerman, 1970, 236).

Thus did the town meeting continue as an instrument primarily of consensus-building rather than conflict airing. What we remember fondly as "direct Democracy," in Greenfield's contemporary phrase "giving voters more direct information than they have ever had before," was less direct than *directed*. As town meetings moved from town halls to TV studios, however, a code of entertainment replaced one of morality as a driving force. H. L. Mencken wrote in his essay "Sound Bite Questions, Buncombe Responses": "I traveled with him on three of his four campaign trips and witnessed his performance at close range. . . . Most of his speeches were not delivered at all; they were simply recited. And what a recitation it was!" (1956, 334).

Mencken, a journalist and satirist, wrote those words about Republican presidential candidate Alf Landon in 1936. Politicians, as far as Mencken was concerned, practiced the art of buncombe—that is, empty and meaningless talk or clap trap aimed not at responding to citizens but masking ambitions. His observations about Landon in 1936 might as easily apply to any of the major contestants in Campaign '92. For if any single point stands out about the performance of presidential and vice-presidential candidates in the electronic town halls it is that their responses to the alleged "give-and-take" of the meetings was recitative, not deliberative.

To explore the recitative and other characteristics of citizen-candidate interaction we turn to the content of a saturation sampling and a substantive coding (Glaser, 1978) of 28 electronic town halls held between February 20 and October 30.[1] The sample exemplifies a variety of formats, rules, and audiences. We turn first to the candidates exploiting the electronic town hall in fullest measure, namely, the Democrats' Bill Clinton and Al Gore, then to incumbents George Bush and Dan Quayle. From there we move to the man who brought Clinton to his town hall four times, Bush twice, and Ross Perot six times (he even provided Libertarian Andre Marrou with his only national forum), Larry King. Finally, we examine the one instance when all three major candidates appeared at the same town meeting, the second televised presidential debate.

"IF THEY HOLD ONE, WE WILL COME"

"I believe in these town meetings and if I become your president, I'll continue to do them." Bill Clinton spoke these words on "Face to Face with Bill Clinton," a regional town hall meeting originating in Dallas on August 25 with questions coming from studio audiences in a four-city hookup. The meeting, sponsored by Times-Mirror Broadcast Stations, was carried on 125 radio stations, a 22-station TV network, and by C-SPAN. The rules, format, audience makeup, questions, and answers made for a vintage Clinton recitation. Local news anchor/hosts in each of the four cities framed the one-hour telecast that foreshadowed the "spontaneous" questions to follow: viewers learned that in Dallas people were worried about the economy, "St. Louis is hurting" for jobs, Austin concerns were "hi tech and the environment," and Birmingham residents worried over education, aging, and crime. Moreover, the applause given Clinton's remarks by each city's studio audience hinted at a pro-Clinton stacking in the manner of the Hillsboro Format of 1968.

During the "Face to Face" there were two dozen questions put to the candidate. With visible restraint the anchor/hosts asked only four questions; the remaining 20 were spread across the studios in each of the four cities on a rotating basis: moving in order from Dallas to St. Louis, Austin, and Birmingham. The questions covered the economy (jobs, employment, lay offs, reconversion of defense industries, and small business); health care, taxes and spending (income and entitlements); education (funding for public and private schools, minority dropouts, student loans); civil rights (racism, gay and lesbian rights); crime; abortion; and

AIDS. Only one foreign policy topic, the pre–Gulf War policy of the Bush administration toward Iraq, produced a question. Questioners appeared as though supplied by Hollywood's central casting: a self-identified physician (African-American male) asked about health care, an AIDS victim asked about AIDS, an African-American identifying herself as a "young voter" asked about student loans, a member of Texans United for Life asked about abortion, a policeman asked about juvenile violence, a member of the National Conference of Christian and Jews asked about racism, and a father standing beside his "family" (wife and children) asked about equal funding for education.

Using the vernacular of journalists, questions asked in town hall meetings can be divided into two categories. Those that are focused, specific, and calling for a direct answer are the "hardball" questions journalists pride themselves in asking. For example, "Governor, if you are elected president will you appoint an AIDS Czar to coordinate the war on AIDS?" That calls for a direct answer. In contrast, "softball" questions are general, unfocused, and ambiguous; they invite the candidate to take off on any tangent he desires, namely, recite in a programmed manner. Thus, "Governor, what will you do to solve the national health crisis?" permits a smooth transition to a rehearsed response. Of the two dozen questions asked in "Face to Face," 10 were hardballs, 14 softballs. Clinton responded in kind. In 11 instances Clinton answered directly confining himself to the topic at hand; in 13 instances he redefined the question, then provided a recitative response.

In many respects the "Face to Face" town meeting had many characteristics of all electronic town halls in 1992. First, although the candidate received instructions to keep his responses brief (in order to maximize the number of questions from the audience), he rarely did so. Thus, regardless of the question asked it was the candidate, not the questioner, who defined the situation. Second, the composition of the audience could be likened to a focus group—diverse but representing stereotypes and special interests. Third, question topics matched the individuals who asked them; hence, senior citizens asked about social security and health care, parents about education, businessmen about small business, and so forth. Finally, the range of topics covered typified those Clinton (and Al Gore) encountered in other town meetings (in some cases questions were even worded the same way). They were precisely the topics emphasized by the Clinton-Gore campaign, namely, the economic recovery, health care, and education; foreign policy was rarely at issue. In short, the town meetings produced recitative questions, recitative responses.

This air of a ritual catechism, although present, was less visible as Bill Clinton and Al Gore, either individually or together, appeared on town halls conducted under the auspices of the three networks' morning shows (*Today, Good Morning America,* and *CBS This Morning*), talk shows (such as *Donahue*), and entertainment shows (*Nashville Now,* MTV's *Choose or Lose*). On those shows the citizen-candidate relationship, essentially direct on "Face to Face with Bill Clinton," was mediated by a third party—the celebrity host. Consider, for example, that of 29 questions asked of Clinton on *Today* (June 30) one-third came from host Bryant Gumbel; of 21 questions asked at "Breakfast with Bill Clinton" on *Good Morning America* (on October 30 from the Candlewick Diner in East Rutherford, NJ), 7 came from host Charles Gibson. And, when Clinton and Gore were on *CBS This Morning* (August 10) the show's producers had a large pool of questioners to draw on: 75 people in the studio audience in New York, questioners located in six cities across the nation, and 2000 questions that had been mailed to CBS. Yet, of 52 questions asked during the two-hour program, only 18 came from the studio audience, 8 from the six cities, and 3 from the mail; the remaining 23 questions came from moderators Paula Zahn (15) and Harry Smith (8). Similarly the sampled town halls held on *Donahue, Nashville Now,* and MTV's *Choose or Lose* featuring Clinton and/or Gore were host/hostess driven. In all sampled town halls featuring one or both members of the Democratic ticket, there were 395 questions asked of the candidate(s), three-fifths by citizens as audience members, callers, or via letters, and two-fifths by celebrity host/hostesses. The "make-believe media" (Parenti, 1992) may pay lip service to contributing to deliberative Democracy, but it is a star-mediated, not direct, Democracy.

Setting aside the star-studded aspects of the Clinton/Gore town halls, citizen participation in them followed the same pattern on network, cable, and syndicated town meetings as observed in "Face to Face with Bill Clinton." Audiences retained their focus group composition, asked questions matching their socio-demographic attributes, focused on domestic (not foreign) issues already stressed by the Clinton/Gore ticket, and, in effect, played roles as supporting cast members to the candidates. Overall softball questions outnumbered hardball questions by a 3:2 ratio. By the same ratio the candidates responded with recitations rather than direct answers.

One of the most widely publicized town hall meeting exchanges illustrated how adept the Democratic presidential candidate became during the campaign at providing recitation responses to catechism questions. In Winston-Salem, North Carolina, at a town hall broadcast by *CBS This Morning,* Clinton encountered a housewife who asked what appeared to be a spontaneous hardball question. She wanted to know, could the nominee name the price of a gallon of gas, a pound of hamburger, a gallon of milk, a loaf of bread, blue jeans, and a doctor's visit? Without hesitation Clinton rattled off: "Gasoline is about $1.20 a gallon," hamburger "a little over $1," a gallon of milk $2, a loaf of bread "about a dollar now," blue jeans "run anywhere from $18 to $50 depending upon what kind you get," and he added, he knew doctors who would charge only $15, "but not many." Host Harry Smith commented, "This is like *The Price Is Right.* How did he do?" "Pretty good," said the questioner.

As Herbert Blumer wrote long before the arrival of the electronic town hall, "the various media are participating in a total evolving process." Hence, to try to sort out the "distinctive influence" of any medium on the "collective definition" that is the electoral outcome is risky (1959, 201). Yet, examining the performance of Clinton and Gore in the sampled town hall formats discussed to this point makes it possible to understand one journalist's assessment. Martin Walker of the *Manchester Guardian Weekly* wrote that Clinton "likes to call it a town-meeting, but [it] is far more like a daytime TV talk show, with a host roaming through the studio audience with a microphone while the celebrity guest chats and answers rather softer questions than professional journalists tend to put" (1992b, 8). Clinton made the talk show/town meeting hybrid "his chosen format" because "he chats easily, is comfortable with the format, and relates swiftly to people." Hence, "his glibness becomes an advantage, his low pitched voice, which often sounds fuzzy and indistinct at rallies, is far more effective in the mock-intimacy of the TV studio."

Contrast the eagerness of the Clinton/Gore ticket to maximize appearances in town hall formats with the reluctance of Bush/Quayle. Aside from appearances on *Larry King Live,* Bush and Quayle confined their appearances to traditional host-guest interview formats on such programs as *Good Morning America,* where Bush appeared seven times during the campaign, or on evening programs such as *Prime Time* or *David Frost* on PBS. Hence, Bush's presence on the July 1 edition of *CBS This Morning* provided a rare opportunity to view his performance in the town hall give-and-take.

However, having convinced the incumbent president to engage in a town hall exchange on the White House lawn with an audience of 100 people plucked out of the White House tour line, CBS producers and co-hosts Paula Zahn and Harry Smith turned the meeting into a celebrity roast. Of 47 questions asked during the two-hour program, 30 were derived from the co-hosts (17 from Zahn, 13 from Smith). Tourists' questions covered social security, education, the economy, trust, taxes, the deficit, the environment, and (2) foreign policy. Although they were tourists, the questioners—as in the case of Clinton/Gore town meetings— were typecast: a black male asked, "What do you tell the black kids?"; a retired white female asked about threats to entitlements; a little boy asked how Bush felt about Quayle-bashing; and a black male asked the president about the possibility of consulting with minority leaders. The softball questions gave Bush the opportunity to redefine the situation to his own advantage; in two-thirds of his answers he recited standard themes from his campaign.

Zahn and Smith, however, pressed the president. Zahn wanted to know why the president had not displayed more leadership on the home front; would there be a litmus test for Supreme Court appointees; was Ross Perot a friend or foe; "what went wrong with the job creation" program; Smith wanted to know why the Bush administration had delayed so long on Bosnia-Herzegovina; would Bush pledge not to raise taxes; why had the United States supported Saddam Hussein; and why had the administration gutted the clean air bill? An amiable but slightly vexed president finally turned to the audience and asked jokingly, "Why do the media ask questions to stir up controversy when you people want to know what I'm doing about the problems?"

THE MEN WHO WOULD BE KING MEET THE MAN WHO WOULD BE KINGMAKER

"Basically, my style is one of utter, it's almost, I'd say, naivete. I'm curious. I want to know why." Talk show host Larry King revealed that self-judgment on October 10 on *60 Minutes* in response to charges made by correspondent Mike Wallace that King asked "softball questions" of candidates on *Larry King Live*. Wallace was repeating a charge he had made when he phoned King's show on the evening of September 30, a night when Ross Perot was the guest. (Wallace's phone call was included on the *60 Minutes* profile of King aired on October 30, along with Perot's response that King did not ask softball questions.)

Softball questions or not, for many observers of Campaign '92 *Larry King Live* epitomized the electronic town hall format. On his call-in show, King gave more airtime with the presidential and vice-presidential candidates than did any other news or talk show on TV. He had interviewed so many of the candidates that toward the close of the campaign America's town hall moderator was looked to for his assessments of the candidates. King obliged: Bush "is the most thoughtful. [He] has the best memory"; Quayle "has taken a lot of bum raps"; Clinton "is one of the most relaxed guys I have been around"; Perot "never told me a lie. . . . He's direct, and he doesn't bear fools easily" (Swertlow, 1992, 41).

Although the candidates eagerly entered what Ross Perot called King's "electronic town hall," allegedly to talk directly with the American people, the conversation was one-sided. King asked questions; candidates talked *to* not *with* the audience. In 14 sampled *Larry King Live* programs with presidential and vice-presidential candidates, some programs running 60 minutes and others 90 minutes, there were only 102 questions asked by callers. Of those there were questions repeated from show to show, others phoned in by supporters of King's guest that permitted the candidate to recite a standard speech, others from backers of the guest's opponent aimed at provoking an untoward response, and a few from noncitizen overseas callers. Moreover, many shows featured a "mystery caller" (King's words). Thus, Bill Clinton heard from his mother; Al Gore from his wife; Ross Perot from singer-actress Cher (twice), military analyst David Hackworth, Republican national chairman Rich Bond, and Mike Wallace.

With callers relatively few, screened, stage managed, and prepared with token queries, it remained for King to act as both town hall modera- tor and town crier. Given his command of airtime, on an average he asked 8 to 10 questions for every one taken from a caller. As Anthony Pratkanis and Elliot Aronson noted, "Question-asking can be a subtle form of pre- persuasion—a carefully crafted question can be used to define the issue at hand, to suggest subtly what the 'right' answer may be, and to organize the way we think about an issue" (1991, 63). King's habit of asking lead- ing questions containing their own recitative answers simplified matters for guests. Typical examples: Of Clinton, "Would President Clinton sub- mit a balanced budget soon?" or, "I asked the president last night if he dis- liked you and he said no. He likes you. Do you dislike him?" Of Bush, "Do you think CBS, NBC, ABC are prejudiced against you?" or "Why is foreign policy hardly ever discussed in this campaign?" And of Perot, "Couldn't a good, forceful effective leadership president change things?" or "You wouldn't pollute the sky to rebuild the industrial base?"

This is not to say that King did not ask direct questions demanding direct answers. He did. But his use of leading questions and irrelevant questions (of Bush, "When was the last time you drove [an automobile]?" and of Perot, "When will we see your wife again?") left ample opportu- nity for the candidates to move the conversation in the direction they wished, address repeatedly the issues their managers deemed key, avoid close scrutiny, and appear relaxed, confident, and congenial.

Thus, each major presidential candidate exploited appearances on *Larry King Live* to mobilize consensus around issues and themes stressed repeatedly throughout the campaign, not to deliberate with citizens. Clin- ton used King's program, first, to drive home his recitations on "trickle- down economics" and health care. Second, when confronted with the "trust" and "character" issues via Bush's attacks, Clinton used the King forum to deflect the thrust. Bush used King's town hall to reassert the trust issue, deflect the charge that he was not compassionate, and respond to charges regarding his alleged complicity in the Iran-Contra guns-for-hostages plan. Perot exploited *Larry King Live* to float his phantom candidacy, keep it alive after not entering the race, and explain his foot-in-mouth charges of "dirty tricks." In sum, *Larry King Live,* as with other town hall formats, served the campaign purposes of the candidates. Only marginally did the number and tenor of callers' questions offer opportunities for consultation with potential voters, or even require responding to voters in other than recitative ways.

THREE IN A BOOTH: THE ELECTRONIC TOWN HALL DEBATE

On one occasion the three candidates confronted one another in a single town meeting, the second presidential debate. Three weeks earlier George Bush blamed Bill Clinton for the absence of debates in the campaign. Choosing radio talk show host Rush Limbaugh's widely syndicated program as his venue Bush declared, "I want to debate, but I'm not going to let this new man dictate the terms" (Feeney and Lewis, 1992, 19-A). He was to regret that remark, although not as much as his 1988 invitation to "read my lips." For it was Clinton's managers who influenced the choice of the town hall terms of the second debate—a single moderator roaming through a large studio audience, sticking a microphone in each questioner's face in the manner of *Donahue.* That choice worked to the Arkansas governor's advantage. Through weeks of town hall meetings, sitting on a stool, strolling forward to engage the audience, smiling amiably, and smoothly segueing from posed question into practiced recitation, Clinton had sharpened his skills for just such a setting. Clinton's pictured ease was in marked contrast with Bush's distracted glances at his watch and Perot's failures to reach closure on questions (Golson, 1992, 31).

Although widely acclaimed by many political observers as the ideal debate format (Walker, 1992a, 10), it was typical of all entertainment-oriented, moderator-driven TV talk shows that marked Campaign '92. The issues were the standard ones: educational reform, the budget and trade deficits, crime, gun control, health care, retirement plans, racism, term limits (once), the "New World Order." From the 209 "uncommitted voters" that made up the studio audience came 14 questions (plus 8 more from moderator Carole Simpson), the majority addressed to all three candidates and encouraging recitative responses. Not surprisingly, the candidates faced the same questions from earlier town meetings and gave the same pat responses. The debate thus afforded the opportunity for the three contenders to forge a consensus as best each could.

If instant polls are to be believed, Clinton managed that task better than his opponents. A CBS poll of 1,145 voters reported 53 percent declaring Clinton the "winner," 25 percent Bush, and 21 percent Perot. An ABC poll also announced Clinton as victor (Walker, 1992a, 10). However, this may have been an example of the medium being the message (McLuhan and Fiore, 1967); that is, the format, not the candidate, shapes viewers' perceptions. Two incidents stand out, and both disadvantaged Bush. First, early in the debate Bush undertook a recitation attacking Clinton on the trust issue. He was quickly brought up short by comments/questions posed from the audience. Why not address "complexities, not trash"; "can we focus on issues and needs," crossing "your hearts" and promising "no more mud?" Thus ended attack politics for the evening.

The second incident involved a question from a young black woman, "How has the national debt personally affected each of your lives? And if it hasn't, how can you honestly find a cure for the economic problems of common people if you have no experience in what's ailing them?" Bush's recitation ("Well, I think the national debt affects everybody") was cut short by Simpson's intervention: "You personally?" The town meeting then took a moderator-candidate turn: First, Bush: "Obviously it has a lot to do with interest rates." Then, Simpson: "She's saying, 'You personally.' *You* on a personal basis. How has it affected you?" Again Bush: "I'm sure it has. I love my grandchildren." Once more, Simpson: "How?" Bush went on to talk about education costs, a worry for every parent. Then: "If the question . . . maybe I . . . get it wrong. Are you suggesting that if somebody has means that the national debt doesn't affect them?" The questioner returned to the exchange, but Bush again professed confusion. Once again Simpson intervened: "But how has it affected you, and if you have no experience in it, how can you help us, if you don't know what *we're* feeling?" Bush rambled about being in the White House, "and hear what I hear and see what I see and read the mail and touch the people that I touch from time to time." Finally, "Everybody cares if people aren't doing well. But I don't think it's fair to say, you haven't had cancer, therefore, you don't know what it's like."

By contrast Clinton's response, an echo from earlier town meetings, was a polished one: "I've been governor of a small state for 12 years. . . . In my state when people lose their jobs there's a good chance I'll know them by their names. When a factory closes, I'll know the people who ran it. And I've been out here for 13 months in meetings just like this ever since October, with people like you all over America, people that have lost their jobs, lost their livelihood, lost their health insurance." The cause of it all? "We have had 12 years of trickle-down economics."

AVOIDING THE BOREDOM OF RECITATIONS

In a letter drafted to Piero Soderini in 1513, Niccolo Machiavelli warned that princes must always beware the "first law of politics," namely, *boredom* (Minogue, 1972, 156). Faced with humaneness, honesty, and conviction in politicians, people first like it, grow accustomed to it, then are bored by it. They are then ripe for cruelty, treachery, and deceit. But, having acquiesced to that, they are again bored and yearn for a "gentler and kinder" nation. And so the cycle goes. The task of politicians is to deal with the popular proclivity for boredom by orchestrating appeals at a sufficient level of commonality and generality to reduce boredom or to exploit it.

The electronic town hall meetings of 1992 served the candidates well, particularly Bill Clinton, in their efforts to overcome citizens' boredom with campaign techniques of the past: standardized campaign speeches, press conferences, evening news sound bites, negative political ads, airport fly-ins, and pep rallies. By returning to a basic function of America's early town meetings, namely, they "solved the problem . . . by evading it" (Zuckerman, 1970, 93), candidates were able to have their cake and eat it too. They continued their recitations, that is, their buncombe, but via an entertaining rather than boring format.

Whether the electronic town hall has become a permanent feature of the electoral landscape remains to be seen. Politicians trying not to be boring must strike a balance between two political adages, namely, "Don't follow a banjo act with a banjo act," and "Dance with the one that brung ya." If town meetings return it might be well for future observers to inquire about them. The list is by no means exhaustive, but here are a few questions to ask:

- Who are the sponsors of each town hall meeting and what special pleading are they up to?
- How is the studio/call-in audience for each town meeting selected and what is its partisan, ideological, socio-demographic composition?
- How are audience questions screened, who are the gatekeepers and what are their interests?
- Are the questions leading questions designed to "set up" a candidate's recitations/responses?
- Are questions "plants," disinforming allegations later publicized as factoids along with candidates' responses?
- What drives the format—information, news, entertainment, and to what end?
- Who is the star of the show: moderator, candidate, or we the people?

- Does the content of town hall "exchanges" enlighten public understanding and provoke public participation, or is the town hall just another forum for obfuscation and public frustration?

Walter Cronkite's prophesy cited earlier, namely, *"It will not stand! There will be a backlash,"* may be the future of the electronic town hall. Remember, however, another TV news anchor, David Brinkley, who went out on a similar limb about televised political ads in 1970. Speaking to a conference of 6,000 teachers he said, "People just can't be fooled by those sly, tricky, cute little clips of film. I think they're dead because they didn't work. Frankly, I'm sick of looking at these things" (Dye, 1970, A-3). If Cronkite's prophesy goes the way of Brinkley's, the electronic town hall of 1992 may well have ushered in a new era of political boredom.

NOTE

1. The following electronic town halls were sampled for this study.

Bill Clinton: *Larry King Live.* CNN. June 4, 1992; *Today.* NBC. KFOR, Oklahoma City, OK. June 9, 1992; *CBS This Morning.* CBS. KWTV, Oklahoma City, OK. June 15, 1992; *Good Morning America.* "Breakfast with Bill Clinton." ABC. KOCO, Oklahoma City, OK. June 23, 1992; *Today.* NBC. KFOR, Oklahoma City, OK. June 30, 1992; "Face to Face with Bill Clinton." Times Mirror Broadcasting Stations. KDFW, Dallas/Fort Worth. August 25, 1992; *CBS This Morning.* CBS. KWTV, Oklahoma City. October 26, 1992; *Larry King Live.* CNN. October 28, 1992; *Good Morning America.* "Breakfast with Bill Clinton." ABC. KOCO, Oklahoma City, OK. October 30, 1992.

Bill Clinton and Al Gore: *Nashville Now.* TNN. August 8, 1992; *CBS This Morning.* CBS. KWTV, Oklahoma City, OK. August 10, 1992; *Larry King Live.* CNN. October 5, 1992; *Donahue.* Syndicated. KOCO, Oklahoma City, OK. October 6, 1992.

Al Gore: *Larry King Live.* CNN. September 9, 1992; "Choose or Lose." MTV. October 21, 1992.

George Bush: *CBS This Morning.* CBS. KWTV, Oklahoma City, OK. July 1, 1992; *Larry King Live.* CNN. October 7, 1992; *Larry King Live.* CNN. October 30, 1992.

Dan Quayle: *Larry King Live.* CNN. October 27, 1992.

Ross Perot: *Larry King Live.* CNN. February 20, 1992; *Larry King Live.* CNN. April 16, 1992; *Larry King Live.* CNN. June 24, 1992; *Peter Jennings Special.* "National Town Meeting." ABC. KOCO, Oklahoma City, OK. June 29, 1992; *Larry King Live.* CNN. July 7, 1992; *Larry King Live.* CNN. August 30, 1992; *Larry King Live.* CNN. October 29, 1992.

Andrew Marrou: *Larry King Live.* CNN. October 10, 1992.

George Bush, Bill Clinton, and Ross Perot: *Second Presidential Debate.* C-SPAN. October 15, 1992.

REFERENCES

Bark, E. 1992a. "ABC Asks, 'Who is Ross Perot?'" *Dallas Morning News,* June 23, 9-A.

————. 1992b. "Clinton Cancels TV Buy; Spate of Free Air Time Cited." *Dallas Morning News,* June 20, 18-A.

Blumer, Herbert. 1959. "Suggestions for the Study of Mass Media Effects." In *American Voting Behavior,* Eugene Burdick and Arthur J. Brodbeck, eds., 197–208. Glencoe, IL: Free Press.

Carter, Reginald, and David Beiler. 1992. "Jerry's World." *Campaign* 7, no. 7: 24–25.

Daley, Steve. 1992. "TV's 'New News' Shook Some Old Political Notions." *Chicago Tribune,* Nov. 1, 4-1, 4-4.

de Tocqueville, Alexis. 1969. *Democracy in America,* J. P. Mayer, ed.; George Lawrence, trans. New York: Anchor Books.

Dye, Robert M. 1970. "Brinkley Predicts End to TV Political Ads." *Kansas City Star,* Nov. 6, A-3.

[Editorial.] 1992. "Softball Interviews: Even Talk Show Hosts Should Throw Curves." *Dallas Morning News,* Oct. 12, 20-A.

Feeney, Susan, and Kathy Lewis. 1992. "Bush, Clinton Spar on Credibility Issue." *Dallas Morning News*, Sept. 22, 19-A.

Glaser, Barney G. 1978. *Theoretical Sensitivity.* Mill Valley, CA: Sociology Press.

Golson, Barry. 1992. "*What* Historic Debate?" *TV Guide,* Oct. 31, 31.

Golson, Barry, and Peter Ross Range. 1992a. "Clinton on TV." *TV Guide,* Nov. 21, 14–18.

————. 1992b. "Wotta Year!" *TV Guide,* Nov. 7, 16–21.

Goodman, Walter. 1992. "And Now, Heeeeeeeeere's a Referendum." *New York Times,* June 21, H-25.

Greenfield, Jeff. 1992. "Hardball or Beanball?" *New York Times Book Review,* Sept. 27, 11.

Kolbert, Elizabeth. 1992. "For Talk Shows: Less News Is Good News." *New York Times,* June 28, 2-E.

McGinnis, Joe. [1969] 1992. *The Selling of the President 1968.* New York: Trident Press (reprint).

McLuhan, Marshall, and Quentin Fiore. 1967. *The Medium Is the Message.* New York: Bantam Books.

Mencken, H. L. 1956. *A Carnival of Buncombe.* Baltimore: Johns Hopkins University Press.

Minogue, K. R. 1972. "Theatricality and Politics: Machiavelli's Concept of Fantasia." In *The Morality of Politics,* B. Pareth and R. N. Benk, eds., 148–62. London: George Allen & Unwin.

Parenti, Michael. 1992. *Make-Believe Media: The Politics of Entertainment.* New York: St. Martin's Press.

Pratkanis, Anthony, and Elliot Aronson. 1991. *Age of Propaganda.* New York: W. H. Freeman and Co.

Range, Peter Ross. 1992. "Walter Cronkite Is Mad as Hell." *TV Guide,* July 11, 15–18.

Sly, John Fairfield. 1930. *Town Government in Massachusetts (1620–1930).* Cambridge, MA: Harvard University Press.

Summers, Dana. 1992. Cartoon. *Dallas Morning News,* June 27, 30-A.

Swertlow, Frank. 1992. "Larry King Reigns over TV's Political Scene." *TV Guide,* Oct. 24, 41.

TV Guide. 1992. "Cheers and Jeers." Jul. 4, 7.

Walker, Martin. 1992a. "Bush Administration Gets that Sinking Feeling." *Manchester Guardian Weekly,* Oct. 25, 10.

————. 1992b. "Plane Tales of Clinton's Time-Zone Travelers." *Manchester Guardian Weekly,* Nov. 8, 8.

Zuckerman, Michael. 1970. *Peaceable Kingdoms: New England Towns in the Eighteenth Century.* New York: Alfred A. Knopf.

10

Video Verité: C-SPAN Covers the Candidates

Janette Kenner Muir

What C-SPAN does is give everybody a seat at the event. . . . [It] fulfills one of the great dreams of the people who invented TV—that you can see an event while it's happening, unvarnished, without any commentary, so that people can make up their own minds.

Newton Minnow[1]

The 1992 presidential campaign was unique in ways that scholars will study for years to come. There were the obvious differences—a governor from a small southern state overcoming serious credibility challenges, a billionaire running as a third-party candidate mobilizing thousands of people across the country, and a highly popular incumbent president experiencing substantial reversals in public attitudes. There were also differences in the Democratic process itself, including increased participation from citizens through town hall meetings, call-ins, and interactive technologies. One of the most significant changes in the 1992 campaign was the impact of cable television in defining the pivotal moments of the campaign. CNN's *Larry King Live* served as a centerpiece for cable coverage, providing a forum for each candidate unlike any in previous campaigns. C-SPAN (Cable-Satellite Public Affairs Network) provided another important dimension of the election: its live coverage of candidates, coupled with the *Road to the White House* series, marked a coming of age for the young network in its contribution to the political process. This coming of age is chronicled in this chapter, with a brief description of the C-SPAN network itself, an analysis of the coverage of the 1992 presidential campaign, with implications and cautions for the future.

THE C-SPAN NETWORK

Founded in 1979, C-SPAN began as the cable network that carried the daytime proceedings of the U.S. House of Representatives. Since its inception, the network has evolved into a two-channel, 24-hour operation that covers both the House and Senate when in session, and public events of all kinds, from National Press Club and White House speeches, to small news conferences and rallies. C-SPAN I continues to focus primarily on the House of Representatives; C-SPAN II focuses on covering the Senate.

The mission of the network is to broadcast public events without the typical commentary one would see on the major networks. Brian Lamb, C-SPAN's founder and CEO, sees the absence of a mediator as one of the network's true strengths: "We strive to show people what is happening without telling them what to think about it. We're an alternative, a kind of balance on your dial" (Wyckoff, 1993, A7).

Balance is an important goal of the network. Though some audience members will, on occasion, criticize C-SPAN's coverage as biased toward some ideological view, C-SPAN programmers are quick to note that balance in perspectives is eventually achieved during the course of a week. For example, during the 1992 campaign, C-SPAN aired campaign speeches and events for major candidates, and provided a forum for over thirty other presidential candidates. Some of these candidates included Leonora Fulani of the New Alliance Party, Andrew Marrou of the Libertarian Party, and Howard Phillips of the U.S. Taxpayers Party (*C-SPAN Digest*, 1993, 2).

The Audience

A common question asked about the network is "who watches C-SPAN?" When the network first began, it was transmitted to approximately 3.5 million households. It can now be seen in almost 60 million homes. Anyone who subscribes to a cable company that agrees to carry the network can watch C-SPAN. Thus, the audience tends to be widely mixed, consisting of homemakers, government officials, high school students, and senior citizens, to name only a few.

Since the network is entirely funded by the cable industry, it cannot tabulate ratings in the way that networks supported by advertising revenue can. In order to better understand who its audience is, C-SPAN commissioned Statistical Research, Inc., to conduct a national survey to see how viewers use C-SPAN and to better understand the network's overall impact (*C-SPAN Digest*, 1993, 1).

The survey randomly sampled 1,400 respondents nationwide about their C-SPAN viewing habits. Since 1988, the number of households subscribing to the network has increased from 43 to 58 million, and the number of viewers who say they tuned in to watch some part of the election grew by 80 percent when compared to past election viewing. Although a wide range of viewer backgrounds exist, there are some general tendencies apparent from the survey research. Seventy-seven percent of the C-SPAN audience range from 18 to 49 years of age; and male-female viewership is split—52 percent men and 48 percent women. In terms of education, 40 percent report that they have completed college, and 14 percent have gone on to graduate school.

Perhaps the most interesting, yet unsurprising, result of the survey is that C-SPAN viewers tend to be more politically active and better informed than the average television viewer. Of those viewers registered to vote, 98 percent reported voting in the 1992 presidential election. Reported political affiliations were fairly balanced: 28 percent Democrats, 29 percent Republicans, 31 percent political independents. The survey also indicated that C-SPAN viewers are twice as likely as nonviewers to contact a senator or House member, make a financial contribution to a political organization or campaign, or volunteer to work on a campaign. Likewise, C-SPAN viewers tend to be more informed about public affairs. Sixty-four percent of C-SPAN viewers read a newspaper every day, compared with 51 percent of nonviewers; 69 percent of the viewers also watch a television newscast daily, compared with 60 percent of nonviewers (*C-SPAN Digest*, 1993, 2–3).

Overall, the profile of the typical C-SPAN viewer is a varied one, but those who watch the network appear to be more informed, more politically active, and some describe themselves as "political news junkies." Additionally, political leaders use C-SPAN for public affairs information. Throughout the Capitol, televisions can be found in various representative's offices, tuned to the network to catch a session of Congress or a significant hearing. Those who are interested in politics—both the process and the end results—watch the network.

Public Participation

Another way C-SPAN is able to gauge public interest in its programming is by hosting call-in programs. C-SPAN's live call-in programming began in 1980, the first programming offered to complement coverage of the House of Representatives. In 1992, call-in programming accounted for approximately 900 hours in the 6,000 hours of first-run public affairs programs shown that year (Ringel, 1992, 12).

C-SPAN devotes two 45-minute segments each morning and evening to call-ins. These programs generally feature a guest such as a Congressional member, a journalist, or a special interest group representative. The topics discussed are usually timely and contemporary. For example, during the 1992 campaign, C-SPAN featured a program every Monday evening with guests discussing the presidential or Congressional campaigns.

At times, open phone lines will be provided where a host takes calls from the audience without a guest present to define the agenda. During the first week of the Persian Gulf War, C-SPAN opened its lines round-the-clock for people to express their concerns. Thousands of calls came from people throughout the country—and from other nations as well. By opening phone lines to the public in this manner, C-SPAN was able to monitor the pulse of the nation, including the fears and apprehensions of America at war (Muir, 1993). And in keeping with the goal of encouraging public input, C-SPAN opened phone lines to get viewer reactions many times during the course of the 1992 election.

Call-in programming is an affirmation of the network's philosophy to show viewers the process of government and allow them to decide for themselves how they feel about what they are viewing. Providing a forum for viewers to call in, enabling them to ask questions and make comments, is a direct way to empower the public. By allowing this programming to exist as an integral part of the network, C-SPAN provides an important contribution to enhancing citizen participation in the affairs of the public and revitalizing the traditional notions of Democratic government. The network's commitment to its viewers and its overall mission for fair and balanced coverage of events can easily be seen in its focus on the 1992 campaign.

THE 1992 PRESIDENTIAL CAMPAIGN

In December 1992, C-SPAN was named the recipient of the Golden CableACE Award, "the industry's highest honor for a special project or program that distinguishes cable communications by its unique contribution to the viewing public" (Carmody, 1992, D8). This award was due, in large part, to the extensive coverage of the 1992 presidential election, managed with an operating budget of $2 million, an astounding feat when compared with CNN, which spent $10 million on election coverage, including $4 million on the conventions alone (Piccoli, 1992, E1). By the end of the campaign, C-SPAN had collected over 1,200 hours of election coverage. This section shows the evolution of C-SPAN's coverage during the presidential election, following the three major stages of campaigning: the preprimary/primary stage, the nominating conventions, and the general election.

The Preprimary/Primary Stage

C-SPAN began its coverage of the presidential campaign with its *Road to the White House* program in April 1991, when Paul Tsongas announced his intention to run as the first presidential candidate. With this announcement, C-SPAN cameras began to follow Tsongas as he campaigned from town to town in New Hampshire. With a wireless microphone and a limited number of cameras for a shoot, the network managed to collect hours of coverage for each candidate who announced his or her intentions to run, and particularly those who were considered the front-runners. Highlights were then placed into an hour-and-a-half format shown on C-SPAN I each Friday evening and re-aired on Sunday evening.

As the campaign progressed, the *Road to the White House* moved beyond the weekly format, airing more coverage, often devoting entire weekends and prime time slots to covering events with the candidates, especially those that could be aired live. The network's flexibility with programming when the House and Senate are not in session enables a candidate's speech to be aired several times during the course of a week. Thus, the public had many opportunities to see candidates in action.

Video Verité. During the preprimary stages of the campaign process, candidates realize that media coverage is essential to their political survival, hence they tend to be more flexible and accessible to the media. C-SPAN took advantage of this, and traveled with many of the candidates one-on-one, giving the audience a chance to get to know them beyond the traditional campaign sense. Steve Scully, producer to the *Road to the White House* series, and a regular interviewer and call-in moderator, noted that the idea of the program was "to bring the campaign home to the people" (1993). He further described his personal goal for the program:

I always envision my family sitting at home watching television. What would interest them? Seeing Bill Clinton at a cheesecake factory in Chicago eating cheesecake, or seeing him in New Hampshire eating sea urchins and campaigning along the Portsmouth fisherman's harbor, seeing Paul Tsongas swim at Dartmouth College in Hanover, New Hampshire, or seeing Bob Kerrey in Colorado on the horses right before the primary. What you do is you try to make these people human beings. And you do that by following them around and giving people a sense of who they are and what makes them tick. (1993, 1)

Bringing the candidates to the people, watching them engage in the everyday facets of the campaign process—waving flags, talking to workers, chatting with diners—is the core of what C-SPAN does. These long, sometimes tedious hours of coverage, especially during the preprimary period, reveal important information about a candidate's ability to withstand the continual scrutiny of the American public.

Many moments stand out during the preprimary and primary season. There were two memorable events that Scully described that offered poignant depictions of the candidates in their quests for the presidency. The first notable event was when Paul Tsongas went swimming in Hanover, New Hampshire, with the C-SPAN cameras running. Knowing that he would have to satisfy public concerns about his health following his bout with cancer, Tsongas needed to present a strong, physical presence to the public. His diminutive stature and soft voice added to public apprehension about his ability to appear "presidential." Tsongas's decision to let C-SPAN cover his exercise routine was an important political move to deal with his image. Scully described the experience and its impact as it was aired on *Road to the White House*:

I thought it was unusual that a presidential candidate would allow people to show him swimming, but it seemed interesting and we put it on the air. But once it became a television event, it seemed to become almost a symbol of his campaign because C-SPAN kept airing it. (1993)

Given Tsongas's front-runner status before the New Hampshire primary, a scene as simple as swimming laps could produce dramatic results in shaping one's perception of the candidate. When seen on C-SPAN, coupled with political advertising that depicted a similar scene, the candidate could visually negate any concerns about his health.

Another significant event that occurred prior to the New Hampshire primary was George Bush's trip to Exeter, New Hampshire, a political venture necessary because of the challenge of Patrick Buchanan. Bush needed to convince the New Hampshire voters that he cared about their needs and concerns, and improve his credibility as an involved president. A poignant moment occurred when President Bush stood in a receiving line, greeting anyone who wanted to shake his hand. Scully tells the story about how this moment came to be:

It was freezing cold in Exeter, and the secret service were being real tough about getting in there to cover this event. We got set up, shot the speech, and then the rest of the press leaves. Since Bush was still there we continued to role the cameras. I had my shotgun mike in the crowd because I wanted to get some of the questions asked to Bush. As he started to shake hands I put the mike up, thinking somebody would definitely kick me out. Twenty minutes later I'm still up there with the shotgun mike and we're the only camera shooting; everyone else had left. You see this kind of campaigning everyday, yet don't realize the power that it has. When it's put on television, there's something about that that just made it different. This event showed Bush as the president, a real person, deeply concerned about New Hampshire, because he spent so much time shaking hands with each of these people. This hadn't been seen before. The leader of the free world, in New Hampshire, spending 20 to 25 minutes just talking to voters. (1993, 3)

These vignettes are just two examples of C-SPAN's capacity for "video verité." Each bring the event and the candidate into the viewers' homes, allowing a glimpse of those human elements that help to determine a candidate's ability to be president.

Candidate-Created Messages. In addition to providing daily coverage of the leading presidential candidates, C-SPAN also covered all announcement speeches and most political advertisements aired by each candidate. The staging of the announcement is generally dramatic and visually engaging (Trent and Friedenberg, 1991). For example, in 1983 Gary Hart climbed a Colorado mountain to proclaim his candidacy, and in 1991 Bill Clinton surrounded himself with family and friends to announce his intentions to run. Knowing that only a few seconds will be aired on the nightly newscast, the phrasing and visual depictions are crucial for getting media attention (Jamieson, 1992). C-SPAN cameras air the announcements in their entirety, often followed by open phones for viewers to voice their reactions.

It was during these early stages of the campaign that billionaire businessman H. Ross Perot introduced himself to the American public, announcing his interest in the presidency in a speech at the National Press Club in March 1992. During the primary season alone, Perot made over seven major appearances, all broadcast on C-SPAN, and his interviews and speeches are some of the most-requested transcripts for the network (Range, 1992, 13).

Adding another element to the political campaign process, advertising played an important role in getting the audience's attention and setting the tone of the campaign. C-SPAN aired as many political advertisements as they had access to. Scully noted that as the campaign season unfolded viewers could get a feel for how the various candidates were progressing—the negative tone of the Tsongas ads, Clinton's targeting of Tsongas (Clinton had been expected to target Kerrey), and so forth. The network found that viewers were interested in the advertisements of the candidates and kept airing them throughout the primary season (Scully, 1993, 6).

Political advertisements provided important information for viewers especially during the primary season. In addition to advertisements from the 1992 campaign, C-SPAN aired historic ads with the help of the political archives at the University of Oklahoma. These ads provided an important political context to the current campaign, and provided historical background to the presidential campaign process.

Media Coverage. As a way to provide another perspective on the 1992 election, C-SPAN turned to both the local and national media covering the race. One way C-SPAN was able to focus on the process of campaigning was by carrying local network coverage of the campaign during the primary season. More than fifteen simulcasts of local television news programs from across the country gave C-SPAN viewers a unique perspective on how candidates respond to regional concerns (Pollack, 1992, 2). For example, prior to the New Hampshire primary, C-SPAN presented coverage from WMUR, a local New Hampshire station. These programs provided viewers with ways to see how local networks responded to the campaign process—who was leading in the state and the issues most salient for its citizens. The simulcasts started as a way for C-SPAN to air programming that would show other sides of life in New Hampshire and other primary states, but they also provided a way to get primary results from the races.

The programming initially worked by taking the political story from WMUR—usually the third, fourth, or fifth story in the newscast—editing it, and putting it on at 8 o'clock in the evening in order to build excitement in the race. During the last eight to ten days before the New Hampshire primary, C-SPAN simulcast the news program live since politics would be the top story on the newscast (Scully, 1993, 5).

This process worked in at least a dozen other states. On the nights of the Georgia and Illinois primaries, for example, C-SPAN devoted six hours of coverage to the election returns. What began as a way to fill a niche ended up creating a demand, and people enjoyed watching it. The television stations were responsive to C-SPAN because it provided them with an opportunity for national television exposure. When viewers scanned the dial for political information, C-SPAN assumed that many viewers would be attracted to the local news from another area of the country. Scully noted that although viewers did not necessarily know the players, "they could get results on specific house races in New Hampshire, Illinois, Pennsylvania and all the other states we decided to go to" (1993, 5).

When it seemed that people would tire of the incessant campaign process, the same stump speeches, and multicandidate debates, C-SPAN cameras turned to those who covered the candidates: the journalists themselves. Coverage of all parts of the public affairs process has long been a part of C-SPAN's philosophy, and there have been numerous examples where C-SPAN has sought contributions from all the players in the process. Journalist round tables, panel presentations, and call-in programs have provided self-reflective moments about how to cover campaigns, how to better scrutinize evidence, and how to be more responsible in the reporting. Actual coverage of these journalists in action enables viewers to see that theory can be put into practice.

C-SPAN has been successful not only in covering the events and processes of the campaign, but in providing an awareness to the public of the campaign as a "meta-event," or as a crafted "pseudo event." Video verité, along with coverage of the media, has in this sense contributed to the public's understanding of and critical response to the campaign as a wholly mediated event.

The Nominating Conventions

C-SPAN's commitment to gavel-to-gavel coverage of the House and Senate naturally transfers to the presidential arena, and the coverage of any event that is deemed relevant to public affairs. Complete coverage of the national party conventions was an expected part of C-SPAN's programming and had a direct impact on the coverage provided by the three major networks.

C-SPAN transmitted both party conventions from the Call-to-Order to the final Benediction, with no commentary or cut-aways to news taking place elsewhere. When the conventions were not in session, C-SPAN devoted much of the remaining airtime to viewer call-in programs, round-table discussions, and interviews.

The Democrats. The interesting difference in media coverage of the 1992 national party conventions was the amount of time scheduled by the major networks, especially compared to what was carried on cable. All three major networks cut back their coverage to approximately an hour each night, continuing to air situation comedies and nighttime dramas, justifying the move with the rationalization that the real campaign news does not occur at political conventions (Schram, 1992; Kurtz, 1992).

When the conventions were covered, viewers were forced to contend with endless discussion about the unfolding drama. Jim Milavsky criticized the commentary inherent in the coverage, praising C-SPAN's gavel-to-gavel coverage of the events:

Whether it was CNN, ABC, NBC, PBS, or the PBS-NBC joint venture, the problem was the same: anchormen, reporters and pundits who too often tried to make themselves the stars of the show. . . . They spent too much time telling us whether a speech was good or bad—assuming that we couldn't decide that for ourselves—and not enough time giving us information about what this "revital-ized" Democratic Party was all about. As it turned out, C-SPAN's uninterrupted, unfiltered coverage of everything that went on at the podium was in many ways more satisfying and revealing than the interviews and analysis provided by higher-budget networks. (1992, 3)

In his critique of the media's coverage of the Democratic National Convention, Martin Schram described the highlights missed in the major network coverage:

On Wednesday, ABC and NBC missed Mario Cuomo's impressive, message-defining speech nominating Clinton; it was live on CNN, PBS, C-SPAN and CBS, which showed flexibility by starting earlier than planned. Finally, all networks except C-SPAN cheated families out of a genuine civics moment—the uninterrupted roll call of the states. Parents and children everywhere deserved to watch their state cast its votes in this culmination of the presidential nomination process. But the networks kept cutting away to dish stale punditry and chase fresh rumors. (1992, 110)

The critiques of the major networks underscore what C-SPAN did best in providing the most direct way audiences could watch the presidential selection process in action. Although one could easily tire of the glitz and glamour of the Democratic convention and the dramatic staging of events, the historical transitioning of a new era in governance—the ushering in of Bill Clinton and Al Gore—marked the convention as an important historical moment.

The dramatic staging of the convention, held in Madison Square Garden, began with a tribute to the "Year of the Woman." After an introduction by Barbara Mikulski, each woman running for political office spoke from the floor. Diane Feinstein, Barbara Boxer, Patty Murray, and Lynn Yeakel were but a few of the women covered by C-SPAN and CNN. This defining moment, along with Barbara Jordan's closing keynote address, set the tone for the convention, introducing a new era of diversity in leadership, of new, fresh voices in government.

Taking advantage of its programming flexibility, C-SPAN was able to solicit ongoing feedback from audience members during the convention. Throughout the week C-SPAN featured key convention players such as Ann Richards, campaign consultants such as James Carville and David Wilhelm, as well as representatives and media personalities, opening phone lines so that viewers could call in and talk directly with the guests. Occasional open phones were scheduled where audience members could set the agenda. These programs were often facilitated by Brian Lamb or Susan Swain, C-SPAN's senior vice president. The emphasis was less on interpreting and rephrasing the opinions of the experts for the public, and more on putting the public directly in touch with the experts.

One newsworthy item that was featured on C-SPAN during the convention week was Perot's withdrawal from the presidential race, and the subsequent reactions of viewer call-ins. This announcement naturally paved the way for the new Democrats, and shattered the hopes of those citizens who had been working to get Perot on the ballot in all fifty states.

The Republicans. The coverage of the 1992 Republican convention worked in much the same way as the coverage of the Democrats. C-SPAN cameras carried the event in its entirety, and like before, major network coverage was limited. James J. Kilpatrick lamented the lack of substantive coverage on the part of the major networks:

On my doctor's advice, I didn't go to Houston. I stayed home and watched C-SPAN. From time to time I switched to the networks. On Thursday night, Bob Dole introduced the president. You would not have heard Dole's excellent speech if you relied on the networks. (1992, 10)

Kilpatrick criticized the subjective network coverage and dismal mood that prevailed in reporting the events, a criticism that remained with media coverage, in general, throughout the remainder of the campaign.

The Republican convention did have several noteworthy highlights, many of which were carried by all major networks. Ronald Reagan's Monday night speech set a nostalgic tone for the convention, Patrick Buchanan's family values speech set the defining one. Marilyn Quayle and Barbara Bush did much to underscore the party's definition through a tribute to families on Wednesday evening, culminating in appearances by all of Bush's grandchildren, and the president himself. These events framed the final evening of acceptance speeches by Dan Quayle and George Bush, leaving many to believe that the party, and Bush in particular, were catching a second wind for the final push of the campaign (Kilpatrick, 1992). C-SPAN cameras, of course, were there to cover these defining moments, absent commentary about the quality of the speeches and the dramatic staging of the events.

A fascinating aspect of the C-SPAN coverage at both conventions was the tendency to leave the cameras running during breaks and after the speeches were over. This gave viewers an "after hour" perspective on the conventions, a chance to see what goes on when most other networks have switched to commentary and commercials.

The General Election

With the redefinition of both the Democratic and Republican parties, the rejoining of Ross Perot, and the shift to new media forms of coverage, the final months of the presidential campaign were unparalleled in the amount of information available and the renewed enthusiasm for electoral politics. C-SPAN continued to offer its steady view of all candidates, the campaign process itself, and the media that covered the process.

As the Clinton/Gore team embarked on their famous bus trip into America's heartland, Quayle traveled his own bus route, and Bush boarded a train in the tradition of the old Whistlestop tours of Harry Truman. Everywhere the candidates went, C-SPAN cameras were there to cover the entire event live. While the major party candidates traveled around, C-SPAN also re-aired Perot's 30-minute infomercials, and the occasional public events he attended.

The Dornan Speeches. In addition to the candidates' numerous public appearances, surrogate spokespersons also took center stage. One person who understood C-SPAN's philosophical commitments and could use them to his advantage was California Representative Bob Dornan. Several nights at the end of September and beginning of October, Dornan and a few of his conservative colleagues used the empty House chamber floor for an hour, issuing "special orders" by which to criticize the Democratic ticket. Dornan's words were recorded in the Congressional Record and his appearances were seen across the country on C-SPAN.

The rules of the House forbid personal attacks on the president, members of Congress, and presidential contenders while the House is in session. During special orders, House members have more latitude to criticize and challenge their opponents. Dornan's vitriolic rhetoric gained a great deal of attention when he accused Clinton of going to Moscow as a guest of the KGB. Although he had no evidence to support his claim, Dornan surmised that Clinton was hiding something: "Why doesn't he just say 'I was against the war and the draft?' He's been hiding something all these years. . . . Nobody got into Russia without being invited. . . . I couldn't do it. I tried" (Waldman, 1992, 16).

When George Bush appeared on *Larry King Live* shortly after Dornan's speeches, King directly asked the president about these claims. Bush's response was noncommittal, but he did suggest that the story was, at least, worth looking into. While attempting to separate himself from the Republican House members, Bush tried to use the charges, with little success, to set the agenda for media focus. Political expertise at using media is evident in Dornan's use of C-SPAN coverage of the House.

The Presidential Debates. As the days progressed, suspense built regarding the presidential debates. Would George Bush debate Bill Clinton? Should Ross Perot be invited to participate? What kind of format would focus the discussion best? How many debates should be held? As the answers to these questions unfolded, the American public was presented with four different debate formats, a variety of networks on which to watch them, and appearances by the three major presidential and vice-presidential candidates.

The most interesting aspect of C-SPAN's coverage was the reaction following the debates. Whereas the usual reaction by the major networks is to go immediately to the surrogate speaker or network commentator to clarify the issues and tell the audience who won the debate, C-SPAN let the cameras roll, showing each debate scene as it wound down. When newsmakers gave their spin on the debates, C-SPAN would cover the spinning, and then show viewers the journalist who provided additional commentary. In between this coverage, phone lines were opened for viewers to call in and voice opinions about who won each debate, and what issues seemed important.

In addition to regular debate coverage, C-SPAN aired previous debates between presidential candidates. Anticipating the 1992 debates, audiences were given a historical view of the election process—the leaders, the issues, and the evolution of media coverage.

The Final Days. As the 1992 presidential campaign came to a close, the American public had received a tremendous amount of information about the candidates running for president. Campaign coverage inundated television, radio, and newspapers. The cable networks, and C-SPAN in particular, offered a plethora of information, which was in turn synopsized on the major networks. *Larry King Live* and morning talk shows displayed the candidates without the filter of news commentators, and C-SPAN offered round-the-clock live coverage of speeches and events for each major candidate.

On election eve and election night, C-SPAN continued to provide open phone lines for public input about the campaign process and the final election. Each candidate's final address was featured, including the conciliatory speech of Ross Perot and his celebratory dance with his wife and daughters to a rendition of Patsy Cline's "Crazy." As the band played on, other networks went to Dan Quayle's speech, and then on to George Bush. By midnight, Bill Clinton, the nation's new president, was able to speak, and C-SPAN cameras were, naturally, running live.

TOWARD FUTURE CAMPAIGNS

Approximately 1,200 hours of presidential campaign coverage was aired by C-SPAN and collected by the Purdue University Public Affairs Video Archives, the repository for most programming aired on C-SPAN I and C-SPAN II. Anyone truly interested in the political process can watch the unfolding drama of the election. When asked to speculate on how C-SPAN may cover the next presidential election, Scully responded by identifying the three principles that guide his choice:

(1) Always remember what we do best, that is, bringing events to the people, gavel-to-gavel; (2) Continue to do live programming as much as possible. That's what makes things interesting for viewers; and (3) Try to keep the calls going, putting everything in perspective with the call-in shows and other major programming. (1993, 3)

These principles frame the network's commitment to opening the election process to the entire public, letting viewers watch and decide for themselves. "There's no secret in what we do," Scully added, "we always try to be fair and not deviate from our continual mission" (1993, 3).

These principles guide the choices C-SPAN makes in covering the presidential election cycle and, in turn, yield important insights regarding the campaign process. Looking at the 1992 coverage, three major benefits can be derived from C-SPAN's focus.

First, the network offers a different perspective on events by allowing viewers to see how the pseudo events are staged. Watching candidates prepare for speeches, wait for workers outside factories, pose in front of heavy machinery or on a harbor dock, the C-SPAN viewer is able to get a better sense not only of the candidate, but of the process that goes into "staging" an event. The opportunity to see comparatively unstaged coverage, to understand the differences in how campaign rhetoric is mediated, helps to demystify the process.

Second, C-SPAN's direct line to the public through call-in programming puts people in touch with the experts who directly participate in the campaign process. Where major networks might feature these experts in talk show formats, few programs allow direct access to these people, and most simply rephrase the experts' views for the audience. Allowing opportunities for the public to call in and speak directly with James Carville or Mary Matalin creates a better flow of communication and gives callers a sense of directly participating in the political process.

A third benefit of C-SPAN's coverage is that it allows viewers to participate in American political power by providing an after-hours, behind-the-scenes view of what is taking place. When the cameras continue to roll following a presidential debate and viewers watch the cliques, the media celebrities, and the players all in conversation, jockeying for position, a bemused observer can better understand the political machinations. This perspective is a defining characteristic of C-SPAN in action, and provides a direct sense of engagement and participation in American political power.

Whereas there are many benefits to be gained from watching the C-SPAN network, it is also important to mention a few cautionary notes, particularly as the network looks toward the next presidential campaign. C-SPAN's continued mission is to bring public affairs to the people and let the people speak for themselves. After such accolades for the 1992 coverage, it will be interesting to see whether or not C-SPAN's mission shifts with its increased popularity. With notoriety often comes more demands from more powerful voices.

What was seen in the 1992 presidential campaign marked an important transition in the way politicians make news and use television as the primary way to campaign, especially new types of media forums. Jim Wooten described the impact of these new forums on more traditional forms of campaign coverage:

Voters now want contact without the media middleman. They want to judge for themselves, to look at a candidate and determine whether he's principled and can be trusted. C-SPAN and "Larry King Live" and "Donahue," therefore, become the primary tools of political communication. (1992, A10)

Cable television had a dramatic impact on the 1992 campaign, especially with regard to the talk-show explosion that evolved over the course of the election cycle. The ability to reach specific audiences, much the way radio is used, allows candidates to fine-tune messages, to "narrowcast" issues into succinct messages for targeted audiences (Cummings, 1992, C4). One major impact that this kind of "free media" has had is to limit the role political advertising plays in the campaign. Jamieson notes that prior to the 1992 election, ads were the primary source of information for the uninvolved viewer; however, other important forums were utilized in 1992, dramatically changing the role of presidential campaigning in the 1990s (Cummings, 1992, C4).

Any wise politician will realize that appearing on C-SPAN provides him or her with direct access to the public. Given the costs of political campaigning, it would seem prudent to use this vehicle as much as possible as a conduit for getting one's platform and issues to the citizens who make up a large part of the voting constituency. Knowing C-SPAN cameras will be covering an event live and will likely re-air it a number of times increases the likelihood that politicians will use the network to create different types of pseudo events, staging dramatic scenes that may appeal to the viewers. Although C-SPAN cameras can continue to roll after the event and hence show the process of staging that has developed, there is still some potential for abuse on the part of the campaigner attempting to get as much coverage as possible.

Perhaps this abuse is most evident in the role Representative Dornan played in the 1992 campaign. Knowing that C-SPAN cameras would be there to cover his "special orders," Dornan took advantage of this "free media time" to make unsubstantiated claims against Bill Clinton. Although these claims ultimately did more to damage the Republican party than the Democrat running for president, they did set much of the agenda for several weeks during the general election. Whether the voices are dominated by campaigners, representatives, or even cable operators, C-SPAN must be wary of the potential for abuse in the future.

Along these same lines, let us hope that C-SPAN can avoid the enticements that affect the usual journalist who follows the campaign. The network proclaims to be a type of "video verité," a window on what is directly happening, at the moment it is happening. Yet, given the confines of a television screen, C-SPAN cannot avoid its role in both selecting and reflecting what occurs, rather than acting as an all-seeing eye on reality itself. Camera angles, subject choice, number of cameras covering an event, all play significant roles in helping to shape the event one sees on his or her television screen. The reflection of reality is still dependent on the lenses of a selective group. This select group, nevertheless, is guided by a professional team of people who seem to be truly dedicated to C-SPAN's mission to serve the public. Although it is as close as anything can be to "reality television," one must remember that even in its purist form, C-SPAN is a mediated message, still prone to agenda setting and gatekeeping. The network carries a powerful potential, and a significant obligation, to shape messages for the audience in a responsible way.

Major networks also need to rethink how they cover the presidential election. Budgetary crises during the 1992 campaign directly impacted the quality of coverage by the major networks (May, 1991, A1). As early as December 1991, the networks were outlining ways to cut costs and provide more responsible coverage during the 1992 election. Cooperative ventures were proposed between networks. NBC and PBS developed the first partnership to cover the national party conventions together. Network executives also promised to improve traditional coverage by providing more analysis from studios and closer attention to the issues and the qualifications of various candidates (A1).

   Whereas some would argue that media coverage did improve during the 1992 campaign, Kathleen Jamieson's observations about network coverage during the 1988 campaign still held true to a great degree in 1992. In *Dirty Politics,* Jamieson argues that network coverage tends to focus on the strategic machinations of the campaign process rather than simply reporting what takes place (1992, 165–66). To the extent that one only watches a major network for political information, the lopsided nature of what one receives underscores the poor state of network news coverage in American society. Thus, networks do voters a serious disservice by shifting focus from substantive issues to the dramatic elements of campaigning (1992, 198).

   The fixation on the drama is mitigated by the little amount of time networks did spend covering the presidential campaign of 1992. Though one could easily argue about how *much* coverage there seems to be on the air, what is truly devoted to the candidate's words (as opposed to the network commentary) is a minimal amount of time. This was evident, of course, in the coverage of the nominating conventions. Judgments were made regarding what the public would consider newsworthy and dramatic, an insinuation of what citizens wanted to hear and what they seemed to care about. Kilpatrick's observation about the tone of media coverage of the Republican National Convention underscores the abusive nature of media commentary. Even with the strong conservative message dominating the convention, coverage still focused on how poorly Bush was doing in the polls, the lack of a solid message, and dissension among the ranks (Goodman, 1992).

   One would hope that the advent of C-SPAN's popularity, especially in covering the election process, will not be an excuse for major networks to sacrifice quality information for what may be even more daring. The move should be toward more responsible reporting and less of the dramatic and titillating. A 24-hour political network should *encourage* responsible coverage, not serve as a rationale to reduce it.

   A final cautionary note comes more as a direct message to the C-SPAN network. Buried within all this coverage of the 1992 presidential election are numerous pearls symbolizing the campaign, if only one is willing to dig through the ennui of continual coverage. Peter Range aptly described the tedium that comes with watching long segments on C-SPAN: "An afternoon of C-SPAN can feel like a life sentence in the gulag of windowless Sheraton banquet rooms, surrounded by a punishment brigade of earnest men and women in dark suits. It's torture by white tablecloth. The pace is glacial. The pace is real" (1992, 15). Although the pace may quicken somewhat during an election cycle, it is easy to feel overwhelmed and breathless upon its conclusion. Few may want to recapture the campaign by wading through the quagmire, but the fact that over one thousand hours have been captured should satisfy anyone's political appetite for a historical retrospective look at 1992. Scholars have already begun to mine C-SPAN's coverage, and conferences are now being held on the functions and effects of C-SPAN coverage.[2] It is clear that C-SPAN is making an important contribution to the study of the presidency and political communication.

With this contribution, however, it is important that C-SPAN realize the amount of information overload possible in watching the political campaign unfold on the network, and that it make continual efforts to reach out to the population through education. The philosophy of purity in presentation should not take away from progress toward gaining new, interested, and empowered citizens. Hence, C-SPAN should make continual efforts to expand its audience so that citizens not currently voting will be more willing to watch the network and become involved. Continual outreach to colleges and high schools, along with literature about C-SPAN's services, will help to make the network more accessible to the public and hopefully instill the idea of television as a place to gather information rather than merely be entertained.

New voters in 1996 can be better prepared and better informed if C-SPAN continues to pursue its goals and stay focused on its mission. In that rests the network's greatest service to the American public and its greatest challenge as it brings the political campaign process into our homes.

NOTES

1. P. R. Range, "C-SPAN: The Little Network that Could." *TV Guide,* July 18, 1992, 15.

2. For example, the Public Affairs Video Archives at Purdue University held a research conference immediately after the close of the presidential campaign in November 1992. C-SPAN coverage was central to research efforts in both political science and communication. Copies of the abstracts from this conference can be obtained from the Purdue Archives, Purdue University, Stewart Center G-39, West Lafayette, IN 47907.

REFERENCES

Carmody, John. 1992. "The TV Column." *Washington Post,* Dec. 3, D8.

C-SPAN DIGEST: A Biweekly Newsletter from Cable's Public Affairs Network. 1993. January.

Cummings, J. 1992. "Election '92 TV's Starring Role: Cable Allows Candidates to Target Their Messages." *Atlanta Constitution,* Nov. 1, C4.

Goodman, W. 1992. "Republicans Play a Dissonant Tune." *New York Times,* Aug. 19, C14: 5.

Jamieson, Kathleen H. 1992. *Dirty Politics: Deception, Distraction, and Democracy.* New York: Oxford University Press.

Kilpatrick, James J. 1992. "Prediction: Bush Will Win Despite Biased Media." *Atlanta Journal and Constitution,* Aug. 24, A10.

Kurtz, H. 1992. "For Big Three Networks, Party Conventions Lose Their Luster." *Washington Post,* July 5, A6.

May, A. L. 1991. "Will TV Do More with Less in '92?: Shrinking Budgets May Refocus Presidential Race." *Atlanta Constitution,* Dec. 15, A1.

Milavsky, J. R. 1992. "Temper-Tantrum Hunt by TV News a Waste of Time." *Atlanta Constitution,* July 19, 3.

Muir, J. K. 1993. "C-SPAN's Coverage of the Gulf War: Television as Town Square." In *Media and the Persian Gulf War,* Robert Denton, ed. Westport, CT: Praeger.

Perot, H. R. 1992. National Press Club Speech. Public Affairs Video Archives.

Piccoli, Sean. 1992. "Voting by Numbers: In the Digital Age, Toting up Campaign '92." *Washington Times,* Nov. 3, E1.

Pollack, Rayne. 1992. "C-SPAN Awareness and Use Up Dramatically." News release, December.

Range, P. R. 1992. "C-SPAN: The Little Network that Could." *TV Guide,* July 18, 12–15.

Ringel, Jonathan. 1992. "Behind the Scenes of a Live Viewer Call-In." *C-SPAN Quarterly,* Summer.

Schram, M. 1992. "Networks Go to the Convention—Barely." *Newsday,* July 30, 110.

Scully, Steve. 1993. Personal Interview, Jan. 12.

Trent, Judith S., and Robert V. Friedenberg. 1991. *Political Campaign Communication: Principles and Practices,* 2d ed. Westport, CT: Praeger.

Waldman, M. S. 1992. "28 Days Campaign Countdown." *Newsday,* Oct. 6, 16.

Wooten, Jim. 1992. "Our Civilization Will Survive Perot's Candidacy." *Atlanta Constitution,* June 10, A10.

Wyckoff, W. 1993. "C-SPAN's Founder, CEO Strives to Strike Balance on TV Dial." *Fairfax Journal,* Feb. 4, A1, A7.

Selected Bibliography

Abelson, Robert P., Donald R. Kinder, Mark D. Peters, and Susan T. Fiske. 1982. "Affective and Semantic Components in Political Person Perception." *Journal of Personality and Social Psychology* 42: 619–30.

Altheide, David. 1976. *Creating Reality: How Television News Distorts Events.* Beverly Hills: Sage.

Altheide, David L., and Robert P. Snow. 1991. *Media Worlds in the Postjournalism Era.* New York: Aldine De Gruyter.

Arterton, F. Christopher. 1978. "Campaign Organizations Confront the Media-Political Environment." In *Race for the Presidency,* James D. Barber, ed., 3–24. New York: Prentice-Hall.

———. 1993. "Campaign '92: Strategies and Tactics of the Candidates." In *The Election of 1992,* Gerald Pomper et al., eds., 74–109. Chatham, NJ: Chatham House.

Asher, Herbert. 1980. *Presidential Elections and American Politics,* rev. ed. Homewood, IL: Dorsey Press.

Atkin, Charles K., Lawrence Bowen, Oguz B. Nayman, and Kenneth G. Sheinkopf. 1973. "Quality versus Quantity in Televised Politics Ads." *Public Opinion Quarterly* 37: 209–24.

Baker, Ross. 1993. "Sorting Out and Suiting Up: The Presidential Nominations." In *The Election of 1992,* Gerald Pomper et al., eds. Chatham, NJ: Chatham House.

Bartels, Larry M. 1988. *Presidential Primaries and the Dynamic of Public Choice.* Princeton, NJ: Princeton University Press.

Becker, Samuel L. 1971. "Rhetorical Studies for the Contemporary World." In *The Prospect of Rhetoric,* Lloyd F. Bitzer and Edwin Black, eds., 21–43. Englewood Cliffs, NJ: Prentice Hall.

Bennett, W. Lance. 1992. "White Noise: The Perils of Mass Mediated Democracy." *Communication Monographs* 59: 401–6.

Berkowitz, David. 1987. "TV News Sources and News Channels: A Study in Agenda Building." *Journalism Quarterly* 64, no. 1: 61–95.

———. 1992. "Non-Routine News and Newswork: Exploring What-a-Story." *Journal of Communication* 42, no. 1: 84–95.

Bertelsen, Dale A. 1992. "Media Form and Government: Democracy as an Archetypal Image in the Electronic Age." *Communication Quarterly* 40: 325–37.

Black, Edwin. 1970. "The Second Persona." *Quarterly Journal of Speech* 56: 109–19.

Blumenthal, Sidney. 1980. *The Permanent Campaign.* New York: Touchstone Books.

Blumer, Herbert. 1959. "Suggestions for the Study of Mass-Media Effects." In *American Voting Behavior,* Eugene Burdick and Arthur J. Brodbeck, eds., 197–208. Glencoe, IL: Free Press.

Blumler, J. G. 1987. "Election Communication and the Democratic Political System." In *Political Communication Research: Approaches, Studies, Assessments,* David L. Paletz, ed. Norwood, NJ: Ablex.

Brummett, Barry. 1991. *Rhetorical Dimensions of Popular Culture.* Tuscaloosa: University of Alabama Press.

Buchanan, Bruce. 1991. *Electing a President: The Markle Commission Research on Campaign 88.* Austin: University of Texas Press.

Burnham, Walter. 1993. "The Legacy of George Bush: Travails of an Understudy." In *The Election of 1992,* Gerald Pomper et al., eds. Chatham, NJ: Chatham House.

Caddell, Patrick, and Richard Wirthlin. 1981. "Face Off: A Conversation with the Presidents' Pollsters." *Public Opinion,* Dec./Jan., 2–12.

Chagall, David. 1981. *The New Kingmakers.* New York: Harcourt, Brace, Jovanovich.

Cundy, Donald T. 1986. "Political Commercials and Candidate Image." In *New Perspectives on Political Advertising.* Lynda Lee Kaid, Dan Nimmo, and Keith R. Sanders, eds., 210–34. Carbondale: Southern Illinois University Press.

David, P. T., R. M. Goldman, and R. C. Bain. 1960. *The Politics of National Party Conventions.* Washington, DC: Brookings Institution.

de Tocqueville, Alexis. 1969. *Democracy in America.* J. P. Mayer, ed., George Lawrence, trans. New York: Anchor Books.

Dennis, Everette, et al., eds. 1993. *The Finish Line: Covering the Campaign's Final Days.* New York: Freedom Forum Media Studies Center.

Denton, Robert E. 1988. *The Primetime Presidency of Ronald Reagan.* New York: Praeger.

Denton, Robert E., and Gary Woodward. 1990. *Political Communication in America,* 2d ed. Westport, CT: Praeger.

Devlin, L. Patrick. 1989. "Contrasts in Presidential Campaign Commercials of 1988." *American Behavioral Scientist* 32: 389–414.

———. 1993. "Contrasts in Presidential Campaign Commercials of 1992." *American Behavioral Scientist* 37 (2): 272–90.

Diamond, Edwin, and Stephen S. Bates. 1988. *The Spot: The Rise of Political Advertising on Television,* 2d ed. Cambridge, MA: MIT Press.

DiClerico, Robert E., and Eric Uslaner. 1984. *Few Are Chosen: Problems in Presidential Selection.* New York: McGraw-Hill.

Edwards, George C., and Stephen Wayne. 1990. *Presidential Leadership: Politics and Policy Making,* 2d ed. New York: St. Martin's Press.

Fenno, Richard. 1978. *Home Style: House Members in Their Districts.* Boston: Little, Brown.

Foley, John, et al., eds. 1980. *Nominating a President: The Process and the Press.* New York: Praeger.

Frankovic, Kathleen. 1993. "Public Opinion in the 1992 Campaign." In *The Election of 1992,* Gerald Pomper et al., eds., 110–31. Chatham, NJ: Chatham House.

Friedenberg, Robert. 1990. *Rhetorical Studies of National Political Debates.* Westport, CT: Praeger.

Gamson, William A. 1992. *Talking Politics.* New York: Cambridge University Press.

Garramone, Gina M. 1985. "Effects of Negative Political Advertising: The Role of Sponsor and Rebuttal." *Journal of Broadcasting and Electronic Media* 29: 147–59.

Garramone, Gina M., and Stephen J. Smith. 1984. "Reactions to Political Advertising: Clarifying Sponsor Effects." *Journalism Quarterly* 61: 771–75.

Garramone, Gina M., Charles K. Atkin, Bruce E. Pinkleton, and Richard T. Cole. 1990. "Effects of Negative Political Advertising on the Political Process." *Journal of Broadcasting and Electronic Media* 34: 299–311.

Geiger, Seth F., and Byron Reeves. 1991. "The Effects of Visual Structure and Content Emphasis on the Evaluation and Memory for Political Candidates." In *Television and Political Advertising, Volume 1: Psychological Processes,* Frank Biocca, ed., 125–43. Hillsdale, NJ: Lawrence Erlbaum Publishers.

Germond, Jack, and Jules Witcover. 1988. *Whose Broad Stripes and Bright Stars: The Trivial Pursuit of the Presidency 1988.* New York: Warner Books.

Gormley, W. T., Jr. 1978. "Television Coverage of State Government." *Public Opinion Quarterly* 42, no. 3: 354–59.

Graber, Doris A. 1984. *Processing the News: How People Tame the Information Tide.* New York: Longman.

———. 1992. "News and Democracy: Are Their Paths Diverging?" *Roy W. Howard Public Lecture in Journalism and Mass Communication Research,* no. 3 (Indiana University).

Gronbeck, Bruce. 1984. "Functional and Dramaturgical Theories of Presidential Campaigns." *Presidential Studies Quarterly,* 14: 487–98.

Gurevitch, Michael, and Anandam P. Kavoori. 1992. "Television Spectacles as Politics." *Communication Monographs* 59: 415–20.

Hellweg, Susan A., George N. Dionisopoulos, and Drew B. Kugler. 1989. "Political Candidate Image: A State-of-the-Art Review." In *Progress in Communication Sciences* 9, Brenda Dervin and Melvin J. Voight, eds. Norwood, NJ: Ablex.

Hemphill, M., and L. D. Smith. 1990. "The Working American's Elegy: The Rhetoric of Bruce Springsteen." In *Politics in Familiar Contexts: Projecting Politics through Popular Media,* Robert L. Savage and Dan Nimmo, eds., 199–213. Norwood, NJ: Ablex.

Hershey, Marjorie. 1989. "The Campaign and the Media." In *The Election of 1988,* Gerald M. Pomper, ed. Chatham, NJ: Chatham House.

The Hotline. 1991–1992. Vol. 4, no. 224–vol. 6, no. 68.

Husson, William, Timothy Stephen, Teresa M. Harrison, and B. J. Fehr. 1988. "An Interpersonal Communication Perspective on Images of Political Candidates." *Human Communication Research* 14: 397–421.

Jamieson, Kathleen Hall. 1988. *Eloquence in an Electronic Age: The Transformation of Political Speechmaking.* New York: Oxford University Press.

———. 1992. *Dirty Politics: Deception, Distraction, and Democracy.* New York: Oxford University Press.

Johnston, Deirdre D. 1989. "Image and Issue Information: Message Content or Interpretation." *Journalism Quarterly* 66: 379–82.

Joslyn, Richard A. 1980. "The Content of Political Spot Ads." *Journalism Quarterly* 57: 92–98.

———. 1984. *Mass Media and Elections.* Reading, MA: Addison-Wesley.

———. 1986. "Political Advertising and the Meaning of Elections." In *New Perspectives on Political Advertising,* Lynda Lee Kaid, Dan Nimmo, and Keith R. Sanders, eds. Carbondale: Southern Illinois University Press.

Just, Marion, Ann Crigler, and Lori Wallach. 1990. "Thirty Seconds or Thirty Minutes: What Viewers Learn from Spot Advertisements and Candidate Debates." *Journal of Communication* 40: 120–33.

Kaid, Lynda Lee. 1981. "Political Advertising." In *Handbook of Political Communication,* Dan Nimmo and Keith R. Sanders, eds., 249–71. Beverly Hills, CA: Sage.

———. 1991. "The Effects of Television Broadcasts on Perceptions of Political Candidates in the United States and France." In *Mediated Politics in Two Cultures: Presidential Campaigning in the United States and France,* Lynda Lee Kaid, Jacques Gerstlé, and Keith R. Sanders, eds., 247–60. Westport, CT: Praeger.

Kaid, Lynda Lee, and John Boydston. 1987. "An Experimental Study of the Effectiveness of Negative Political Advertisements." *Communication Quarterly* 35: 193–201.

Kaid, Lynda Lee, Mike Chanslor, and Mark Hovind. 1992. "The Influence of Program and Commercial Type on Political Advertising Effectiveness." *Journal of Broadcasting and Electronic Media* 36: 303–20.

Kaid, Lynda Lee, Robert H. Gobetz, Jane Garner, Chris M. Leland, and David K. Scott. 1993. "Television News and Presidential Campaigns: The Legitimization of Televised Political Advertising." *Social Science Quarterly* 74.

Kaid, Lynda Lee, and Kathleen H. M. Haynes. 1991. *The Political Commercial Archive: A Catalog and Guide to the Collection.* Norman, OK: Political Communication Center.

Kaid, Lynda Lee, and Ann Johnston. 1991. "Negative Versus Positive Television Advertising in U.S. Presidential Campaigns, 1960–1988." *Journal of Communication* 41: 53–64.

Kaid, Lynda Lee, Chris Leland, and Susan Whitney. 1992. "The Impact of Televised Political Ads: Evoking Viewer Responses in the 1988 Presidential Campaign." *Southern Communication Journal* 57: 285–95.

Kaid, Lynda Lee, and Keith R. Sanders. 1978. "Political Television Commercials: An Experimental Study of Type and Length." *Communication Research* 5: 57–70.

Kaniss, Phyllis. 1991. *Making Local News.* Chicago: University of Chicago Press.

Keeter, Scott, and Cliff Zukin. 1983. *Uninformed Choice.* New York: Praeger.

Kendall, Kathleen, and June Ock Yum. 1984. "Persuading the Blue-Collar Voter: Issues, Images, and Homophily." *Communication Yearbook* 8.

Kendall, Kathy, and Judith Trent. 1989. "Presidential Surfacing in the New Hampshire Primary." *Political Communication Review* 14, 3.

Kern, Montague. 1989. *30-Second Politics: Political Advertising in the Eighties.* New York: Praeger.

Kernell, Samuel. 1986. *Going Public: New Strategies of Presidential Leadership.* Washington, DC: Congressional Quarterly Press.

Kessel, John. 1988. *Presidential Campaign Politics: Coalition Strategies and Citizen Response.* Chicago: Dorsey.

Kinder, Donald R. 1986. "Presidential Character Revisited." In *Political Cognition: The 19th Annual Carnegie Symposium on Cognition,* Richard R. Lau and David O. Sears, eds. Hillsdale, NJ: Lawrence Erlbaum.

Kinder, Donald R., Mark D. Peters, Robert P. Abelson, and Susan T. Fiske. 1980. "Presidential Prototypes." *Political Behavior* 2: 315–37.

Kurtz, Howard. 1993. *The Media Circus.* New York: Random House.

Lacy, Stephen, and James Bernstein. 1992. "The Impact of Competition and Market Size on the Assembly Cost of Local Television News." *Mass Communication Review* 19, nos. 1 and 2: 41–48.

Ladd, Everett, and John Benson. 1992. "The Growth of New Polls in American Politics." In *Media Polls in American Politics,* Thomas Mann and Gary Orren, eds., 19–31. Washington, DC: Brookings Institution.

Lang, Annie. 1991. "Emotion, Formal Features, and Memory for Televised Political Advertisements." In *Television and Political Advertising, Volume 1: Psychological Processes,* Frank Biocca, ed., 221–43. Hillsdale, NJ: Lawrence Erlbaum.

Lichter, S. Robert, et al., eds. 1988. *The Video Campaign: Network Coverage of the 1988 Primaries.* Lanham, MD: American Enterprise Institute.

McGinnis, Joe. 1992. *The Selling of the President 1968.* New York: Trident Press.

McLuhan, Marshall, and Quentin Fiore. 1967. *The Medium Is the Message.* New York: Bantam Books.

Marcus, George E. 1988. "The Structure of Emotional Response: 1984 Presidential Candidates." *American Political Science Review* 82: 737–61.

Miller, A. H., M. P. Wattenberg, and O. Malanchuk. 1986. "Schematic Assessments of Presidential Candidates." *American Political Science Review* 80: 521–40.

Miller, Arthur H., Martin P. Wattenberg, and Okasana Malanchuk. 1985. "Cognitive Representations of Candidate Assessments." In *Political Communication Yearbook, 1984,* Keith R. Sanders, Lynda Lee Kaid, and Dan Nimmo, eds. Carbondale: Southern Illinois University Press.

Muir, Janette. 1993. "C-SPAN's Coverage of the Gulf War: Television as Town Square." In *Media and the Persian Gulf War,* Robert E. Denton, ed., 123–44. Westport, CT: Praeger.

Napolitan, Joseph. 1976. "Media Costs and Effects in Political Campaigns." *Annals of the American Academy of Political and Social Science* 427: 119.

Neumann, Russell, Marion Just, and Ann Crigler. 1992. *Common Knowledge: News and the Construction of Political Meaning.* Chicago: University of Illinois Press.

Nimmo, Dan. 1976. "Political Image Makers and the Mass Media." *Annals of the American Academy of Political and Social Science* 427: 33–44.

North, Robert C., Ole Holsti, M. George Zaninovich, and Dina A. Zinnes. 1963. *Content Analysis: A Handbook with Applications for the Study of International Crisis.* Evanston, IL: Northwestern University Press.

Owen, Diana. 1991. *Media Messages in American Presidential Campaigns.* Westport, CT: Greenwood.

Page, Benjamin I., and Robert Y. Shapiro. 1992. *The Rational Public: Fifty Years of Trends in American Policy Preferences.* Chicago: University of Chicago Press.

Parenti, Michael. 1992. *Make-Believe Media: The Politics of Entertainment.* New York: St. Martin's Press.

Patterson, Thomas E. 1980. *The Mass Media Election: How Americans Change Their President.* New York: Praeger.

Patterson, Thomas E., and Robert D. McClure. 1976. *The Unseeing Eye.* New York: G. P. Putnam.

Pfau, Michael, and Michael Burgoon. 1988. "Inoculation in Political Campaign Communication." *Human Communication Research* 15: 91–111.

Pfau, Michael, Roxanne Parrott, and Bridget Lindquist. 1992. "An Expectancy Theory Explanation of the Effectiveness of Political Attack Television Spots: A Case Study." *Journal of Applied Communication Research* 20, no. 3: 235–54.

Polsby, Nelson, and Aaron Wildavsky. 1980. *Presidential Elections: Contemporary Strategies of American Electoral Politics,* 7th ed. New York: Free Press.

Popkin, Samuel L. 1991. *The Reasoning Voter: Communication and Persuasion in Presidential Campaigns.* Chicago: University of Chicago Press.

Postman, Neil. 1986. *Amusing Ourselves to Death: Public Discourse in the Age of Show Business.* New York: Penguin Books.

Postman, Neil, and Steve Powers. 1992. *How to Watch TV News.* New York: Penguin Books.

Pratkanis, Anthony, and Elliot Aronson. 1991. *Age of Propaganda.* New York: W. H. Freeman.

Ratzan, Scott. 1989. "The Real Agenda Setters." *American Behavioral Scientist,* 451–63.

Roddy, Brian L., and Gina M. Garramone. 1988. "Appeals and Strategies of Negative Political Advertising." *Journal of Broadcasting and Electronic Media* 32: 415–27.

Sabato, Larry J. 1981. *The Rise of the Political Consultants: New Ways of Winning Elections.* New York: Basic Books.

Savage, Robert. 1986. "Statesmanship, Surfacing, and Sometimes Stumbling: Constructing Candidate Images During the Early Campaign in America's New Political Era." *Political Communication Review* 11: 5–9.

Schram, Martin. 1987. *The Great American Video Game: Presidential Politics in the Television Age.* New York: William Morrow.

Selnow, Gary. 1991. "Polls and Computer Technologies: Ethical Considerations." In *Ethical Dimensions of Political Communication,* Robert E. Denton, Jr., ed., 171–98. New York: Praeger.

Sigelman, Lee. 1992. "There You Go Again: The Media and the Debasement of American Politics." *Communication Monographs* 59: 407–10.

Sigelman, Lee, and D. Bullock. 1991. "Candidates, Issues, Horse Races, and Hoopla: Presidential Campaign Coverage, 1888–1988." *American Politics Quarterly* 19: 5–32.

Simons, Herbert W., and Don J. Stewart. 1991. "Network Coverage of Video Politics: 'A New Beginning' in the Limits of Criticism." In *Television and Political Advertising, Volume 2: Signs, Codes, and Images,* Frank Biocca, ed. Hillsdale, NJ: Lawrence Erlbaum.

Smith, Carl. 1988. "News Critics, Newsworkers and Local Television News." *Journalism Quarterly* 65, no. 2: 99–102.

Smith, L. D. 1987. "The Nominating Convention as Purveyor of Political Medicine: An Anecdotal Analysis of the Democrats and Republicans of 1984." *Central States Speech Journal* 38: 252–61.

———. 1988. "Narrative Styles in Network Coverage of the 1984 Nominating Conventions." *Western Journal of Speech Communication* 52: 63–74.

———. 1989. "A Narrative Analysis of the Party Platforms: The Democrats and Republicans of 1984." *Communication Quarterly* 37: 91–99.

———. 1990. "Convention Oratory as Institutional Discourse: A Narrative Synthesis of the Democrats and Republicans of 1988." *Communication Studies* 41: 19–34.

————. 1992a. "How the Dialectical Imperative Shapes Network News Content: The Case of CNN vs. the Entertainment Networks." *Communication Quarterly* 40: 338–49.

————. 1992b. "The Party Platforms as Institutional Discourse: The Democrats and Republicans of 1988." *Presidential Studies Quarterly* 22: 531–44.

Smith, Larry David, and Dan Nimmo. 1991. *Cordial Concurrence: Orchestrating National Party Conventions in the Telepolitical Age.* Westport, CT: Praeger.

Traugott, Michael. 1992. "The Impact of Media Polls on the Public." In *Media Polls in American Politics,* Thomas Mann and Gary Orren, eds., 125–49. Washington, DC: Brookings Institution.

Trent, Judith. 1978. "Presidential Surfacing: The Ritualistic and Crucial First Act." *Communication Monographs* 45: 281–92.

Trent, Judith S., and Robert V. Friedenberg. 1991. *Political Campaign Communication: Principles and Practices,* 2d ed. Westport, CT: Praeger.

Walsh, Edward. 1992. "The More Seed Money, the Better the Harvest." In *The Quest for National Office,* Stephen Wayne and Clyde Wilcox, eds., 50–56. New York: St. Martin's Press.

Wayne, Stephen. 1992. *The Road to the White House 1992.* New York: St. Martin's Press.

Wayne, Stephen, and Clyde Wilcox, eds. 1992. *The Quest for National Office.* New York: St. Martin's Press.

West, Darrell M. 1993. *Air Wars: Television Advertising in Election Campaigns, 1952–92.* Washington, DC: Congressional Quarterly Press.

Zarefsky, David. 1992. "Spectator Politics and the Revival of Public Argument." *Communication Monographs* 59: 411–14.

Index

About the Editor and Contributors

ROBERT E. DENTON, JR., is Professor and Head of the Department of Communication Studies at Virginia Polytechnic Institute and State University. He is the editor of two Praeger Series, Political Communication and Presidential Studies, and is the author, coauthor, or editor of nine books, including *The Media and the Persian Gulf War* (Praeger, 1993), *Ethical Dimensions of Political Communication* (Praeger, 1991), and *Political Communication in America* (2d edition) (Praeger, 1990).

ROBERT V. FRIEDENBERG is Professor of Communication at Miami University in Ohio. He is the editor of *Rhetorical Studies of National Political Debates: 1960–1968* (Praeger, 1990) and coauthor of *Political Campaign Communication: Principles and Practices,* 2d ed. (Praeger, 1991). In 1989 he received the "Outstanding Book of the Year Award" from the Religious Speech Communication Association for *"Hear O Israel": The History of American Jewish Preaching 1654–1970.* He has served as a communication consultant for the Republican National Committee and has been involved in over seventy political campaigns.

RACHEL L. HOLLOWAY is Assistant Professor in the Department of Communication Studies at Virginia Polytechnic Institute and State University. She teaches in the areas of public relations, issue management, and political communication. She is the author of *In the Matter of J. Robert Oppenheimer: Character, Rhetoric, and Politics* (Praeger) and *America's Quest for Security and the Hydrogen Bomb Controversy* (forthcoming).

LYNDA LEE KAID is Professor of Communication at the University of Oklahoma, where she also serves as Director of the Political Communication Center and supervises the Political Commercial Archive. She is co-editor of the *Political Communication Review.* She teaches and conducts research in the areas of political advertising and news coverage of political events. She is coauthor of *Political Campaign Communication: A Bibliography and Guide to the Literature,* and coeditor of *Mediated Politics in Two Cultures* (Praeger), *New Perspectives on Political Advertising, Massenmedien im Wahlkampf,* and *Political Communication Yearbook, 1984.* Her articles have appeared in numerous books and journals, including *Journalism Quarterly, Communication Research, Social Science Quarterly, Journal of Communication,* and *Communication Quarterly.*

MONTAGUE KERN is Assistant Professor of Political Communication at the Department of Journalism and Mass Media, School of Communication, Information and Library Science, Rutgers University. She was a spring 1992 Fellow at the John F. Kennedy School of Government. She is author of *30-Second Politics* (Praeger) and coauthor of *The Kennedy Crisis: The Press, the Presidency, and Foreign Policy.*

ALAN LOUDEN is Associate Professor in the Department of Speech Communication at Wake Forest University, where he serves as Director of Debate. He serves on several editorial boards and has published in the area of political communication.

JANETTE KENNER MUIR is Basic Course Director and Assistant Professor in the Department of Communication at George Mason University. She has published articles in a variety of communication journals as well as several book chapters. She is currently editing a volume on the uses of C-SPAN in the communication classroom.

DAN NIMMO is Professor in the Department of Communication at the University of Oklahoma. He is author or coauthor of more than two dozen books in political communication. More recent titles include: *Newsgathering in Washington, Candidates and Their Images* (with Robert Savage), *Government and the News Media: Comparative Dimensions* (with Michael Mansfield), *Handbook of Political Communication* (with Keith Sanders), and *Mediated Political Realities* (with James Combs). Among those examining the relationship of politics and the news media are *Cordial Concurrence* (with Larry David Smith), *The Political Pundits* (with James Combs), and *The New Propaganda.*

LARRY DAVID SMITH is Assistant Professor in the Department of Communication at Purdue University. His articles on presidential nominating conventions, presidential rhetoric, political and product advertising, and popular culture have appeared in a variety of scholarly journals such as *Communication Quarterly, Communication Studies, Southern Communication Journal,* and *Political Communication Review.* He is coauthor (with Dan Nimmo) of *Cordial Concurrence: Orchestrating National Party Conventions in the Telepolitical Age* (Praeger).

MARY E. STUCKEY is Assistant Professor in the Department of Political Science at the University of Mississippi. She teaches courses on the presidency and political communication. She is the author of *Getting Into the Game: The Pre-Presidential Rhetoric of Ronald Reagan* (Praeger), *Playing the Game: The Presidential Rhetoric of Ronald Reagan* (Praeger), and *The President as Interpreter-in-Chief.*

DAVID M. TIMMERMAN is a doctoral candidate in the Department of Speech Communication at Purdue University and a visiting lecturer in Speech Communication at Indiana University at Kokomo. His research interests include homiletics, political communication, and classical rhetoric. His writings have appeared in *Argumentation and Advocacy* and *Journal of the American Academy of Ministry.*

JUDITH S. TRENT is Professor of Communication and Associate Vice President for Research and Advanced Studies at the University of Cincinnati. She has written and spoken widely on the subject of political campaign communication. She is coauthor of *Political Communication: Principles and Practices,* 2d ed. (Praeger).

ROBERT H. WICKS is Assistant Professor in the School of Journalism at Indiana University. His research areas include political communication and social cognition as applied to media information processing. His scholarly articles have appeared in *Communication Research, American Behavioral Scientist, Journal of Broadcasting and Electronic Media, Journalism Quarterly,* and *Journal of Advertising Research.* He has also worked professionally as a television and radio reporter and editor.

www.ingramcontent.com/pod-product-compliance
Lightning Source LLC
Chambersburg PA
CBHW070240290326
41929CB00046B/2117